THE CATHOLIC REFORMATION

Savonarola to Ignatius Loyola

JOHN C. OLIN

Fordham University Press
New York

LC 92–29865
ISBN 0–8232–1477–X (clothbound)
ISBN 0–8232–1478–8 (paperback)
Originally published by Harper & Row, 1969
First Fordham edition, 1992

Library of Congress Cataloging-in-Publication Data

The Catholic Reformation : Savonarola to Ignatius Loyola : reform in
the Church, 1495–1540 / [compiled and commented on] by John C. Olin.
 p. cm.
 Originally published: New York : Harper & Row, 1969. With new
introd.
 "A selection of documents in English translation."
 Includes bibliographical references and index.
 ISBN 0–8232–1477–X.—ISBN 0–8232–1478–8 (pbk.)
 1. Counter-Reformation—Sources. I. Olin, John C.
BR430.C38 1992   92–29865
                                                         CIP

Printed in the United States of America
10 9 8 7 6

THE CATHOLIC REFORMATION
Savonarola to Ignatius Loyola

1. La Navicella, or the Bark of Peter. Drawing by Parri Spinelli (d. 1453).

Contents

Illustrations

1. La Navicella, or the Bark of Peter. Drawing by Parri Spinelli (d. 1453) after Giotto's mosaic in the old basilica of St. Peter in Rome. The episode depicted is in Matthew 14, 22–33, and is symbolic of troubled times in the Church. *Courtesy of the Metropolitan Museum of Art. frontispiece*

2. Woodcuts of Savonarola preaching in the Duomo at Florence and writing in his cell at the convent of San Marco. These cuts originally illustrated two of Savonarola's published works, *Compendio di revelatione* (1495) and *Della semplicità della vita christiana* (1496). *Courtesy of the Metropolitan Museum of Art.* page 2

3. John Colet. Drawing by Hans Holbein after a portrait bust by Torrigiano in St. Paul's in London (destroyed in the Great Fire of 1666). The drawing is in the Royal Library at Windsor Castle. *By gracious permission of H.M. the Queen.* page 28

4. The Fifth Lateran Council in session. Woodcut used as the frontispiece for the original printing of the bull *Supernae dispositionis arbitrio* in Rome in 1514 (under the title *Bulla Reformationis*). *Courtesy of the Union Theological Seminary Library.* page 42

5. Erasmus. Sixteenth-century copy of Quentin Metsys' portrait of Erasmus by Cornelis Visscher. In the Royal Collection at Hampton Court. *By gracious permission of H.M. the Queen.* page 66

6. Title page of Froben's 1518 edition of Erasmus' *Adagiorum Chiliades.* page 70

7. Title page of the Cologne edition of 1541 of Lefèvre's *Commentaries on the Four Gospels.* *Courtesy of the Bodleian Library, Oxford.* page 108

8. Tomb of Pope Adrian VI. In the church of Santa Maria dell' Anima in Rome. The marble relief under the sepulcher proper depicts Adrian's entry into Rome in August, 1522. The Latin inscription above it reads: "Alas, how much does the power of even the best of men depend upon the times in which they live!" page 120

9. Pope Paul III. Portrait by Titian, painted in 1543, at the Pinacoteca in Naples. page 184

viii THE CATHOLIC REFORMATION

10.   Cardinal Gasparo Contarini. A contemporary portrait in the Uffizi Gallery in Florence. Reproduced from Giuseppe Alberigo, *I vescovi italiani al concilio di Trento* (Florence, 1959).   page 192

11.   Profession of vows by Ignatius Loyola and companions, made at the basilica of St. Paul in Rome, April 22, 1941. Ignatius' profession (top half of document) reads as follows:

I the undersigned promise to Almighty God and to the supreme pontiff, His vicar on earth, before His virgin mother and the entire court of heaven, and in the presence of the society, perpetual poverty, chastity, and obedience, according to the manner of life set forth in the bull of the society of the Lord Jesus and in its constitutions promulgated or to be promulgated. Moreover, I promise special obedience to the supreme pontiff with regard to the missions mentioned in the bull. Also, I promise to see to it that children are instructed in the rudiments of faith, according to the same bull and constitutions.   page 200

Courtesy of the Central Archives of the Society of Jesus in Rome.

12.   St. Ignatius Loyola. Copy of a portrait by Alonzo Sánchez Coello, painted in 1584 under the direction of Pedro Ribadeneira, a former associate of the saint and his first biographer. The original was destroyed in a fire in Madrid in 1931. Reproduced from George E. Ganss, S.J., *Saint Ignatius' Idea of a Jesuit University* (Milwaukee, 1956).   page 206

Preface to the Fordham Edition

I am happy that Fordham University Press is republishing this volume which Harper & Row originally brought out in 1969. Its value lies primarily in the fifteen documents relating to Catholic reform that it makes available, and for that reason, I feel sure, it continues to be useful. I have not revised or updated the headnotes or bibiographical references in the original edition, and I ask pardon on that score. These, however, present substantial information that remains basic and, I trust, they will still be helpful. My recent *Catholic Reform from Cardinal Ximenes to the Council of Trent* which Fordham published in 1990 to some extent updates the subject, though that slim volume is quite a different book. It may be said nevertheless to supplement or complement this earlier and present volume. I had originally intended to carry the story of the Catholic Reformation through the era of the Council of Trent in a second volume of documents comparable to this one, but, alas, distractions arose, and I failed to do so.

Let me note that I recognize there are differences of attitude and approach with regard to "Catholic reform" in the sixteenth century. I put the term in quotes because the notion itself is sometimes questioned and from different points of view. I believe, however, that the term expresses a valid conceptualization, though I do not mean to use it in a narrow or excessively specific sense. I know the picture of Catholicism in the sixteenth century is complex and has different phases and various aspects, and I acknowledge that my own treatment covers only a part of the broader story. It is a part, however, that has often been ignored or dismissed and has sometimes been denied. It fully deserves, I believe, an historian's attention.

In my earlier preface I thank a number of people who helped me with the volume. The years have passed. Some have moved on to other posts and responsibilities, some remain colleagues and friends, and some have died. I have them all in mind, and I again express my gratitude for their generous assistance.

June 22, 1992   JOHN C. OLIN

Preface

This volume presents a selection of documents in English translation which illustrate the character and thrust of Catholic reform in the early sixteenth century. The period it spans—from 1495 to 1540, from the days of Savonarola's predominance in Florence to the time when Ignatius Loyola and his early companions came to Rome and won the approval of Paul III for their new Order—was an age of great religious ferment and upheaval. It is marked historically by that crisis we call the Protestant Reformation, but in reality this development, as major as it is, constitutes only one aspect of the story. Underlying it and even encompassing it was a tremendous surge for religious renewal and reform. "The world thirsts for the Gospel truth," wrote Erasmus. This volume focuses on another and lesser-known aspect of that phenomenon, that is, on the movement for renewal and reform which remained within the Catholic Church and which sought to reform the life of that existing hierarchical institution and renew devotion within the framework of its teaching and authority.

In this perspective Catholic reform must be distinguished from Protestant reform, and it must also be distinguished from what is called the Counter-Reformation. The latter (at least in the original or literal sense of the term) came as a response and reaction to the Protestant challenge and is to be seen in a relationship of hostility and opposition to Protestantism. Reform within the Catholic Church had a different origin, purpose, and basic character. After 1517 the varied currents of this age of religious ferment and crisis inevitably began to cross and intermingle. Catholic reform was influenced and given new urgency and force by the Protestant challenge, and regeneration came about only after widespread revolt and disruption had occurred. In fact one may wonder how effective Catholic reform would have been without the pressure of cataclysmic events. "We should refrain," Hubert Jedin warns us, "from viewing Catholic attempts at reform in the period of the Middle Ages as a mighty stream which, by its own momentum, would have led to a general reform even if there had been no schism." Yet a distinction between spontaneous reform and defensive reaction within the Church can be maintained. And the aim of this volume is to reveal something of the nature and impulse of this spontaneous reform. Our understanding of the surge for renewal which stirred all of Christendom in the sixteenth century will thereby be enlarged, as will also our understanding of the life and fortunes of the Catholic Church in this critical time. A subsequent volume, I hope, will carry the story through the era of the Council of Trent and will perforce deal more extensively with Counter-Reformation manifestations and problems.

In addition to a general introduction on the background of my subject, I have prefaced each document with a brief introduction of its own, and I have included fairly extensive bibliographical references in each chapter. My intention was threefold: to aid in the reading and study of the specific documents, several of which are here made available in English translation for the first time, to convey some sense of the course and continuity of the movement as a whole, and to encourage further inquiry into the various facets of Catholic reform. That the movement is a vital and significant one from both the standpoint of the historian and that of the Christian is a theme we hardly need to emphasize, and it is to be hoped it will be more adequately appreciated and explored. The texts and notes here presented are offered with that in mind, though with the knowledge that they are but a small contribution to the study of a subject that is large and complex.

Finally there are many whose great assistance and kindness I must acknowledge, especially in the work of translation. I have indicated in the notes for each selection whence came my text and to whom must be given the credit for the English version I have used, but here let me express my formal and heartfelt thanks to those who undertook on my behalf an arduous translation task: to my colleagues Alfred E. Vecchio for Savonarola's Renovation sermon, Alfeo Marzi for the Chapters of the Oratory of Divine Love, and James F. Brady, Jr., for his collaboration on Giberti's *Constitutions,* and to former students at Fordham Charles W. Lockyer, Jr., John Monfasani, John Marrone, Joseph Leahey, and John Higgins for their very considerable aid and diligent work on several of the Latin documents. In most of the latter instances I corrected and revised their basic drafts and ascribed the translation to both of us. I also want to thank Margaret Mann Phillips for her gracious permission to use her translation of Erasmus' *Sileni Alcibiadis* and the Reverend Mark Stier, O.F.M. Cap., for his kind permission to use his translation of the Capuchin Constitutions of 1536. I am also grateful to the B. Herder Book Company, the Bruce Publishing Company, and Newman Press for generously permitting me to reprint texts that were originally published under their imprints. Last but far from least, not a few of my friends and colleagues assisted me with encouragement and advice and scholarly help during the course of my labors, and these I cannot forget. To Fathers John W. Bush, George S. Glanzman, Albert J. Loomie, Robert E. McNally, and Herbert A. Musurillo, all of the Society of Jesus, to Joseph O'Callaghan and Roger Wines of Fordham University's History Department, to Peter Pouncey of Classics at Columbia University, and to Richard Pacella of Union Theological Seminary Library I offer thanks.

February 16, 1969   JOHN C. OLIN

INTRODUCTION:

The Background of Catholic Reform

The Church in the late Middle Ages endured what may be called a "time of troubles"—a time marked by challenge and dissent, manifesting the symptoms of spiritual and institutional decline, climaxed by the great crisis and disruption that broke in the sixteenth century. The pattern is large and complex and its texture is uneven, but the observer can hardly fail to perceive that trial and peril beset the vast ecclesiastical structure of the West in the fourteenth and fifteenth centuries. Its organization and authority as well as the integrity of its inner life and mission seem to have been placed in prolonged jeopardy by the events and currents of that age. And it was not simply a matter of external forces beating against the Church and taking their toll of its power and substance. Within the religious community itself there were ominous signs of weakness and disorder: the schism resulting from the double papal election of 1378 and continuing down to 1417, the exaggeration of papal power and a concomitant opposition to it both in practice and in theory, the worldliness and secularization of the hierarchy that reached to the papacy itself in the High Renaissance, ignorance and immorality among the lower clergy, laxity in monastic discipline and spiritual decay in the religious life, theological desiccation and confusion, superstition and abuse in religious practice. The picture should not be overdrawn (there were many instances of sanctity, dedication, and even spiritual renewal during this time), but in general, Catholic life in the late Middle Ages seems grievously depressed—hollowed out, to use Lortz's image[1]—and the evidence of deep-seated trouble is inescapable.

A considerable body of contemporary comment and observation can be cited to this effect, and indeed the texts presented in this volume bear frank witness to the ills that afflicted the Church. But at the outset two voices may be allowed to speak to lend credence and confirmation to the state of affairs we have described. Lorenzo de' Medici, *Il Magnifico*, wrote a letter of paternal advice in early 1492 to his son Giovanni, who at the age of sixteen was about to go to Rome and take up his residence as a cardinal. The youth is the future Pope Leo X. Lorenzo urged him to virtue and an exemplary life, and he added: "I well know, that as you are now to reside at Rome, that sink of all iniquity, the difficulty of conducting yourself by these admonitions will be increased. . . .

---

[1] Joseph Lortz, *How the Reformation Came*, trans. O. M. Knab (New York, 1964), pp. 105, 111. See also the judgment of Ludwig Pastor in *The History of the Popes from the Close of the Middle Ages*, trans. F. I. Antrobus, R. F. Kerr, *et al.* (40 vols.; St. Louis, 1891–1953), V, 226, and VII, 292 ff.

You will probably meet with those who will particularly endeavor to corrupt and incite you to vice."[2] From north of the Alps the German scholar and versifier Sebastian Brant gave a broader and more public warning. In his moralistic poem *Narrenschiff*, first published in Basel in 1494, he wrote the following quatrain:

> St. Peter's ship is swaying madly,
> It may be wrecked or damaged badly,
> The waves are striking 'gainst the side
> And storm and trouble may betide.[3]

Such voices can be multiplied, and it must also be stressed that the plight of the Bark of Peter evoked a fuller response than the mere advertisement of its fitful course or the castigation of its crew. There arose the call for remedying the evils that had come to pass. There was counsel and advice on restoring the vessel to its former efficiency and its original progress. Nor were efforts lacking in the attempt to achieve these goals. This response, constructive and restorative, to the condition of the Church is generally what we mean when we use the words reform and reformation. And it is of course the subject of our study.

Basically the two terms reform and reformation mean a return to an original form or archetype or ideal and imply the removal or correction of faults which have caused deformation. The object of reform is restored to its original character, its essential mode of being. Applied to the Church and to religious faith and practice, the significance of these words is obvious. They mean a return to the original purity and splendor of Christ's Church and indeed to Christ himself, the model of Christians and the very *form* of the Church. Dante's words in *De Monarchia* come to mind:

> Now the form of the Church is nothing else than the life of Christ in word and in deed. For his life was the idea and pattern of the Church militant, especially of its shepherds and most especially of its chief shepherd, whose duty it is to feed the sheep and lambs. He himself said, in John's Gospel, as he bequeathed the form of his life to us, "I have given you an example that as I have done to you, so you do also." And specifically to Peter, after he had assigned him the post of shepherd, he said, "Peter, follow thou me."[4]

The call for such reform may be said to arise from the nature of things— from the disparity between the ideal and the reality that to a lesser or greater degree is ever present in man's history. With respect to the Church, as Jedin points out, it "originated in the consciousness that Christ's foundation, as historically realised in its individual members, no longer corresponded to the

---

[2] William Roscoe, *The Life of Lorenzo de' Medici* (10th ed.; London, 1851), pp. 285–86. Lorenzo's low estimate of the College of Cardinals was "unfortunately only too well founded," says Pastor, *op. cit.*, V, 361.

[3] Sebastian Brant, *The Ship of Fools*, trans. Edwin H. Zeydel (New York, 1944), p. 333.

[4] Dante, *On World Government (De Monarchia)*, trans. Herbert W. Schneider (2d ed.; New York, 1957), p. 76. The quote is from Bk. III, Chap. 15, of *De Monarchia*.

ideal—in other words, that it was not what it should be."⁵ And so the disparity must be ended and the historical Church brought into conformity with the ideal. It must strive to be what it should be—faithful to Christ and the mission He enjoined, drawing close to that glorious Church of which St. Paul speaks, "without spot or wrinkle or any such disfigurement."⁶

Because of conditions in the late Middle Ages the consciousness of a contrast between the contemporary Church and the primitive form and ideal was particularly acute. Dante is expressing it in the chapter we have quoted from the *De Monarchia,* and in several striking passages of the *Paradiso* he observes the grave discrepancy between the Church of his day and that of Christ and the Apostles and the saints.

> Barefoot and lean came Cephas, came the great
> Vessel of the Holy Ghost; and they would sup
> At whatsoever house they halted at.
>
> Pastors today require to be propped up
> On either side, one man their horse to lead
> (So great their weight!) and one their train to loop.
>
> Over their mounts their mantles fall, full-spread;
> Two beasts beneath one hide behold them go!
> O patience, is thy meekness not yet fled?⁷

Thomas à Kempis in his *Imitation of Christ*—the title of which is a reform program—also marks the difference, though in more personal moralistic terms. "Behold the living examples of the old fathers in which shineth true perfection, and thou shalt see how little it is and almost naught that we do. Alas, what is our life compared to them?" And, after describing their life of sanctity and virtue, he exclaims: "O how great was the fervor of religion in the beginning of its institution!"⁸ Savonarola is likewise deeply conscious of the discordance between present ways and the model of the early Church. "In the primitive Church the chalices were of wood, the prelates of gold; in these days the Church hath chalices of gold and prelates of wood."⁹

Given this awareness, the task then was correcting what was wrong and restoring the Church to her pristine state. However, we have perhaps said enough in general terms about the nature and occasion of Catholic reform in the late Middle Ages. Let us now look briefly at the historical development of the notion of reform and at some of its specific manifestations in the life

---

⁵ Hubert Jedin, *A History of the Council of Trent,* trans. Dom Ernest Graf (2 vols.; St. Louis, 1957–61), I, 6–7.

⁶ Ephesians 5, 27.

⁷ *Paradiso,* XXI, 127–35, quoted from the Dorothy L. Sayers and Barbara Reynolds translation (Penguin Classics; Baltimore, 1962), pp. 244–45.

⁸ Thomas à Kempis, *The Imitation of Christ,* Pt. I, Chap. XVIII (Everyman's Library ed.; London, 1910), p. 30.

⁹ Savonarola's Advent sermon XXIII of 1493, quoted in Pasquale Villari, *Life and Times of Girolamo Savonarola,* trans. Linda Villari (London, 1896), p. 184.

of the Church. Our perspective on the Catholic Reformation in the sixteenth century will thereby be enlarged.

The original concept of Christian reform is one of the reform of the individual—of his personal renewal and the restoration in him of the image of God, the *form* of his creation. It is the concept found in Holy Scripture and in the Fathers of the early Church, and it has been studied very thoroughly by Gerhart Ladner in his work *The Idea of Reform*.[10] The Church as such was not the object of a reform endeavor, but rather the inner man who was to be remade *ad imaginem et similitudinem Dei*. This original and fundamental concept never disappears, for it is an integral part of the Christian message. "If then any man is in Christ, he is a new creature: the former things have passed away; behold, they are made new!"[11] Erasmus underlined this doctrine in the introduction to the New Testament he published in 1516. "What else is the philosophy of Christ," he asks, "which He himself calls a rebirth, than the restoration of human nature originally well formed?"[12] Rebirth (the Latin term Erasmus used is *renascentia*), restoration, and reform refer then to the very basic personal renewal that Christianity entails.

By the eleventh century, however, the idea of reform had also come to include the correction and renewal of the Church at large. This expanded concept found expression in the Gregorian reform of that time.[13] So-called because Pope Gregory VII (1073–85) was its leading figure, it sought to end the feudal lay domination of the Church and restore her freedom and her spiritual mission. It centered chiefly on the clergy or *sacerdotium*, and its thrust was what we would call institutional. Papal primacy and authority were forcefully asserted; elections to ecclesiastical office were to be freely and properly conducted; old canons governing the Church were renewed; bad customs and practices were to be abolished. The Church, in short, was to be reformed in line with its original and authentic constitution so that its true apostolate might be realized.

But such institutional reform is not to be conceived apart from the reform of the individual Christian. "Gregory VII and the Gregorians," writes Dom Leclercq, "many of them monks and all of them influenced by St. Augustine, conceived of reform as an essentially spiritual matter. For them, as for their master, there could be no reform of the Church without reform of the Christian."[14] The latter is the primary goal, and the Church reformed is actually the Church made more effective in the *cura animarum*—in the work of teach-

---

[10] (Cambridge, Mass., 1959; Harper Torchbook ed., 1967.)

[11] II Corinthians 5, 17.

[12] From the *Paraclesis*, in *Christian Humanism and the Reformation: Selected Writings of Erasmus*, ed. John C. Olin (New York, 1965), p. 100.

[13] Ladner, *The Idea of Reform*, pp. 277, fn. 147, 401–2, 423–24; idem, "Reformatio," in *Ecumenical Dialogue at Harvard: The Roman Catholic-Protestant Colloquium*, eds. Samuel H. Miller and G. Ernest Wright (Cambridge, Mass., 1964), pp. 172 ff.; and Jean Leclercq, "The Bible and the Gregorian Reform," in *Historical Investigations* (Vol. 17 of *Concilium*; New York, 1966), pp. 63–77.

[14] *Ibid.*, p. 74.

ing, guiding, and sanctifying her members. Vatican II formulated that in a memorable way when it declared that "every renewal of the Church essentially consists in an increase of fidelity to her own calling."[15] Her reform and renewal, however, must come in some way through her members, and this presupposes their own personal conversion and commitment. The institution per se does not reform itself but is reformed by men who are reformed. In this sense the Church needs saints, that is, men who truly are reformed and whose example and efforts are the means for further reformation.

The life of St. Francis of Assisi (1181/2–1226) is particularly instructive in this regard. His own conversion was accompanied by those symbolic words he heard in the chapel of San Damiano: "Repair my house which, as you see, is being totally destroyed." And his remarkable life was lived in such close imitation of Christ that it became an inspiration and strength for the whole Church. Of him the Cardinal of Santa Sabina reported to Pope Innocent III: "I have found a man of most perfect life, that is minded to live conformably with the Holy Gospel, and to observe in all things Gospel perfection: through whom, as I believe, the Lord is minded to reform throughout the whole world the faith of Holy Church."[16] The Pope himself saw in Brother Francis "the holy man by whom the Church of God shall be uplifted and upheld."[17]

The two kinds of reform—institutional and personal—thus are closely related, and, as Ladner suggests, the Gregorian and Franciscan movements are complementary phases and aspects of the same idea.[18] It is also clear that St. Francis moves at the deeper level, more in keeping with the original and fundamental concept of Christian renewal. Yet thereby the Church and Christendom were renewed.

> He'd not long risen when the earth was stirred
> By touches of invigorating power
> From his great strength . . .[19]

The expanded concept of reform is also in a sense expressed in the formula *reformatio in capite et in membris* which gained currency in the late Middle Ages. Attributed to William Durandus at the time of the Council of Vienne (1311–12), its most famous usage perhaps is in the decrees and pronouncements of the Council of Constance (1414–18).[20] The decree *Sacrosancta* of

[15] From the Decree on Ecumenism, in *The Documents of Vatican II*, ed. Walter M. Abbott (New York, 1966), p. 350.

[16] *The Legend of Saint Francis by the Three Companions*, trans. E. G. Salter (London, 1905), p. 78.

[17] *Ibid.*, p. 82.

[18] Ladner, "*Reformatio*," pp. 172, 190. See also David Knowles' portrait "Francis of Assisi," in his *Saints and Scholars* (Cambridge, 1962), pp. 86–87.

[19] Dante's *Paradiso*, XI, 55–57 (Sayers and Reynolds translation).

[20] William Durandus the Younger, *Tractatus de modo generalis concilii celebrandi* (Paris, 1671), Pt. I, Chap. I. For the decrees of Constance, see *Readings in Church History*, ed. Colman J. Barry (Westminster, Md., 1960), I, 504–5. See also Cardinal D'Ailly's reform proposal, *De reformatione ecclesiae*, presented at Constance in 1415 (in the volume containing Durandus' *Tractatus* cited above).

1415, for example, declares the Council's purpose to be the ending of the great schism which had rent the Church since 1378 and the Church's reformation in its head and members. Thus used, the phrase became linked with the conciliar movement that was born of the Western Schism and the plight of the Church at that critical time, and it serves to underline the fact that conciliarism was essentially a reform movement. Asserting the supremacy and active role of the General Council in the government of the Church, the conciliarists sought to limit papal authority and end the abuses connected with papal appointments and papal taxation.[21] This was the heart of their *reformatio in capite* and the first principle of the more general reformation that must follow, for, as Durandus himself had pointed out, "when the head languishes, all the members of the body suffer pain."[22]

The Council of Constance did resolve the Western Schism, but it was not eminently successful in its reform endeavors. Nor did the subsequent Councils of Pavia-Siena (1423–24) and of Basel (1431–49), as provided for by the decree *Frequens* of 1417, achieve that reform and renewal that so many sought. Basel featured from beginning to end a bitter struggle between the conciliarists and the Papacy and climaxed its antipapal legislation in 1439 by deposing the reigning Pope Eugenius IV and electing an antipope Felix V. In this instance a Council had led to schism, and the spectacle thus afforded contributed decisively to the defeat of the conciliar movement and the victory of the papal monarchy in the fifteenth century. The hope too of achieving a *reformatio in capite et in membris* through the agency of a General Council was also ended.[23] It was now incumbent on the Papacy whose primacy had been reasserted and confirmed to give leadership in that cause.

In this heavy responsibility the Papacy failed. Neither its own reform nor that of the Church at large was sufficiently promoted, and therein lies one of the darkest features of the religious scene at the close of the Middle Ages. A deeply moving page of Gordon Rupp's *Luther's Progress to the Diet of Worms* is recalled: "What are the inexorable consequences of the sins of the New Israel? . . . What happens when the successors of the Apostles betray,

21 Jedin, *op. cit.*, I, 9 ff.; E. F. Jacob, *Essays in the Conciliar Epoch* (2d. ed.; Manchester, 1953), pp. 18–23; and Paul de Vooght, *Les Pouvoirs du concile et l'autorité du pape au concile de Constance* (Paris, 1965). See also Joseph Gill, S.J., *Constance et Bâle-Florence* (Paris, 1965), for a general history of the fifteenth century Councils.
22 Durandus, *op. cit.*, p. 241.
23 This must be understood only with reference to the conciliar movement in the fifteenth century. A General Council might still be deemed a necessary and essential means for achieving reform, as indeed the address of Egidio da Viterbo at the Fifth Lateran Council in 1512 clearly shows (see Chap. IV *infra*). As for the consequences of conciliarism on reform in the Church, the argument is tangled. J. N. Figgis, in his *Studies of Political Thought from Gerson to Grotius, 1414–1625* (Cambridge, 1916), pp. 31–32, views the failure of the conciliar movement as making the more violent Protestant Reformation inevitable. Philip Hughes, in *A History of the Church* (3 vols.; New York, 1935–49), III, 282–84, 306–7, 330–33, comes down hard on conciliarism as sponsoring inadequate and misdirected reforms and as creating conditions which made the needed reforms all the more difficult to achieve. Jedin, in the opening chapters of his *History of the Council of Trent*, I, gives the fullest and most nuanced treatment of this difficult question.

deny, forsake their evangelical vocation?"[24] Stern judgment will be rendered, and Rupp, evoking the tremendous vision of Michelangelo in the Sistine Chapel of a Christ risen in wrath, sees the Reformation as an ordeal, the Doomsday of the late medieval Church. Yet an awareness of the need for reform was not lacking in the Roman Curia following its triumph over the rebellious Council of Basel.[25] The *Advisamenta* of Cardinal Capranica during the pontificate of Nicholas V (1447–55)—it "reads like a complete programme of the Catholic reformation," says Jedin[26]—and the reform memorials of Domenico Domenichi and Nicholas of Cusa in the days of Pius II (1458–64) are witness to this fact. And even the notorious Alexander VI, struck by remorse over the assassination of his son, the Duke of Gandia, in 1497 appointed a reform commission which seriously and competently reported on the state of the Church and drafted comprehensive reform measures. But these were all dead letters. Nothing was accomplished, nothing gained. In fact, the Papacy itself in the later decades of the fifteenth century—the "Papacy of Princes," as Father Hughes has called it—entered a period of moral disintegration which culminated in the most scandalous venality and secularization.[27] The *deformatio in capite* was most acute as the hour of judgment began to strike.

But if Council and Pope had eliminated themselves from the quest for reform in the actual circumstances of the time, what other avenues or agencies for Christian renewal and the Church's reformation remained? Here the picture is not quite so dreary; here the signs of regeneration may be discerned. For this perspective, however, we must turn for the moment from our concern with institutional reform, that is, from the *reformatio in capite* which had been obstructed and denied, to the matter of personal reform, that is, to the *reformatio in membris* which could and did have a spontaneous life. The two reformations, as we have said, must be joined in the Catholic concept, and they are of course closely related in their mutual interaction, but there is an obvious difference in their proximate goals and in their spheres of activity and effective means. We must turn then to the reform of the members if we would observe the beginnings—and the wellspring in the immediate sense—of the Catholic Reformation of the sixteenth century. The documents in this volume and the development they represent by the same token are linked very closely to these endeavors.

There are many examples of personal renewal and partial reform in the late Middle Ages. Jedin has given clear indication of this in a substantial

[24] (New York, 1964), p. 49.
[25] Jedin, *op. cit.*, I, Bk. I, Chap. VI; Pastor, *op. cit.*, III, 269 ff. (for Pius II), V, 500 ff. (for Alexander VI); L. Celier, "L'Idée de réforme à la cour pontificale du concile de Bâle au concile du Latran," *Revue des questions historiques*, LXXXVI (1909), 418–35; and *idem*, "Alexandre VI et la réforme de l'église," *Mélanges d'archéologie et d'histoire*, XVII (1907), 65–124.
[26] Jedin, *op. cit.*, I, 121.
[27] Hughes, *op. cit.*, III, 386 ff., and H. O. Evennett, *The Spirit of the Counter-Reformation*, ed. John Bossy (Cambridge, 1968), pp. 103–5.

chapter in his *History of the Council of Trent*.[28] The Church was not without religious communities or prelates or zealous men and women who sought to live by the highest spiritual ideals. The Charterhouse of Cologne, the Augustinian Canons of Windesheim, Jean Gerson, chancellor of the University of Paris, the scholarly Cardinal Nicholas of Cusa, St. Antoninus, Archbishop of Florence, Thomas à Kempis, the great preacher St. Bernadino of Siena are but a few of the instances—notable ones, to be sure—the fifteenth century affords. And these are characterized not only by their own individual virtue and dedication but by the wider influence their labors bore. A movement broader than any single individual or community can also be cited as witnessing and in turn contributing to the religious renewal so needed at this time. This was the *Devotio moderna*, originating in the Netherlands and associated primarily with the Brothers of the Common Life and the congregation of Windesheim, but casting wide its net of inspiration and revival. It was, to quote Margaret Aston, "probably the most generative religious movement of the whole century," and it forms a major source of Catholic reform in the following era.[29]

The *Devotio moderna* was a spirit of personal piety, based above all on the following of Christ and the cultivation of a simple and fervent interior life. It centered its doctrine on Christ and the Gospels; it stressed meditation and methodic prayer; it aimed at a life of practical virtue. Gerard Groote of Deventer (1340–1384) was its father, and his life and preaching—*docuit sancte vivendo*—were the inspiration for two religious societies—the Brothers of the Common Life and the Canons Regular of Windesheim—that continued and expanded its spiritual ideals. Florence Radewijns was Groote's most important disciple and the actual founder in 1387 of the Windesheim congregation. A canon in the monastery of Mount St. Agnes near Zwolle, Thomas à Kempis, wrote (*c.* 1411) its most celebrated and characteristic work, *The Imitation of Christ*. From the end of the fourteenth century on, the influence of this new spirituality spread widely in Europe. Its schools and convents multiplied, and its writings circulated everywhere (more than 600 manuscripts and 55 printed editions of the *Imitation* date from the fifteenth century). Nicholas of Cusa and Erasmus were its pupils; Jacques Lefèvre and St. Ignatius Loyola came within its orbit.[30] There is no question that we are in the presence of a reform current of the utmost importance.

[28] Vol. I, Bk. I, Chap. VII.

[29] Margaret Aston, *The Fifteenth Century: The Prospect of Europe* (New York, 1968), p. 157; Evennett, *op. cit.*, pp. 9, 18, 33; and L.-E. Halkin, "La 'Devotio moderna' et les origines de la réforme aux Pays-bas," in *Courants religieux et humanisme à la fin du XVe et au début du XVIe siècle* (Paris, 1959), pp. 45–51. On the Devotio moderna, see Albert Hyma, *The Christian Renaissance, a History of the 'Devotio Moderna'* (2d ed.; Hamden, Conn., 1965); Jacob, *op. cit.*, Chaps. VII and VIII; R. R. Post, *The Modern Devotion* (Leiden, 1968); and *Dictionnaire de spiritualité*, III, cols. 727–47 (article *Dévotion moderne*, by Pierre Debongnie).

[30] On the very interesting question of the influence of the Devotio moderna on St. Ignatius Loyola, see I. Rodriguez-Grahit, "La Devotio moderna en Espagne et l'influence française," *Bibliothèque d'Humanisme et Renaissance*, XIX (1957), 489–95, and *idem*,

It is also frequently pointed out that the *Devotio moderna* represents, at least to some extent, a "lay" spirituality, an assertion of the layman's need for spiritual life and renewal in the face of an ecclesiasticism that had become decadent and corrupt.[31] Too much of a thesis or dichotomy should not be made of this, but there seems little reason to doubt that the *Devotio* does signalize a quest for a more personal religious experience on the part of laity and clergy alike as against the merely formal or traditional practices of piety and prayer. Evennett's judgment that "we see here the individualism of the age taking its appropriate form in Catholic spirituality" would seem to go the heart of its particular historical derivation and significance.[32] And at this juncture and in this sense we can also connect the *Devotio moderna* with other efforts toward personal sanctification and renewal during this time—with the revival preaching of St. Bernadino, St. John of Capistrano, and Savonarola, with lay confraternities like the Oratory of Divine Love, with the devout humanism of so many of the scholars of the Renaissance. The age itself served to stir the need, mold the shape, and impel the surge of religious reform.

Our reference to humanism brings us to another important movement, parallel to the *Devotio moderna*, different in character and spirit from it but nevertheless manifesting basic reform features and certainly contributory to actual Catholic reform in the sixteenth century. Humanism is the name given to the so-called classical revival in Renaissance Italy. There are controversies regarding its origins, nature, significance, and influence, but the view that it was a pagan or anti-Christian movement is no longer tenable.[33] Indeed a contrary evaluation seems much closer to the mark. As a literary and scholarly movement it bore from the beginning a very prominent ethical character and a lively awareness of the problem and task of reconciling an authentic classicism with Christian values and beliefs. In fact, there are signs that in its origin and impulse humanism was a profound regenerative movement within the context of the classical and Christian tradition, that it was, in short, what we can at least loosely call a reform.[34] Its emphasis on rhetoric or philology or

---

"Ignace de Loyola et le collège Montaigu. L'influence de Standonck sur Ignace," *ibid.,* XX (1958), 388–401. One of Evennett's main themes in *The Spirit of the Counter-Reformation* is this influence; see Chaps. II and III and John Bossy's comments in the Postscript, pp. 126–28.

[31] Aston, *op. cit.,* pp. 157–61. See also the closely related view in Friedrich Heer, *The Intellectual History of Europe,* trans. Jonathan Steinberg (2 vols.; New York, 1968), I, 260, 274–75.

[32] *Op. cit.,* p. 36.

[33] P. O. Kristeller, *Renaissance Thought* (New York, 1961), Chap. IV. On the interpretation of humanism, see William J. Bouwsma, *The Interpretation of Renaissance Humanism* (an A.H.A. pamphlet; Washington, 1959), and P. O. Kristeller, "Studies in Renaissance Humanism during the Last Twenty Years," *Studies in the Renaissance,* IX (1962), 7–30. On humanism, see also *idem, Renaissance Thought II* (New York, 1965); Eugenio Garin, *Italian Humanism,* trans. Peter Munz (New York, 1965); R. Weiss, *The Spread of Italian Humanism* (London, 1964); and A. Renaudet, "Autour d'une définition de l'humanisme," in his *Humanisme et renaissance* (Geneva, 1958), pp. 32–53.

[34] Garin lays great stress on this, as do Federico Chabod, *Machiavelli and the Renaissance,* trans. David Moore (London, 1958), pp. 191–95, and Heer, *op. cit.,* I, Chap. XII.

classical learning should not blind us to its deeper hopes and implications. The important humanists were convinced that the study of classical letters, the *studia humanitatis,* was the foundation for the education and development of the whole man, and they held this conviction as Christian scholars and Christian educators.[35] And they believed too that this heralded a new day, a return to a golden age.

In quite a different way humanism also had very great bearing on religious renewal and reform. This relates to its scholarly approach and method. The humanists sought to discover the authentic texts of the ancient classics, to read them in their original language, and to understand them in their original context and meaning. When this "return to the sources" together with the critical scholarship and the historical perspective such a "return" entailed were applied to the Christian classics, that is, to Holy Scripture and the early Fathers, the way was opened for a theological and religious reorientation, the dimensions of which encompass both Catholic and Protestant reform in the sixteenth century. "To be able to read the book of God in its genuine meaning is to be a genuine theologian."[36] This extension of classical humanism we are accustomed to call Christian humanism and to associate with the northern humanists—Colet, Erasmus, Lefèvre—but it must be remembered that biblical and patristic study was "a real and very extensive phenomenon" in the Italian Renaissance.[37] Lorenzo Valla's *Adnotationes in Novum Testamentum* (c. 1444), the first printing of which Erasmus arranged in 1505, Gianozzo Manetti's Latin translations of the New Testament and the Psalms (c. 1450?), and Pico della Mirandola's Genesis commentary called the *Heptaplus* (1489) are monuments to this scholarly endeavor. Nor must one forget the related contribution—indeed the life's work—of the great Florentine Platonist Marsilio Ficino (1433–1499), who sought to restore a *docta religio* in the guise of a Neoplatonic Christian theology.[38] His mission and purpose at least were primarily religious, apologetic, and reformative.

By the turn of the sixteenth century Renaissance humanism was beginning to have a galvanizing effect throughout Europe. *Ad fontes* was becoming more and more a guiding principle for those who sought religious renewal and reform, and the return to Scripture and the Fathers was seen as the means of reforming theology and revivifying Christian life. Erasmus is usually cited

[35] This seems clear enough from W. H. Woodward, *Vittorino da Feltre and Other Humanist Educators* (Cambridge, 1897; repr., New York, 1963).

[36] Garin, *op. cit.,* pp. 70–71. On scriptural humanism in its late medieval and Reformation context, see Werner Schwarz, *Principles and Problems of Biblical Translation* (Cambridge, 1955), and Henri de Lubac, S.J., *Exégèse médiévale,* Second Part, II (Paris, 1964), Chap. X.

[37] P. O. Kristeller, *Le Thomisme et la pensée italienne de la renaissance* (Montreal, 1967), pp. 65–66. See also Raymond Marcel, "Les perspectives de l'apologétique de Lorenzo Valla à Savonarole," in *Courants religieux et humanisme à la fin du XVe et au début du XVIe siècle* (Paris, 1959), pp. 83–100, and E. Harris Harbison, *The Christian Scholar in the Age of the Reformation* (New York, 1956), Chap. II.

[38] Kristeller, *Renaissance Thought II,* Chaps. IV and V; Garin, *op. cit.,* pp. 88–100; and Nesca A. Robb, *Neoplatonism of the Italian Renaissance* (London, 1935), Chap. III.

as the leader and exemplar of this European-wide humanist reform move-ment.[39] There is no need to challenge his preeminence in this regard, but it should be pointed out that just as Erasmus was not the first to move in this direction, so humanism's influence on reform can be observed in many other instances and in many diverse ways. Not a few of the documents in this volume bear this out, though they do not by any means exhaust the subject. Its spectrum is vast indeed, and Protestant reform as well as Catholic reform comes within its range.[40] There is, however, a striking example which we have not otherwise recorded of actual reform within the Church in the early sixteenth century closely associated with the expansion of humanism. This is the undertaking and achievement of the great Cardinal of Spain, Francisco Ximenes de Cisneros (1436–1517).

From 1495 on, this remarkable man, the most important figure perhaps in the reign of Ferdinand and Isabella, held the primatial see of Toledo.[41] From that post and in close cooperation with the Catholic monarchs he pursued the task of reforming the Spanish Church and restoring its discipline and spiritual zeal. In his synods of Alcalá (1497) and Talavera (1498) he set down the program his priests must follow in their own consecrated lives and in preaching the Gospel and caring for the souls entrusted to them.[42] Soon afterward he founded the University of Alcalá—the original college of San Ildefonso was opened in 1508—for the education of a clergy who would constitute, in the words of Bataillon, "the cadres of a Church more worthy of Christ."[43] Alcalá was from the start the center of humanism in Spain. The greatest humanist scholars were invited there; the three languages—Latin, Greek, and Hebrew—were studied; Scripture and the Fathers as well as the pagan classics were engaged, though there were also chairs in Thomist, Scotist, and Nominalist theology. Unquestionably the crown of this enterprise was the preparation of the famous Complutensian polyglot Bible by the scholars Ximenes had gathered at Alcalá. Begun in 1502 under the Cardinal's direction and printed in the years from 1514 to 1517, its six large volumes are "the greatest achievement of early Spanish humanism."[44] They are also a witness

[39] See Chap. VI infra.

[40] For an introduction to at least part of that spectrum, see Lewis W. Spitz, The Religious Renaissance of the German Humanists (Cambridge, Mass., 1963), and Alain Dufour, "Humanisme et Réformation," in Histoire politique et psychologie historique (Geneva, 1966), pp. 37–62.

[41] The major study is L. Fernandez de Retana, Cisneros y su siglo (2 vols.; Madrid, 1929–30). There are several works in English, including Reginald Merton, Cardinal Ximenes and the Making of Spain (London, 1934), and Walter Starkie, Grand Inquisitor (London, 1940). Marcel Bataillon, Erasme et l'Espagne (Paris, 1937), Chap. I, is devoted to Ximenes' reforms. On the role of Ximenes and the development of a "Spanish thesis" concerning the origins of the Catholic Reformation, see the discussion in Evennett, op. cit., Chap. I.

[42] Cisneros, Sinodo de Talavera (Madrid, 1908). The parallel with Giberti's regulations at Verona (see Chap. XI infra) is striking.

[43] Bataillon, op. cit., p. 14.

[44] The New Cambridge Modern History, Vol. I: The Renaissance, 1493–1520 (Cambridge, 1964), p. 124.

of the orientation and the increasing momentum of the early Catholic Reformation.

There was much amiss within the Church and within Christendom at the close of the Middle Ages. There was serious and urgent need for religious reform. But there were attempts also to achieve it in various places and in various ways. These efforts in turn form the background—the preliminaries, so to speak—of the movement we seek to document in the pages that follow. A most serious crisis within the Church, however, was destined soon to intervene. Involving basic questions of doctrine, practice, and authority, this severe trial was to put in jeopardy the very life of the existing Catholic Church. Needless to say, it had major, nay decisive, effect on the course of reform in the Catholic Church. The pattern of that reform nevertheless had been indicated, the foundations laid.

THE CATHOLIC REFORMATION
Savonarola to Ignatius Loyola

CHAPTER I

Savonarola on the Renovation of the Church, 1495

Girolamo Savonarola stands as a great prophetic figure on the eve of the religious crisis of the sixteenth century. Calling for repentance and reform in an age of moral decadence and ecclesiastical corruption, this charismatic preacher announced the imminent judgment of God on a sinful world. His life and his message are intimately bound up with the circumstances of the Italy of his day, but they also have a universal significance, as is clear from the sermon on the renovation of the Church that is presented here. "Had his voice been listened to," writes Roberto Ridolfi, "perhaps beyond the Alps Luther would not have arisen, or his influence would have been less; and Reform, of which every Christian heart felt the need, would then have been born in the very bosom of the Church of Rome."[1]

Savonarola was of a prominent family of Ferrara, where he was born in 1452. A serious student, his mind was turned to religion and the sad plight of the Church from his adolescence. He entered the Dominican Order at Bologna in 1475 against the wishes of his parents, and he soon won distinction as a fervent and learned friar and a forceful and inspired preacher. He was first in Florence, "the city of his destiny," from 1482 to 1484, and he returned there, to the convent of San Marco, for the final, dramatic eight years of his life in 1490. He became Prior of San Marco in 1491, began preaching in the Duomo that same year the great sermons that were the instrument of his influence and power, and rose meteorlike to a dominance in the city few others ever attained.

This dominance coincided with events—the death of Lorenzo the Magnificent in 1492, the invasion of Italy by Charles VIII of France in 1494, the ensuing downfall of the Medici—that were both the occasion for his leadership and the apparent vindication of prophecies he had made.[2] The fateful French in-

---

[1] Roberto Ridolfi, *The Life of Girolamo Savonarola*, trans. Cecil Grayson (New York, 1959), p. 272. Ridolfi's is the best life in English. The older biography of Pasquale Villari, *Life and Times of Girolamo Savonarola*, trans. Linda Villari (London, 1896), is still a most useful and exciting work. For a selection of Savonarola's sermons and writings, see Savonarola, *Prediche e scritti*, ed. Mario Ferrara (2 vols.; Florence, 1952). For further bibliography, consult Mario Ferrara, *Bibliografia savonaroliana* (Florence, 1958).

[2] Guicciardini, in his *History of Florence*, gives a vivid account of his rise and the role he played at this critical time. Guicciardini, *History of Italy and History of Florence*, trans. Cecil Grayson, ed. John R. Hale (New York, 1964), pp. 34–38, 47–50. On

2. Savonarola preaching in the Duomo at Florence and writing in his cell at the convent of San Marco.

vasion he saw as the scourge of God that must precede the eventual renewal and reform of the Church. The political implications of his preaching and his role in the great Renaissance city soon led to opposition, and this, even more than his lashing out at clerical and papal wickedness, provoked his excommunication in 1497. The climactic act in his life's drama is his contest with the notorious Borgia Pope then reigning, Alexander VI (1492–1503), whose immoral life stands in startling contrast to that of the saintly friar.[3] Defiant of this Pope and overcome by his enemies at home, he was arrested, tried, and brought to the scaffold in the spring of 1498. "The wicked were stronger than the good," to quote the contemporary judgment of Luca Landucci.[4]

Despite the political circumstances that involved him, Savonarola was an authentic religious reformer, whose deep spirituality was rooted in the great ascetical and theological tradition and whose consuming aim was the revival of Christian virtue and the renewal of Christian life. "He can be viewed," writes Joseph Lortz, "as the expression or the incarnation of the best attempts at reform in the fifteenth century."[5] His mission profoundly engaged him; it was of and for his times, though the life that sustained it and the ideals that inspired it are ageless in their Christian relevance. Such indeed is suggested by Guicciardini's moving appraisal of the fallen prophet in his History of Florence. "Those who long observed his life and habits," he tells us, "found in them not the slightest trace of avarice or lust or any other sort of greed or weakness; on the contrary they saw in him a most religious life, full of charity and prayer and strict observance not of the outward forms of religion but of its very essence."[6] He was brought to the scaffold and his body was burned and destroyed, but the memory of his life and the impact of his words by no means disappeared.

The following sermon, "On the Renovation of the Church," is one of Savonarola's most famous addresses.[7] It was delivered in the Duomo in Florence on January 13, 1495, shortly after the fall of the Medici regime and at the height of the friar's predominance. It was immediately printed in pamphlet form, the first of Savonarola's sermons to be thus circulated.

---

the prophetic message of Savonarola, see Donald Weinstein, "Savonarola, Florence, and the Millenarian Tradition," *Church History*, XXVII (1958), 291–305.

[3] Accademia d'Oropa, *Alessandro VI e Savonarola, Brevi e lettere* (Turin, 1950). See also the interesting analysis and the judgment sustaining Savonarola of Charles Journet, now Cardinal Journet, in his edition of two meditations of Savonarola on the Psalms, *Dernière méditation de Savonarole* (Brussels, 1961), pp. 111–28.

[4] Luca Landucci, *A Florentine Diary from 1450 to 1516*, trans. A. de R. Jervis (London, 1927), p. 101.

[5] Joseph Lortz, *The Reformation: A Problem for Today*, trans. John C. Dwyer (Westminster, Md., 1964), p. 167.

[6] Guicciardini, *op. cit.*, p. 80.

[7] The original Italian text, slightly abridged, is in Savonarola, *Prediche e scritti*, I, 237–63. This English translation, the first to be published, as far as the editor is aware, was made by Alfred E. Vecchio.

OUR INTENTION this morning is to repeat everything that we have been saying and preaching in Florence these past years about the renovation of the Church, which, to be sure, will soon take place. We shall repeat this, so that those who have not heard it in the past may understand and know that the renovation will come about with certainty and dispatch; so that those who have heard it and are listening this morning may be confirmed; so that those who neither have believed nor do believe may be converted; and so that those who do not want to believe and who still remain stubborn may at least remain confused and bewildered by the reasons I shall give. . . .

Come, brother, what is it that you want to say by this? The things that you predicted four years ago, where did you get them? There is no need to tell you that, because your mind is not prepared for understanding it. I have made it very clear to a few, one or two at the most, of my closest friends. But I must make it very clear to you so that you do not think that I am mad and that I act without reason. I, too, in the past would ridicule these things; but God permitted this in me, so that I may be compassionate towards you when you would not believe them. But you must in truth believe, because those things about which I predicted and preached to you have to a great extent and to this very day come about. I tell you that the rest will come true, that not one iota will fail to come true: and I am more certain of it than you are that two and two make four, and I am more certain of it than I am of touching the wood of this pulpit, because that light [of prophetic inspiration] is more certain than the sense of touch. But I want you to understand well that this light, however, does not justify me. Balaam prophesied that, despite his possession of this light, he was nevertheless a sinner and a wretch.[8] But I tell you, Florence, that this light was given me for you and not for me, because this light does not justify

[8] Numbers 22–24.

man before God. And I want you to know that I began seeing these things already more than fifteen years ago, perhaps twenty; but I began telling of them in the past ten years. First, when I preached to you at Brescia I began to tell you something[9]; after that God permitted that I come to Florence, which is the navel of Italy, so that you may give the news to all the other cities of Italy.

But you, Florence, heard with your ears not me but God, whereas other Italians always heard the words of others; and, therefore, you, Florence, will not have the slightest excuse, if you do not mend your ways. Believe me, Florence, that it is not me but God who is saying these things. You can understand this, for you have heard how many people were on the wrong path and returned to repent; and believe that this result could not have been wrought by a poor little friar, if God were not in him. Believe it then, Florence, and change your ways, and do not believe that your flagellation is ended, for I see the sword behind it. The stone by its nature must fall and does not know it; the swallow makes its nest of dirt and does not know why, but does this because of natural instinct and does not know the reason why it functions in this way. But man is led by a free will. Yet there have been some who because of their simplicity predicted many things and did not know the reason why. And there have been some others who predicted many things not out of simplicity, but have known the reason why. Therefore, in whatever of these two ways you want to say a thing can be predicted, I have predicted it for you: that all of Italy must be turned upside down, Rome as well, and then the Church must be renewed. But you do not believe! You should believe, however, for God has said it to you rather than I.

Now, let us begin with the reasons that I have cited to you in the several years that have passed until now, which demonstrate and prove the renovation of the Church. Some of the reasons are probable and can be contradicted; some are demonstrable and cannot be contradicted, for they are based on Holy Scripture.

The first is *propter pollutionem praelatorum* [because of the pollution of the prelates]. When you see a good head, you know that the body is well; when the head is wicked, woe to that body. However, when God permits that there be at the head of government ambition, lust and other vices, believe that God's flagellation is near. . . . Therefore, when you see that God permits the heads of the Church to be weighed down by evils and simonies, say that the flagellation of the people is near. I am not saying that this condition is found in the heads of the Church, but I am saying "when you will see it."

The second is because of the assumption [i.e. the death] of the good and the just. Every time that God takes away saints and good people, say that the flagellation is near. . . . Behold the number of men that can be found today who can be called just and good! Say, therefore, that the flagellation is near, and that the wrath and the sword of God are in motion.

The third is *per exclusionem iustorum* [through the exclusion of the just].

[9] See Ridolfi, *op. cit.*, pp. 26–27.

When you see that some lord or head of government does not want good and just men near him, but drives them away, because he does not want to hear the truth, say that the flagellation of God is near.

The fourth is *propter desiderium iustorum* [because of the desire of the just]. When you see that all good men desire and call for the flagellation, believe that it is soon to come. See whether there is anyone today whom you think is calling for the flagellation! And believe me, Florence, that your punishment would have already come, were it not for the prayers and sermons of the good. Believe me, today you would have been a garden.

The fifth is *propter obstinationem peccatorum* [because of the stubbornness of sinners]. When sinners are stubborn and do not want to turn to God and do not value or appreciate those who call them to lead good lives, but always proceed from bad to worse and are obstinate in their vices, say that God is angry. And yet, Florence, wait for the flagellation, for you know how long it has been said to you that you should mend your ways, and you have always been obstinate. And it has also been said to you, Rome, and you too remain obstinate; yet you wait for God's anger.

The sixth is *propter multitudinem peccatorum* [because of the multitude of sinners]. It was because of David's pride that the plague was sent. See if Rome is full of pride, lust, avarice, and simony! See if in Rome the wicked are not always multiplying! And then say that the flagellation is near and that the renovation of the Church is near.

The seventh is *propter excussionem primorum, scilicet, charitatis et fidei* [because of the driving out of the chief virtues, that is to say, charity and faith]. In the time of the primitive Church one lived only with complete faith and complete charity. Look, how many there are in the world today who live thus! You, Florence, also seek your ambition, and everyone exalts himself. Believe, there is no cure except in repentance, for the flagellation of God is near.

The eighth is *propter negationem credendorum* [because of the denial of the articles of faith]. Look, today it seems as though no one believes and has faith, and everyone says: "What will happen afterwards?"

The ninth is *propter perditum cultum divinum* [because of the ruin of sacred worship]. Go, see what is done for the churches of God and what devotion is there, for the worship of God seems and is today lost. You will say: "Oh, there are so many religious and so many prelates, more than there have ever been!" Would that there were fewer of them! O tonsured ones, tonsured ones! *per te orta est haec tempestas* [through you this tempest has arisen]! You are the cause of all this evil! And nowadays everyone thinks he is holy, if he has a priest in his house; and I say to you that the time will come when it will be said: "Blessed is that house that does not have a shaved head!"

The tenth is *propter universalem opinionem* [because of universal opinion]. Look at everyone who seems to be preaching and waiting for the flagellation and the tribulations; and to each one it seems that it is a just thing that the punishment of so many iniquities must come. The abbot Joachim and many others preach and announce that this flagellation is to come at this time.[10]

It is for these reasons that I have preached the renovation of the Church. Now let us speak of examples [from Scripture] that demonstrate it. . . .

The second example that I spoke to you about was that one when it was prohibited in Jerusalem that no arms be kept for whatever reason and no smith could make any arms.[11] Even the goading of the oxen had to cease. The smith who always stands at the fire represents the fire of charity which must always exist and burn within us; the striking hammer represents continuous prayer which must always reach God. *Pulsate et aperietur vobis* [Knock and it shall be opened to you].[12] The goading which ceased was philosophy which no longer has a strong sting, as does the science of Sacred Scripture. And there came, however, King Nebuchadnezzar, and he cruelly flagellated that people who were not armed, that is, who had not charity. This also will soon happen to the Church, in which has remained not an iota of charity. . . .

So much for these examples.

Now I shall speak to you of the parables which signify the renovation of the Church.

The first parable is about a citizen who has a farm in which there are two pieces of land, one adjoining the other. One of them is full of stones, thorns and weeds, and of everything else that does not bear fruit. That citizen does not plow or cultivate this field; the other field he plows and cultivates every year, and he tends it with every care because it looks like land good enough to produce fruit. Nevertheless he sees that that which looks like good land produces little or no fruit. What do you think that this citizen will do who owns these two fields? Certainly, if he is prudent, he will take all those stones and thorns that are in the first field and throw all of them in that other field, and he will begin to plow and cultivate this other field. The citizen is Christ who became a citizen, that is, a man similar to you who has a rocky and thorny field, that is, a land of infidels full of hardness similar to stones and heresies similar to thorns, and He also has the other field, that is, a land of Christians which He has cultivated until now, but which nevertheless does not bear fruit at all. He will, however, convert the infidels and will sow in that land His law, and this land that He has cultivated so much He will abandon, and it will be left full of heresies.

Therefore, the renovation of the Church will come about, and many who are present here at this sermon will see it.

The second parable. A fig-tree was planted which in the first year bore

[10] Joachim of Flora (d. 1202), a Calabrian monk, announced a prophetic-historical vision which foretold the coming of a new age of the Holy Spirit. His doctrine was later adopted and more definitely applied by the Spiritual Franciscans.
[11] I Kings 13, 19–22.
[12] Matthew 7, 7.

many figs without a single leaf, the second year it again bore many figs and a few leaves but very few, the third year it bore as many figs as it did leaves, the fourth year it bore more leaves than figs, the fifth year it bore very few figs and very many leaves, and so it came about that it bore nothing but leaves, so that not only did it not produce fruit, but moreover because of its many leaves it overshadowed other plants so that they could not grow. What do you think the gardener should do with this fig-tree? Certainly he will cut it down and throw it into the fire. This fig-tree is the tree of the Church, which, though in the beginning it bore an abundance of fruit and no leaves, nevertheless is at the point today where it bears no fruit at all, but only leaves, that is, ceremonies and shows and superfluities whereby it overshadows the other plants of the earth—which means that the prelates of the Church because of their bad example are responsible for other men falling into very many sins. The gardener will come, that is, Christ, and will cut down this fig-tree which is fruitless. Therefore, the Church will renew itself.

The third parable. There was a king who had an only son. He came upon a poor, ragged woman, spattered with mud. Moved to compassion he took her and brought her into his house, and made her his lawful bride, and had two daughters by her whom he gave in marriage to his only begotten son. This king's wife, having lived thus for some time, began falling in love and creating a great deal of trouble with commoners and servants. The king came to know of it, and he took her and cast her out, returning her to poverty and to mud, as she had been at first. Afterwards one of her daughters began to sin in ways similar to her mother's and even worse, whereby the angry king sent her away, and drove her from himself and from his son, and ordered that no bread be given to her. The other daughter, not admonished by the sin and the punishment of her mother and her sister, began to sin in a like manner and was even worse than her mother and her sister had been. Tell me, what does this one deserve? Certainly, she deserves much more punishment than the mother and the sister.

I would like now to expound on this parable. This king is God, who took that poor woman for His bride, that is, the synagogue of the Jews for His Church, which sinned; and you know how God drove her away from Him and sent her back into the mud where she first had been, that is, He placed her in servitude and misery and her original blindness. The two daughters are the Church of the East, of the Greeks, and the Roman Church, given as brides by God to His only begotten son Christ Jesus crucified, in which we must serve. The Church of the East sinned because of its heresies, and God ordered that she be banished from Him and from His Son Christ Jesus, and commanded that no bread be given her, that no preachers go there anymore, that none give her spiritual food or enlighten her. The other Church is the Roman one, full of simony and evils, which has sinned more than the first or the second. What do you think that she deserves? Do you not think that God wants to punish her? Of course you think so, and even more harshly than the mother and the sister, for they might justly complain to God saying: "If we have sinned, you have made us penitent, but this other one who has sinned more than we; why do you not punish her?" However, believe that the Church will soon be renewed.

These parables given, we shall now speak of how much of the renovation of the Church we have seen, how we have come to know and predict it. But in order that you may understand better, be informed that there are two ways by which we come to know a thing: the first is when we know by some exterior sign what that sign intrinsically signifies, the second is through visions [per immaginazione].

As for the first, when Pope Innocent died,[13] an event occurred which made you laugh at my actions, for I had said that the Church had to be renewed, and you thought that because of that sign [i.e., the death of the Pope] I was in great error and what I had predicted could not come about; but I saw by that exterior sign that the Church had to be renewed completely, and I based opinions upon what you were saying, which was against me.

As for the second, which is visionary, I saw in a vision a black cross above the Babylon that is Rome, upon which was written: Ira Domini [Wrath of the Lord]; and upon this cross there rained swords, knives, lances and every kind of weapon, and a tempest of hailstones and rocks, and awesome and very great flashes of lightning, and the atmosphere was very dark and gloomy. And I saw another cross of gold over Jerusalem, which reached from heaven to earth, upon which was written: Misericordia Dei [Mercy of God]; and here the atmosphere was serene, very bright, and clear. Wherefore, because of this vision, I say to you that the Church of God must be renewed and soon, because God is angry; and moreover the infidels are to be converted, and it will be soon.

Another vision. I saw a sword poised above Italy, and it was quivering; and I saw angels who were coming and held the red cross in one hand and many white stoles, and they held in the other hand a chalice full to the top of sweet and good wine, but at the bottom there was a residue most bitter like gall.[14] These angels gave this red cross to everyone to kiss and handed out the white stoles. There were some who took these stoles, some who wanted them, some who not only did not want them but encouraged others not to take them. Afterwards these angels offered the chalice to each one, and those who had willingly taken the stoles willingly drank of the wine which on top was sweet, and they delighted in the taste. They gave to the others the very bitter residue, and these did not want to drink any of it, but were repelled by it. Suddenly I saw that sword, which was quivering above Italy, turn its tip downward and with great violence and calamity strike among them, and it scourged everyone. But those who had accepted the white stoles felt this flagellation less and drank the sweet wine; those others perforce drank the very bitter residue

[13] Innocent VIII died on July 25, 1492.
[14] This vision comprises various elements drawn from the Apocalypse. Savonarola first described this vision in Advent, 1492.

and during the flagellation implored the others to give them the stoles, but these did not want to give them, saying that it was not the time.

I shall explain to you this vision. The quivering sword (I wish to tell you, Florence) is the sword of the King of France, which is showing itself to all of Italy.[15] The angels with the red cross and the white stoles and the chalice are preachers announcing this flagellation, and they give you the red cross to kiss, which is the passion of martyrdom, in order that you may sustain this flagellation which must come about for the renovation of the Church. The stole signifies the purification of her conscience and her cleansing from every vice; white signifies purity. The chalice, filled to the top with good wine, signifies the passion, which requires that every man drink of it. But those who have taken the stoles and cleansed their consciences will drink the sweet wine, that is, they will feel little of this flagellation, because of the sweet wine at the top of the chalice; for they shall be the first to be flagellated, but it will be sweet because they will suffer it willingly, patiently, and, if they were to die, they shall enter eternal life. Those others will barely be able to drink that very bitter residue, because it will seem to them bitter as it certainly is. And this sword has not yet turned its tip downward, but will go about showing itself throughout all of Italy, because God still waits for you to repent. Convert, Florence, for there is no other cure but repentance. Put on the white stole while there is time and do not wait any longer, for then you will have no opportunity to repent.

Now we shall speak of this renovation in terms of the intellect [i.e., in terms of its being intellectually understood]; and this comes in two ways. I first spoke of this renovation in "formal" and in "non-formal" words. The "formal" words which I spoke to you, know that I did not derive them from Scripture, nor find them in any place, nor did I make them up out of my own head, nor did I receive them from anyone come from heaven to earth, but from God. I cannot make it clearer to you. Understand me, Florence, God speaks these words:

> Rejoice and exult, you just. Nevertheless prepare yourselves for trials, reading, meditation and prayer, and you shall be freed from the second death. And you wicked servants who are in filth, be filthy still. Let your belly be filled with wine, your loins be broken by luxury, and your hands defiled with the blood of the poor. For this is your portion, and this your fate. But know that your bodies and your souls are in my hands, and after a brief time your bodies will be consumed by the scourge, and I shall hand over your souls to the everlasting fire. Listen, all you who inhabit the earth, says the Lord. I the Lord speak in my holy zeal. Behold, the days will come, and I shall unsheath

---

[15] Charles VIII of France, in pursuit of claims to the Kingdom of Naples, began his invasion of Italy in September, 1494. His armies wheeling south entered Tuscany and occupied Pisa and Florence in November. His arrival involved the downfall of the Medici and the rise to great prominence in Florence of Savonarola, who had prophesied his coming and viewed his mission as providential. After taking Naples in early 1495, Charles was soon forced to withdraw from Italy, but his invasion marks the beginning of long years of strife and disorder in the Italian peninsula.

my sword above you. Therefore turn to me before my fury is fulfilled, for then when anguish comes you shall seek peace, but there will be none.[16]

As for the words that are "non-formal," remember when I told you three years ago already that there will come a wind similar to that represented in the story of Elias,[17] and that this wind will shake mountains. This wind has come, and this has been the news that spread last year throughout Italy, and it was said of this King of France. And this news spread everywhere flying like the wind, and shook mountains, that is the princes of Italy, and has kept everything this year in a state of agitation, not knowing whether this King was to come. And behold he has come! You said: "He'll not come. He doesn't have a cavalry. It is winter." And I, who knew how this matter was to turn out, would laugh at you. And behold he has come, and God changed winter into summer, as I told you at that time.

Remember too that I said to you that God would cross to the other side of the mountains and would take him [the King of France] by the bridle reins and would lead him to this side in spite of and against the opinion of everyone. And behold he has come!

Remember too that I said to you that those great fortresses and great walls would be of no value. See if it has all come true! Tell me, Florence, where are your fortresses? Of what value have your walls of stone been to you?

Remember too that I said to you that your wisdom and your prudence would avail you nothing, and you would take everything wrongly, that is, in a contrary way, and like a drunkard out of his senses, you would not know what to do or what was happening to you. And he has now come, and it is verified; and you never wanted to believe me, and you still do not believe! I say to you, obstinate ones, you will not even believe the rest of it, because God does not want to give you the grace to believe, because your obstinacy does not merit it.

Remember that at times, already three or four years ago, when I preached to you, I had so much breath and so much fervor and so much ardor in speaking that it was wondered that I did not burst a vein in my breast. You did not know why, my sons. It was the only way it could be done.

Remember Lazarus Sunday—three years have already passed—when lightning struck the cupola, remember what I said to you that morning, that I could not rest at all that night, and that I wanted to pick up the Gospel of Lazarus and give a sermon on it, and that it was never possible for me to grasp it imaginatively, and that at the time these words came from my mouth: *Ecce gladius Domini super terram cito et velociter* [Behold the sword of the Lord to come over the earth soon and swiftly]. Then I preached to you that morning and told you that the wrath of God was stirred and that the sword was ready and near at hand. Again I say it to you. You must believe.

Remember too that three years have passed since I began to lecture upon Genesis, and at that time I did not know the reason, but I did everything to

[16] The above passage paraphrases several scriptural texts and is in Latin in Savonarola's sermon.
[17] IV Kings 2, 11: "And Elias went up by a whirlwind into heaven."

renew the old a little. And when we got to the flood, it was not possible to proceed further, so abundant was the material. Later I had to go to preach elsewhere. Then, Lent having ended, I began where I had left off at the flood; and I started to comment upon the Ark, thinking I could finish it in a short time. The material was so rich that I could not finish it for that Lent. And having now taken it up again, I could not finish it, because I had to go to Pisa to the King of France for you,[18] and there remained two sermons in order to complete it and bring it to a close. As soon as this was finished, remember that the flood came and on that day this land was turned upside down by the French. I wish to infer this [from the delay in completing the sermons on the flood]: this was a divine work and mystery and not something ordered or prepared by me. Certainly you must really believe, Florence, and you should not want to be so stubborn in your incredulity.

Remember too that I had told you in the past that I was like a father toward you, and God was the mother, for I had reproached you bitterly and sharply and shouted in a loud voice so that you might mend your ways, as does that father who diligently reproaches his son, and that I wished now to be the mother and God wished to be the father. Since the mother, when she sees her son go astray, threatens him and shouts at him and tells him that she will speak to his father as soon as he comes and will have him punished. Afterwards, when the father has come, she does not accuse her son, but says: "If you ever again fall into bad ways, I will have your father punish you." Thus, even though I reproach you now, I do not reproach you with that vehemence and harshness as I did in the past, because I see that the father, that is, God, has come to punish. And so I say to you and plead with you in a humble and low voice: my little children, do penance!

Remember too, Florence, that I said to you that I gave you an apple, as a mother does when she gives an apple to her son when he cries in order to comfort him; but then when he continues to cry further and she cannot soothe him, she takes the apple away and gives it to another son. Thus I say to you, Florence: God gave you the apple, that is, He elected you to be His own. If you do not want to repent and be converted to God, He will take the apple from you and give it to another. This will come true, as true as I am standing here! Therefore, Florence, do these four things that I have told you,[19] and I promise you that you will be richer than ever, more glorious than ever, more powerful than ever.

But no one today believes that angels participate in the affairs of men and converse with them, or that God speaks to any man. But I say to you that *similitudo est causa amoris*, that is, similarity is the cause of friendship.[20] Therefore the more we draw near to God and to the angels through faith and charity, all the more are we friends of God and of His angels; and they

---

[18] Savonarola was a member of an embassy sent to Pisa in early November, 1494, by the Florentines to negotiate with Charles VIII.

[19] This apparently is a reference to the four reasons Savonarola gives for speaking at the very beginning of his sermon.

[20] St. Thomas Aquinas, *Summa Theologica*, I, 27, 4: "*similitudo est principium amandi.*"

talk and converse with us. I am not saying by this, nor have I ever said, that God talks to me. I say neither yes nor no. You are so far from faith that you do not believe. You would sooner believe some demon who spoke with men and who foretold future things. You are senseless and without faith. Tell me, if you believe that Christ became flesh of the Virgin Mary and that He was crucified, which is more difficult to believe than this [i.e., that God speaks to men], you should also believe even more what is easier, that is, that Christ speaks to men.

Besides, if you are Christian, you have to believe that the Church must be renewed. Daniel says that the Antichrist must come and persecute the Christians there in Jerusalem.[21] Therefore, it is necessary that those who are there be baptized and be Christians. But for this to be other men are needed than there are today. The Church, therefore, must be renewed, so that men become good and go there to convert the infidels to Christianity. Go, read the doctors on that Gospel by Matthew, where he says: "This gospel shall be preached in the whole world, and then will come the end."[22] Believe me, Florence! You should, of course, believe me, because you have not seen one iota fail up until now of what I have told you, nor will you in the future. I predicted several years ago the death of Lorenzo de' Medici, the death of Pope Innocent, also the recent event that has now occurred in Florence regarding the change of government. I also said that on that day the King of France would be in Pisa and that here [in Florence] the renovation of the state would take place. I did not say these things publicly from up here, but I am saying them to those who are present at this sermon, and I have witnesses here in Florence.

I know that this morning I am mad and that I am speaking all these things foolishly, but I want you to know that this light does not justify me, for only if I am humble and have charity will I be justified.[23] And this light was not given for me, nor because of my merit, but for you, Florence, was it given me. And therefore, Florence, this morning I have told you these things so openly, inspired by God to tell them to you in this way, so that you may know everything and will not have any excuse whatever when the flagellation comes and will not be able to say: "I did not know it!" I cannot speak more clearly; and I know that this morning I shall be taken for a madman, for many have come here to accuse me. If you say that I am mad, I shall be patient. I have spoken to you in this way because God wished that I speak to you thus.

From the time that I began this Apocalypse we have had much opposition: some of this you know, some God knows, some His angels know. We must struggle against the lukewarm and against the two-fold wisdom, that is, against the wisdom of the New and Old Testament, against the two-fold knowledge, against the philosophy and knowledge of Sacred Scripture,[24] against the two-

[21] Daniel 7, 19–25.
[22] Matthew 24, 14.
[23] Savonarola quotes and refers here to St. Paul's words in II Corinthians 11 and I Corinthians 13.
[24] These are allusions to the opposition of certain preachers and theologians who used Scripture against Savonarola, e.g., the Augustinian Marino da Gennazzano and the Dominican Tommaso da Rieti. See Villari, op. cit., pp. 133–35, 328–30.

fold evil, that is, against the evil which the lukewarm commit today and which those commit who know they are doing evil and want to do it. It was not this way in the time of Christ, because only the Old Testament existed; and if they went astray, they thought they were doing good. And therefore I say to you that, if Christ were to return down here again, He would again be crucified.

I say to you that I have revealed almost nothing, because I say to you that, if I were to reveal everything, it would take me at least six days. Believe me when I tell you that already I have been in danger of death several times.

I have said to you: *Gladius Domini cito et velociter super terram* [The sword of the Lord comes soon and swiftly over the earth]. Believe me that the knife of God will come and soon. And do not laugh at this word *cito* [soon] and do not say that it is a *cito* as used in the Apocalypse, which takes hundreds of years to come. Believe me that it will be soon. Believing does not harm you at all, as a matter of fact it benefits you, for it makes you turn to penance and makes you walk in God's way; and do not believe that it can harm you rather than benefit you. Therefore believe that it is soon, although the precise time cannot be given, for God does not wish it, so that his elect remain always in fear, in faith and in charity, and continually in the love of God. And so I have not told you the appointed time, in order that you may always do penance and always please God. For example, if I were to say to men: The tribulation is to come here in ten years, everyone would say: I can delay longer before I mend my ways; and it would be almost giving you the license to commit evil in the meantime; it would be harmful. And therefore God does not want the appointed time preached. But I tell you wholeheartedly that now is the time for penance. Do not laugh at this *cito* which I speak to you. If you do not do what I have told you, woe to Florence! Woe to the people! Woe to the man in the street! Woe to the aristocrat!

Lastly, I agree that this morning I have been a madman. You will say it, and I knew before I came up here that you would say it. God wanted it this way. Nevertheless I say to you in conclusion that God has prepared a great dinner for all Italy, but all the foods will be bitter, and He has served only the salad which consisted of a small quantity of bitter herbs. Understand me well, Florence: all the other foods are also to come, and they are all bitter, and the foods are to be many, for it is a great dinner. Therefore I conclude, and keep it in mind, that Italy is now at the beginning of her tribulations.

O Italy, O princes of Italy, O prelates of the Church, the wrath of God is over you, and you will not have any cure unless you mend your ways! *Et a sanctuario meo incipiam* [And I will begin at my sanctuary].[25] O Italy, O Florence, *propter peccata veniunt tibi adversa* [misfortunes befall you because of sins]! O noblemen, O powerful ones, O common people, *manus Domini est super vos et non resistet sapientiae potentia vel fuga* [the hand of the Lord is upon you and neither the power of wisdom nor flight may withstand it]! . . . O princes of Italy, flee from the land of the North![26] Do penance while the

[25] Ezekiel 9, 6.
[26] I.e. Babylon. Zechariah 2, 6.

sword is not out of its sheath and while it is not stained with blood! Flee from Rome! O Florence! Flee from Florence, that is, flee in order to do penance for your sins, and flee from wicked men!

The conclusion is this: I have said all these things to you with reasons divine and human and with modesty tempering my tongue. I have entreated you. I cannot command you, because I am not your lord, but your father. Do your part, Florence! I pray to God that He enlightens you, *cui est gloria et imperium per infinita saecula saeculorum.* Amen.

The Oratory of Divine Love, 1497

As the prophetic figure of Savonarola affords one example—a most dramatic one—of reform effort in the late fifteenth century, the religious confraternity known as the Oratory of Divine Love affords another. This confraternity was founded in Genoa in 1497 by a prominent layman, Ettore Vernazza, and three friends and had as its purpose the personal sanctification of its members through the faithful practice of their religious devotions and through works of charity and benevolence.[1] The goal and character of the Oratory identify it with many comparable associations in Italy during this time, notably the Oratory of St. Jerome founded at Vicenza in 1494 by the saintly Franciscan friar Bernadino da Feltre, and it can certainly be linked with the broad movement of religious revival stimulated by such effective preachers as St. Bernadino of Siena and St. John of Capistrano. Its particular inspiration, however, came from a remarkable Genoese woman, then superior of the hospital of Pammatone, Caterina Fieschi Adorno, whom we know as St. Catherine of Genoa. Vernazza was her disciple, and the Oratory's doctrine of divine love, leading men to the practice of charity and specifically the care of the sick, was drawn directly from her teaching and example.[2]

Sometime between 1514 and 1517 a branch of this Oratory was established in Rome—an event which Pastor and other historians have singled out as marking the beginning of effective Catholic reform in this troubled age.[3] The significance of the Roman Oratory, modeled on that at Genoa, is due not only to the time and place of its foundation, coming as it did on the eve of Luther's protest and

---

[1] On the Oratory see the article by Pio Paschini, "Amour (Compagnie du divin)," *Dictionnaire de spiritualité*, I (Paris, 1937), 531–33; the same author's *La Beneficenza in Italia e le "Compagnie del Divino Amore" nei primi decenni del cinquecento* (Rome, 1925); and A. Bianconi, *L'opera della Compagnie del Divino Amore nella riforma cattolica* (Citta di Castello, 1914).

[2] On St. Catherine of Genoa and her doctrine, see Pierre Pourrat, *Christian Spirituality*, trans. S. P. Jacques (4 vols.; London, 1927), II, 286–90, and III, 264–71. Pourrat sees a relationship between Renaissance Platonism and St. Catherine's doctrine of divine love (III, 234–35), a theme also explored in P. O. Kristeller, "Lay Religious Traditions and Florentine Platonism," *Studies in Renaissance Thought and Letters* (Rome, 1956), pp. 99–122, where an analogy is drawn between Ficino's Platonic Academy and confraternities like the Oratory. In both instances divine love is equated with charity and becomes the great spiritual bond.

[3] Ludwig Pastor, *The History of the Popes from the Close of the Middle Ages*, trans. F. I. Antrobus, R. F. Kerr, *et al.* (40 vols.; St. Louis, 1891–1953), X, 388–92. See also Hubert Jedin, *A History of the Council of Trent*, trans. Dom Ernest Graf (2 vols.; St. Louis, 1957–61), I, 146–47.

amid the corruption of Medicean Rome, but also to the quality of its membership, among whom several were to have careers of great importance in the work
of Catholic renewal. Vernazza apparently was also the organizer of the Roman
group which met regularly in the church of St. Dorothy in Trastevere and
engaged in various charitable works, including the maintenance of a hospital
for incurables. Its members numbered close to sixty and included Gaetano da
Thiene, a curial official, later canonized, and Gian Pietro Carafa, Bishop of
Chieti and papal diplomat, later to reign as Pope Paul IV.[4] Gaetano and
Carafa, together with two other members of the Roman Oratory, in 1524
founded the important Theatine Order, which rightly can be considered an
offshoot of the Oratory of Divine Love.[5]

There was a further expansion of the Oratory and its charitable work from
Rome into northern Italy after 1517—by Bartolomeo Stella to his native
Brescia and notably by Gaetano da Thiene to Vicenza, Verona, and Venice.
The influence of this development, merging with that of the Theatines, was
significant, and in its ambit are to be found in the 1520's and '30's many of the
major figures in Italy of the Catholic revival. The point of departure remains,
however, the Genoese confraternity, whose foundation St. Catherine of Genoa
had inspired back in 1497.

The following document is the original Chapters—or Rule—of the Genoese
Oratory.[6] It will be noted that the confraternity was predominantly a lay association and that its membership as well as their activities were to be kept
strictly secret.

---

[4] A 1524 list of the members of the Roman Oratory may be found in A. Cistellini,
Figure della riforma pretridentina (Brescia, 1948), pp. 282–83. It does not include the
names of Contarini, Giberti, or Sadoleto, who were previously thought to be members
of that confraternity, on the basis of a listing in A. Caracciolo, *De Vita Pauli IV*
(Cologne, 1612), p. 182.

[5] On the Theatines, see Chap. X.

[6] The manuscript text was discovered by the Jesuit scholar Pietro Tacchi Venturi in
the library of the University of Genoa and published in his *Storia della Compagnia di
Gesù in Italia* (2 vols.; Rome, 1910–22), I, 423–32. The English translation was made
from the original Italian by Alfeo Marzi. The comparable Chapters of the Roman Oratory may be found in Cistellini, *op. cit.*, pp. 273–77.

In the name of the Lord Jesus Christ here begin the Chapters of the Fraternity of Divine Love under the protection of St. Jerome.

BRETHREN, this our fraternity is not instituted for any other reason than to root and implant in our hearts divine love, that is to say, charity; and thus it is called the Fraternity of Divine Love. And this is so because charity does not proceed from other than the gentle look of God, who, if He looks upon us, looks upon those who are humble in heart, according to the saying of the prophet: "Whom do I regard if not the lowly and the man who trembles at my word?"[7] Thus let him who would be a brother in this company be humble of heart, to which humility tend all the customs and institutions of this fraternity; and let each direct his mind and hope toward God, placing in Him all his affection; otherwise he is a false brother and a hireling who would bring forth no fruit in this fraternity, which can bear no fruit other than that pertaining to the charity of God and of neighbor. And let this suffice for the title, and let it be understood at the outset that what is in the present Chapters or in others, if such be ordered in the future, is not binding under sin, above all mortal.

CHAPTER II: *Concerning the prior.*

And as in heaven there is one God and upon the earth one pastor, so it is convenient that among you there be one head to whom all members should show obedience, which person will be called father prior, and who will receive your paternal reverence with true obedience. He will hold office for six months only, at the end of which time he will be equal with the other brothers, and he may not before the end of one year and a half be prior nor hold other office. For this election let the greatest precaution be exercised with prayers that the Holy Spirit illumine you to elect that person who has the greatest confidence in God along with the other devout attributes of prudence; and let no one make bold to seek the vote of any of the brothers for himself or for others, and let

[7] Isaiah 66, 2.

the election be held as stated below. The brothers having been congregated on the first day of January and the day of St. Peter, the 28th of June, or on that day and hour which will please the father prior and his council, should it happen that this cannot be done on the appointed days, during which days let not the office be said, but, while the brothers are congregating, let them observe some few devotions; also let the Chapters be read and silence kept, and all at the discretion of the prior.

Let divine help be invoked first, saying the *Veni Creator Spiritus* with the prayer. Then let the syndic read all the names of the brothers who cannot be prior, and let them go to the altar, or where it may seem better to the old father prior, as well as to the eldest among those who cannot be prior; and, should it occur that there be none such in the fraternity, let the oldest priest accompany the prior, and let the brothers one at a time come to these two and give the name of that person whom he feels should be prior written on a ballot, and let the prior and his companion see all the ballots and pick the three names among them occurring most often, and let the prior announce these names to the brothers who will then come one at a time to give his vote to that one among the three whom he prefers; and, if the votes be equal, let the names be put in a biretta, and let the first taken out be prior. And, this being done, let it be known that he who has the greatest number of votes is prior, the other two counselors, and, should it happen that there are more than three who have most of the votes cast, let all the names with equal votes be taken up and put in a biretta, and let them be drawn by one of the brothers who has not seen them, and let the first three become prior and counselors.

The prior and counselors having been announced, let the *Te Deum laudamus* be devoutly said along with the prescribed verse and prayer. After this let the new prior and counselors kneeling before the altar be instructed by the old prior concerning the importance of the office which they hold, and then let the former prior approach the new, give the kiss of peace, and place in his hands the book of the present Chapters and the keys to the oratory, saying: "Thou shalt be watchful and diligent in the service of God." And then let him kneel before the altar in view of his brothers and accuse himself of the failures and negligences committed during his priorate. When the new prior has received the kiss of peace, the Chapters and the keys, let him sit in the place of the prior with his counselors on either side, and the old prior having declared his failings, let the new prior give him the penance of confessing himself within two weeks, and let the former prior from that day when he leaves office for a period of two months take the lowest place in the choir, but before the novices. And he cannot be prior who has been absent from the city or has not belonged to the fraternity for a year and a half.

Let the prior and counselors, with three assistants, elect that day all the other officials, and thus elected and on their knees before the altar may they all be advised by the prior of the importance of their several offices; these offices no one may refuse without the permission of those electing him, under pain of being deprived of our fraternity. And, this being accomplished, let the prior to the best of his ability encourage each one to observe the present Chapters and other honest and holy things. The counselors may not hold the same office before the termination of a year, but may be priors or hold other offices, and, should it happen that they [i.e., a former counselor] are among the three in the election of the prior, let him be prior, and let the counselors be elected by vote.

CHAPTER III: *Concerning the selection of the assistants and other officials.*

The first officials to be selected are three assistants to the counselors, and let it be carried out in this manner. Let all the brethren give one vote to his preference, and let those holding the most votes be the three assistants. And then let there be selected visitors to the infirm, who will be at the same time dispensers of alms, a syndic, a master of novices, and two stewards, all of whom are to be selected by the said prior, the counselors, and the three assistants by ballot.

CHAPTER IV: *Concerning the powers of the prior and the three assistants.*

The prior may call the brothers to the oratory outside the usual time, and may give penance in the saying of Pater Nosters and Psalms, or the making of pilgrimages up to two miles, or the paying of two *soldi* and a half per fault, or imposing any discipline upon whomever he chooses. And the counselors being absent, he may put in their place for that day whatever brother he chooses; and he has the power to tax them once a month, all the brothers, that is, or whomever he chooses, to the amount of three *soldi*, and this to meet the needs of the fraternity. The prior and the counselors may impose a pilgrimage up to five miles or a fine of five *soldi* for some misdeed. The prior and the counselors and the three assistants may do all regarding the fraternity, except sell or transfer any of the property *[beni immobili]*, or receive novices, or acquire a new oratory, or correct any of the present Chapters.

CHAPTER V: *Concerning the number of brethren and religious.*

And inasmuch as where there is a multitude there is confusion, the number of the brothers may not exceed thirty-six lay persons and four priests, unless some of the laity should become religious, and in such an eventuality the laity may include thirty-six, and the priests may stay until some should pass from this life. In the meantime let not the number of laymen who have become priests *[sacerdoti laici]* exceed four, and such a number may not be exceeded unless four-fifths of the brothers, being in the oratory, consent with white ballots.[8]

---

[8] Membership in the Roman Oratory was limited to sixty.

CHAPTER VI: *Concerning the duty of those who visit the infirm.*

And because it would be of little value to be brothers unless one performed the duty of brothers one to another, in spiritual as well as corporal things, "because the test of love is seen in action,"[9] whenever any one of our brothers is infirm, let the visitors, or one of them, graciously visit said brother and help him, above all spiritually, and also, if he is in want, let them provide for his needs at the expense of the fraternity; and being asked let them stay and help him throughout the night, providing doctor and medicines, and above all let them arrange for confession and communion as they would for themselves; and having to pay out let them do as they think best without permission; and let them ask of the brothers, in particular or in general, subsidy for the said brother who is poor and infirm, and, if they are not able to provide for such a necessity otherwise, let them with the consent of the prior sell and transfer movable goods of the fraternity; and finally let them with all diligence try to help him, above all spiritually, in that extreme pass. And beyond this duty the said visitors, or others in their stead, should dispense alms to the poor, especially to those of our fraternity, and for the needy let the assistance of the brothers be asked in particular.

CHAPTER VII: *Concerning the duty of stewards.*

Let the stewards be diligent in opening the oratory each time the brothers must congregate there, in lighting and extinguishing the candles, and in keeping the quarters of the oratory clean and ready, and let them be prompt in all things pertaining to their function.

CHAPTER VIII: *Concerning the office of syndic.*

The syndic will write, either on his own or with the help of others, the book of the fraternity, and keep in a part of the book a record of the monies he receives or pays out; in another part let him write the names of the brothers, and in still another the names of the priors and officials with their years and months of office, and in another the names of brothers who have passed from this life.

CHAPTER IX: *Concerning prayers, offices, and ceremonies.*

And since prayer and devotion is that which unites us with God and causes us to receive all graces, let all those brethren who wish to be earnest take comfort, when they arise in the morning, in turning their hearts to God and

---

[9] *"Quia probatio dilectionis exhibitio est operis,"* from St. Gregory the Great's *Homiliae in Evangelia,* in Migne, *Patrologia Latina,* LXXVI, 1220 c.

offering them up mentally and with great affection, begging Him that all day long He make them walk the path of His good will. And then every day, in memory of the seven canonical hours during which Christ our Lord suffered a cruel death for us, let them say with their heart and mouth seven times the Lord's Prayer and as many times the Angelic Salutation, and every time one goes to table let the Pater Noster and Ave Maria be said. And, when getting up from table, let them say the *Tu autem, Domine, miserere nostri,* and besides this every Monday let them say five Pater Nosters and five Ave Marias for the souls of the deceased brothers. And let these be the ordinary prayers that every one says at least each day. And then each Saturday or Friday or other day decided upon by the prior and counselors, and in addition the vigil of the Purification, the vigil of Pentecost, the vigil of the Assumption of Mary, the vigil of our glorious protector Saint Jerome, and the vigil of All Saints, let them be assembled in the oratory observing the practices prescribed by the Chapter [Chapter X] and saying the proper office. On Holy Thursday, following the meal, let the brethren congregate, and while they are meeting let devout things be read, and then let the washing of the feet take place with the ceremonies contained therein in the book of offices, or others, according to the wish of the prior; and then let the great matins be said and discipline carried out in the customary manner. And when any of our brother will depart from this life, let the office for the dead be said in the oratory on a day appointed by the prior, or at least the first nocturn for his soul; and let each of the priests say a mass for his soul, and let the other brothers say for twelve days the *Miserere* and the *De Profundis* and the *Deus in nomine* with three Pater Nosters and three Ave Marias, or let them put at least once one *soldo* in the treasury for his soul. Beyond which let each, as often as he can, make mention of our deceased brothers, and each year on the eve of All Saints let the brethren assemble in the oratory, and let the office of the dead be said there, or at least the first nocturn for their souls, and let each of the religious among us say a mass within eight days, and let the same be done during a day in Lent, according to the order of the prior. And the office over let all the names of the dead brothers be read, and let each answer: "*Requiescat in pace.*"

CHAPTER X: *Concerning good customs.*

Your fraternity cannot include men who either publicly or secretly lead an evil life, namely a life of concubinage, usury, injustice, blasphemy, and let no one among you gamble, nor stay to watch dice or cards, nor other prohibited games, nor at other licit ones through cupidity; and when in church divine offices are being sung, let no one of you go walking up and down or seek occasion to converse with each other more than is necessary in holy and honest places, always giving good example to each other and to whomever may see you. And in the oratory let each of you address his brother as sir [*mesere*], however inferior he may be in rank; and when learning that a certain brother is in sin, let each try to remove him from the same, and, being unable, let it be known to the prior who will take those steps which he feels necessary to save him. Let each in order to form good habits fast one day a week as he is able, and moreover on the vigil of Saint Jerome our protector or in exchange on the vigil of Saint Michael; I do not speak of [other] vigils and other appointed days, because I presuppose that each will observe the fast then. Let the appointed feasts be spent in spiritual labors, for they are ordained to this end. The other days let each hear Mass when he is able, or at least be present at the Elevation. The day that the brothers congregate let each brother as he enters the oratory, as he goes to seat himself, say *"Pax vobiscum"*; and when four or five will have come together let one of them read some devout passage, until such time as the prior appears, or whoever is sitting in his stead, and then let a sign be given, and let the reader remain and kneel before the prior, and, silence being kept, let the office begin.

And if any of the brothers arrives after the beginning of the office, let him stay kneeling in the midst of the assembly, and not move unless he has received a sign from the prior. And whoever comes after the first Psalm, let him proceed to the place of those who have committed a fault. The office over, let the candles be put out; and let the brother who has read the lesson of the day proceed to the altar and begin the lesson prescribed [for those who have committed faults] and say: *"Aprehendite disciplinam."* And let those brothers undergo discipline, while the other brother says the *Miserere* along with the customary verses and prayers, and let the prior respond according to his discretion and end the discipline. And let the brother while awaiting the prior's wish read something from the Passion. And then the *Nunc dimittis* will be sung, and when *"Lumen ad revelationem"* is heard, one of the stewards will bring forth the hidden light, and then let the hymn of the Sunday at hand be sung, or of the current festivities with verses and prayers corresponding to the feast days.

At the end of the office, the prior being at the altar, the syndic will read the inscribed verses, saying:

Who was not at the first Psalm go to the altar.
Who has failed to come to the oratory once or more.
Who has played at cards or dice, or against the rules.
Who has stayed to watch such forbidden games.
Who has not said the Pater Noster or the Ave Maria upon going to table, or upon rising the *Tu autem, Domine.*
Who has not said on Monday the five Pater Nosters and five Ave Marias for the dead brethren.
Who has not said every day seven Pater Nosters and seven Ave Marias for the seven canonical hours.
Who has not seen the Body of the Lord every day.
Who walked up and down in church during the singing of the office.
Who has not confessed last month.

Who broke silence.
Who has not fasted one day during the week.
Who has not fulfilled the penances imposed by the prior at the due time and place.

CHAPTER XI: *Concerning confession and communion.*

Let each brother confess himself as often as possible, but at least once a month. And let this be obligatory. And let each communicate at least four times a year, besides Easter and Christmas, the first time being the Purification, the second Pentecost, the third the Assumption of Mary, the fourth the day of All Saints; and let this be done in the oratory, if possible, and let each come with devotion and purity of heart, as becomes so great a sacrament, and upon the vigils of the said feast days let the brothers congregate and the usual office be said, as is stated above.

CHAPTER XII: *Concerning novices.*

When there will be a desire to invite some one into the said fraternity, let him who wishes to do so inform the prior and counselors, and let the prior give the name of the candidate to the master of novices, who during the space of a month will conduct diligent investigation. And having obtained all the possible information, let it be given to the prior and the counselors who among themselves will vote as to whether or not to make it known. And if there is a two-thirds vote in favor, the prior will make the request known, and the brothers for two months will seek information about him, and in the meantime the prior will urge the brothers often to furnish the same. And the two months over, it will be put to a vote, and if the vote is for him, the master, or whomever the prior and the counselors wish, will seek to speak with him and show him our Chapters, telling him diplomatically that he has heard that in other places such a brotherhood exists whose Chapters, as it were, have come into his hands, and that, if he is well disposed, such a devotion might also be followed here, so that the brother, should he not wish to accept such a thing, will not understand it to be an actual fact. And this finished, let a vote be taken, if the prior and the counselors wish it; and having won four-fifths of the ballots, let him [the candidate] be conducted to the oratory. But first let the master of the novices have him confessed, and, finding him firm in his proposal, let him be brought that night which pleases the prior, during which let not the ordinary offices be conducted, but let one await only the reception of the novice, according to the procedure for the reception of novices. Let the said novice offer a large candle of about two pounds, and let him take the lowest place in the choir. A minor of less than twenty-two years of age may not be admitted, unless it should seem to the prior, the counselors and the three assistants that his appearance, his habits, and his reputation warrant it, he being at least eighteen years of age; and, in the taking of novices, let one be strongly warned against the admission of unworthy persons.

CHAPTER XIII: *Concerning the general meeting.*

And, as in every ship there is a drainage whereby impurities may be purged, so it is that in every fraternity it is necessary to find a manner and method to purge bad offshoots. And thus every year during Lent let the prior make known the day on which the general meeting is to be held, bidding all the brothers to be confessed. And on such an appointed day let all the brethren be put to a vote, one by one, and let each brother offer his ballot on each one of the brethren. And let each who is to remain be required to obtain three-quarters of the white ballots, and let him who is being judged go out; and let each be obliged to keep secret what is said of him under pain of being deprived of our fraternity, or let the prior be charged with putting him to a vote as one who has revealed [the membership of] one of the brothers outside the fraternity. In the meantime let each relate whatever he knows why such and such a brother who has gone out merits being deprived, and, if any one is deprived, let him not be told at once but a day or so later, and with tact; and let such a person be considered as outside the fraternity. In all voting let the four-fifths prevail, except where there is special mention, meaning the four-fifths of the three-quarters of our brethren within the city or within close to four miles, including the sick. And when the vote is carried among the said three-quarters, let it be considered as though it were among all.

CHAPTER XIV: *Concerning secrecy and the punishment of those who reveal their brethren and other matters.*

And inasmuch as this fraternity has lay members who at times are frightened away from good works through the word of others, let each of the brothers be obliged to maintain secrecy concerning his fellow brothers and the works and ways of the fraternity. And should anyone learn that one of the brethren has revealed something touching upon our fraternity, let him be obliged to tell the same to the prior, who, deeming it to be true, is obliged to investigate the same with the counselors and decide whether or not it should be put to a vote among them; and the vote being carried by three-quarters, let him be deprived of the fraternity, and if not so, let him accept the penance imposed by the prior and counselors as well as the three assistants, who in such a case may exceed their ordinary measures for other penances and moreover may sentence him up to ten *libre*. And to like judgment and sentence may he be bound who should appear disobedient and unwilling to accept the penance administered, but first let him be warned three times by the prior or other brethren commissioned by the prior *ad laudem Dei et totius caelestis curiae*.

Addition concerning the affairs of the Hospice.

And inasmuch as the Company of Saint Mary of the Hospice of the Incurable Poor has been founded by our brethren, being a fruit from this tree, let it be ordered that all those who are protectors of the said Hospice and who belong to our fraternity be obliged, before the election or any change in the number of the protectors or other officials of the said Hospice, to alert the prior and our council about what in a short time must be done concerning said election; and, the issue voted upon and being carried by a majority, let those brethren concerned be obliged with every endeavor to learn what is transpiring among the said protectors; and let every effort be made, as far as possible, that in that number of protectors there be as many of us as possible, if this can be done with ease and for the good of the greater part of our brethren; and above all let us diligently strive that the syndic and scribe of the said protectors be one of our brethren. For, otherwise, it will be difficult to maintain such a company along a true path. Beyond this, let our prior take pains to know how things are being managed in the said Hospice, and let him exhort each of us to perform his duty with regard to the Hospice with great care; and each week let him visit the Hospice, and, if he finds that things are not going well, let him notify our brethren, and let those steps be taken which seem wisest to the majority; and let those of us who are among the protectors follow the order as closely as possible. In this matter let our prior be prompt to give warning, for any disorder occurring in the Hospice would be upon his shoulders, he not having done his duty.

Addition concerning the amendment of the Chapters.

And as all things in this life are in need of continual reformation, every time that it will seem necessary to the brethren, expressly to the four-fifths among them, to add to or subtract from the present Chapters something not contrary to divine or human law, nor contrary to good conduct, let it be licit to do so.

CHAPTER III

Colet's Convocation Sermon, 1512

John Colet, the English scholar, theologian, and dean of St. Paul's, has been heralded as inaugurating a new era of scriptural exegesis and theological study, the first to adapt the method and approach of Italian humanism to the content of Christian Revelation and to employ this technique in the cause of religious revival and reform.[1] His enterprise was both scholarly and practical: he sought to reopen scripture as a guide to life and thereby to renew theology and revivify the Christianity of his day. Considered thus, Colet is a figure of seminal importance, a link between humanism and reform, a pioneer of the movement called Christian humanism, soon to be represented above all by Erasmus, whose own life's aim was decisively influenced by the example and precept of the English scholar.[2]

John Colet, born about 1466, was the son of a prosperous London merchant. He entered Oxford probably in 1483, received his M.A., lectured for a few years, and then from late 1492 to 1496 studied on the Continent. "Like a merchant seeking goodly wares, he visited France and then Italy," Erasmus tells us, where "he devoted himself entirely to the study of the sacred writers."[3] Seebohm and others have suggested that he visited Florence and came

---

[1] Frederic Seebohm, *The Oxford Reformers* (2d ed.; London, 1869), and E. H. Harbison, *The Christian Scholar in the Age of the Reformation* (New York, 1956), pp. 55–67. Too simple a view of Colet's role, however, should not be entertained. Many Italian humanists before him were concerned with scripture and reform, and many English scholars preceded him in the study of the new *studia humanitatis*. On the former, see Raymond Marcel, "Les perspectives de l'apologétique de Lorenzo Valla à Savonarole," *Courants religieux et humanisme à la fin du XVe et au début du XVIe siècle* (Paris, 1959), pp. 83–100, but also the comments of Jedin in his *History of the Council of Trent*, I, 155–56, where the original contribution of Colet is stressed, because for him, unlike the Italian scholars, scripture had prime importance. On the latter, see R. Weiss, *Humanism in England during the Fifteenth Century* (Oxford, 1941), and Cardinal Gasquet, *The Eve of the Reformation* (London, 1927), Chap. II: "The Revival of Letters in England." Also see in this regard A. B. Ferguson, "Reginald Pecock and the Renaissance Sense of History," *Studies in the Renaissance*, XIII (1966), 147–65, where Pecock's exegetical method, though not humanist, is viewed as a predecessor of Colet's.

On Colet, see, in addition to Seebohm, J. H. Lupton, *A Life of John Colet* (London, 1887); E. W. Hunt, *Dean Colet and His Theology* (London, 1956); and Sears Jayne, *John Colet and Marsilio Ficino* (London, 1963). The primary life is that written by Erasmus in a letter to Jodocus Jonas in 1521, and translated and published by J. H. Lupton in 1883. It is reprinted in Erasmus, *Christian Humanism and the Reformation: Selected Writings*, ed. John C. Olin (New York, 1965), pp. 164–91.

[2] Seebohm; Harbison, *op. cit.*, pp. 70–77; and J. Huizinga, *Erasmus of Rotterdam* (New York, 1952), pp. 29–33. On Erasmus, see Chap. VI.

[3] Erasmus, *Christian Humanism and the Reformation*, p. 176.

Iohn Colet Dean of St Paul's

3. John Colet. Drawing by Hans Holbein.

under the influence of Marsilio Ficino and Savonarola during these travels and that he returned to England "not a mere humanist, but an earnest Christian reformer."[4] Be that as it may, shortly after his return to England in 1496 he undertook public lectures at Oxford on the Epistles of St. Paul. It was in the course of these famous lectures on Romans and I Corinthians that the new exegetical method was employed, "the method of examining the historical and grammatical meaning of the text as a whole, relating it to the historical circumstances in which it was written, and explaining Paul's meaning in terms of analogous doctrines from the theology of Platonism."[5] And it was at this time too—in late 1499—that Erasmus first met Colet at Oxford and began his long and very close friendship with him.

Colet was made dean of St. Paul's Cathedral in London in 1504, and he founded there several years later the famous school of St. Paul's, dedicated to the Child Jesus and devoted to the Christian education of young boys. Erasmus composed several works, including his *De copia verborum ac rerum* (1512), with Colet and St. Paul's in mind. The dean also gained renown as a preacher and was invited to speak on a number of important occasions. One of these was the opening of the Convocation of the clergy of Canterbury province at the London Cathedral on February 6, 1512. It is this sermon, the only one of Colet's extant, that is given here. Another memorable sermon, the gist of which we have in Erasmus' letter to Jonas, is one Colet delivered before the royal court on Good Friday, 1513.[6] There, on the eve of an English campaign against the French, he boldly denounced war and urged Christians to fight only under the banner of Christ their proper King. To the great surprise of the courtiers, Henry VIII was not enraged but after a long conversation with Colet declared: "Let every man have his own doctor, and everyone follow his liking, but this is the doctor for me."[7] In failing health toward the close of his life, he died in 1519, one of the men of our age, writes Erasmus, "whom I consider to have been true and sincere Christians."[8]

The Convocation sermon was given at the invitation of Archbishop Warham of Canterbury.[9] Remarkably forthright and incisive, it is the work of a man,

[4] Seebohm, *op. cit.*, p. 14 *et passim.*

[5] Jayne, *op. cit.*, p. 27. Jayne pinpoints this as occurring in the second stage of his work on Romans, i.e., in his lectures on Romans 6–11, and attributes it chiefly to the influence of Pico della Mirandola's Genesis commentary, the *Heptaplus.* The influence of Ficino was also great, though Jayne denies that Colet ever met the renowned Florentine Platonist. Jayne's study of this whole question and relationship, as well as his reconstruction of the order of Colet's Oxford works, is most important.

See also P. A. Duhamel, "The Oxford Lectures of John Colet," *Journal of the History of Ideas,* XIV (October, 1953), 493–510, and Seebohm, *op. cit.*, pp. 33–42. Colet's lectures were not published during his lifetime, nor are they extant as delivered. Commentary and lecture notes on Romans and I Corinthians were published, together with an English translation, by J. H. Lupton in his five-volume edition of Colet's Oxford works (London, 1867–76).

[6] Erasmus, *Christian Humanism and the Reformation,* pp. 189–90.

[7] *Ibid.*, p. 191.

[8] *Ibid.*

[9] The English text reprinted here with some slight modification of spelling is from Seebohm, *op. cit.*, pp. 230–47. The original Latin version, *Oratio habita ad clerum in*

as Colet himself declares, "speaking out of zeal, a man sorrowing for the ruin of the Church." The great injunction from St. Paul's Epistle to the Romans not to conform to this world, but to be transformed or reformed with a new mind, gives him the theme and framework for his address, and it is interesting indeed to see his practical adaptation of it.[10]

convocatione, was published in London in 1512, the only work of Colet to be published in his lifetime. A very early English version, either by Colet or his protégé, Thomas Lupset, was also printed about 1530. It is reprinted as an appendix in Lupton's Life, pp. 293–304. On the sermon, see the excellent essay by H. C. Porter, "The Gloomy Dean and the Law: John Colet, 1466–1519," Essays in Modern English Church History, eds. G. V. Bennett and J. D. Walsh (New York, 1966), pp. 18–43.

[10] The injunction is in Romans 12, 2. For comment on this text and on the Pauline doctrine of reform, see Gerhart B. Ladner, The Idea of Reform (Cambridge, Mass., 1959), pp. 53 ff.

YOU ARE COME together today, fathers and right wise men, to hold a council. In which what you will do and what matters you will handle, I do not yet know, but I wish that, at length, mindful of your name and profession, you would consider of the reformation of ecclesiastical affairs; for never was there more necessity and never did the state of the Church more need your endeavors. For the Church—the spouse of Christ—which He wished to be without spot or wrinkle, is become foul and deformed. As saith Isaias, "The faithful city is become a harlot"; and as Jeremias speaks, "She hath committed fornication with many lovers," whereby she has conceived many seeds of iniquity, and daily bringeth forth the foulest offspring. Wherefore I have come here today, fathers, to admonish you with all your minds to deliberate, in this your Council, concerning the reformation of the Church.

But, in sooth, I came not of my own will and pleasure, for I was conscious of my unworthiness, and I saw too how hard it would be to satisfy the most critical judgment of such great men. I judged it would be altogether unworthy, unfit, and almost arrogant in me, a servant, to admonish you, my masters!—in me, a son, to teach you, my fathers! It would have come better from some one of the fathers—that is, from one of you prelates, who might have done it with weightier authority and greater wisdom. But I could not but obey the command of the most reverend Father and Lord Archbishop, the President of this Council, who imposed this duty, a truly heavy one, upon me; for we read that it was said by Samuel the prophet, "Obedience is better than sacrifice." Wherefore, fathers and most worthy sirs, I pray and beseech you this day that you will bear with my weakness by your patience and forbearance; next, in the beginning, help me with your pious prayers. And before all things, let us pour out our prayers to God the Father Almighty; and first, let us pray for his Holiness the Pope, for all spiritual pastors, with all Christian people; next, let us pray for our most reverend

Father the Lord Archbishop, President of this Council, and all the lords bishops, the whole clergy, and the whole people of England; let us pray, lastly, for this assembly and convocation, praying God that He may inspire your minds so unanimously to conclude upon what is for the good and benefit of the Church, that when this Council is concluded we may not seem to have been called together in vain and without cause. Let us all say the Pater Noster.

As I am about to exhort you, reverend fathers, to endeavor to reform the condition of the Church; because nothing has so disfigured the face of the Church as the secular and worldly way of living on the part of the clergy, I know not how I can commence my discourse more fitly than with the Apostle Paul, in whose cathedral you are now assembled: "Be ye not conformed to this world, but be ye reformed in the newness of your minds, that ye may prove what is the good, and well pleasing, and perfect will of God." This the Apostle wrote to all Christian men, but emphatically to priests and bishops: for priests and bishops are the lights of the world, as the Saviour said to them, "Ye are the light of the world"; and again He said, "If the light that is in you be darkness, how great will be that darkness!" That is, if the priests and bishops, the very lights, run in the dark ways of the world, how dark must the lay people be! Wherefore, emphatically did St. Paul say to priests and bishops, "Be ye not conformed to this world, but be ye reformed in the newness of your minds."

By these words the Apostle points out two things:—First, he prohibits our being conformed to the world and becoming carnal; and then he commands that we be reformed in the Spirit of God, in order that we may be spiritual. I, therefore, following this order, shall speak first of Conformation, and after that of Reformation.

"Be not," he says, "conformed to this world." By the world the Apostle means the worldly way and manner of living, which consists chiefly in these four evils—viz., in devilish pride, in carnal concupiscence, in worldly covetousness, and in worldly occupations. These things are in the world, as St. John testifies in his canonical epistle; for he says, "All things that are in the world are either the lust of the flesh, the lust of the eye, or the pride of life." These things in like manner exist and reign in the Church, and amongst ecclesiastical persons, so that we seem able truly to say, "All things in the Church are either the lust of the flesh, lust of the eye, or the pride of life!

In the first place, to speak of pride of life—what eagerness and hunger after honor and dignity are found in these days amongst ecclesiastical persons! What a breathless race from benefice to benefice, from a less to a greater one, from a lower to a higher! Who is there who does not see this? Who that sees it does not grieve over it? Moreover, those who hold these dignities, most of them carry themselves with such lofty mien and high looks that their place does not seem to be in the humble priesthood of Christ but in proud worldly domination!—not acknowledging or perceiving what the master of humility, Christ, said to His disciples whom He called to the priesthood. "The princes of the nations," said He, "have lordship over them, and those who are amongst the great have power. But let it not be so with you: but he who is great among you let him be your minister; he who is chief, let him be the servant of all. For the Son of Man came not to be ministered unto, but to minister." By which words the Saviour plainly teaches that magistracy in the Church is nothing else than humble service.

As to the second worldly evil, which is the lust for the flesh—has not this vice, I ask, inundated the Church as with the flood of its lust, so that nothing is more carefully sought after, in these most troublous times, by the most part of priests, than that which ministers to sensual pleasure? They give themselves to feasting and banqueting; spend themselves in vain babbling, take part in sports and plays, devote themselves to hunting and hawking; are drowned in the delights of this world; patronize those who cater for their pleasure. It was against this kind of people that Jude the Apostle exclaimed: "Woe unto them! for they have gone in the way of Cain, and ran greedily after the error of Balaam for reward, and perished in the gainsaying of Core. These are the spots in your feasts of charity, when they feast with you, feeding themselves without fear; clouds they are without water, carried about by winds; trees whose fruit withers without fruit, twice dead, plucked up by the roots; raging waves of the sea, foaming out their own shame; wandering stars, to whom is reserved the blackness of darkness forever."

Covetousness also, which is the third worldly evil, which the Apostle John calls the lust of the eye, and Paul idolatry—this most horrible plague—has so taken possession of the hearts of nearly all priests, and has so darkened the eyes of their minds, that nowadays we are blind to everything but that alone which seems to be able to bring us gain. For in these days, what else do we seek for in the Church than rich benefices and promotions? In these same promotions, what else do we count upon but their fruits and revenues? We rush after them with such eagerness that we care not how many and what duties, or how great benefices we take, if only they have great revenues.

O Covetousness! Paul rightly called thee the root of all evil! From thee comes all this piling up of benefices one on top of the other; from thee come the great pensions, assigned out of many benefices resigned; from thee quarrels about tithes, about offerings, about mortuaries, about dilapidations, about ecclesiastical right and title, for which we fight as for our very lives! O Covetousness! From thee come burdensome visitations of bishops; from thee corruptions of law courts, and those daily fresh inventions by which the poor people are harassed; from thee the sauciness and insolence of officials! O Covetousness! Mother of all iniquity! From thee comes that eager desire on the part of ordinaries to enlarge their jurisdiction; from thee their foolish and mad contention to get hold of the probate of wills; from thee undue sequestrations of fruits; from thee that superstitious observance of all those laws which are lucrative, and disregard and neglect of those which point at the correction of morals! Why should I mention the rest?—To sum up in one word: every corruption, all the ruin of the Church, all the scandals of the world, come from the covetousness of priests, according to the saying of Paul, which I repeat again, and beat into your ears, "Covetousness is the root of all evil!"

The fourth worldly evil which mars and spots the face of the Church is the incessant worldly occupation in which many priests and bishops in these days entangle themselves—servants of men rather than of God, soldiers of this world rather than of Christ. For the Apostle Paul writes to Timothy, "No man that warreth for God entangleth himself in the affairs of this life." But priests are "soldiers of God." Their warfare truly is not carnal, but spiritual: for our warfare is to pray, to read, and to meditate upon the Scriptures; to minister the word of God, to administer the sacraments of salvation, to make sacrifice for the people, and to offer masses for their souls. For we are mediators between men and God, as Paul testifies, writing to the Hebrews: "Every priest," he says, "taken from amongst men is ordained for men in things pertaining to God, to offer gifts and sacrifices for sins." Wherefore the Apostles, the first priests and bishops, so shrank from every taint of worldly things that they did not even wish to minister to the necessities of the poor, although these were the greatest works of piety: for they said, "It is not right that we should leave the word of God and serve tables; we will give ourselves continually to prayer, and the ministry of the word of God." And Paul exclaims to the Corinthians, "If you have any secular matters, make those of you judges who are of least estimation in the Church." Indeed from this worldliness, and because the clergy and priests, neglecting spiritual things, involve themselves in earthly occupation, many evils follow. First, the priestly dignity is dishonored, which is greater than either royal or imperial dignity, for it is equal to that of angels. And the splendor of this high dignity is obscured by darkness when priests, whose conversation ought to be in heaven, are occupied with the things of the earth. Secondly, the dignity of priests is despised when there is no difference between such priests and laymen; but (according to the prophet Hosea) "as the people are, so are the priests." Thirdly, the beautiful order of the hierarchy in the Church is confused when the magnates of the Church are busied in vile and earthly things, and in their stead vile and abject persons meddle with high and spiritual things. Fourthly, the laity themselves are scandalized and driven to ruin, when those whose duty it is to draw men from this world, teach men to love this world by their own devotion to worldly things, and by their own love of this world are themselves carried down headlong into hell. Besides, when priests themselves are thus entangled, it must end in hypocrisy: for, mixed up and confused with the laity, they lead, under a priestly exterior, the mere life of a layman. Also their spiritual weakness and servile fear, when enervated by the waters of this world, makes them dare neither to do nor to say anything but what they know will be grateful and pleasing to their princes. Lastly, such is their ignorance and blindness, when blinded by the darkness of this world, that they can discern nothing but earthly things. Wherefore, not without cause our Saviour Christ admonished the prelates of His Church, "Take heed lest your hearts be burdened by surfeiting or banqueting, and the cares of this world." "By the cares," He says, "of this world!" The hearts of priests weighed down by riches cannot lift themselves on high, nor raise themselves to heavenly things.

Many other evils there be, which are the result of the worldliness of priests, which it would take long to mention; but I have done. These are those four evils, O fathers! O priests! by which, as I have said, we are conformed to this world, by which the face of the Church is marred, by which her influence is destroyed, plainly, far more than it was destroyed and marred, either at the beginning by the persecution of tyrants, or after that by the invasion of heresies which followed. For by the persecution of tyrants the persecuted Church was made stronger and more glorious; by the invasion of heresies the Church, being shaken, was made wiser and more skilled in Holy Scriptures. But after the introduction of this most sinful worldliness, when worldliness had crept in amongst the clergy, the root of all spiritual life—charity itself— was extinguished. And without this the Church can neither be wise nor strong in God.

In these times also we experience much opposition from the laity, but they are not so opposed to us as we are to ourselves. Nor does their opposition do us so much hurt as the opposition of our own wicked lives, which are opposed to God and to Christ; for He said, "He that is not with me is against me." We are troubled in these days too also by heretics—men mad with strange folly—but this heresy of theirs is not so pestilential and pernicious to us and the people as the vicious and depraved lives of the clergy, which, if we may believe St. Bernard, is a species of heresy, and the greatest and most pernicious of all: for that holy father, preaching in a certain convocation to the priests of his time, in his sermon spoke in these words: "There are many who are catholic in their speaking and preaching who are very heretics in their actions, for what heretics do by their false doctrines these men do by their evil examples; they seduce the people and lead them into the error of life; and they are by so much worse than heretics as actions are stronger than words." These things said Bernard, that holy father of so great and ardent spirit, against the faction of wicked priests of his time; by which he plainly shows that there be two kinds of heretical pravity—one of perverse doctrine, the other of perverse living—of which the latter is the greater and more pernicious; and this reigns in the Church, to the miserable destruction of the Church, her priests living after a worldly and not after a priestly fashion. Wherefore do you fathers, you priests and all of you of the clergy, awake at length, and rise up from this your sleep in this forgetful world: and being awake, at length listen to Paul calling unto you, "Be ye not conformed to this world."

This concerning the first part.

Now let us come to the second—concerning Reformation.

"But be ye reformed in the newness of your minds." What Paul commands us secondly is that we should "be reformed into a new mind"; that we should savor the things that are of God; that we should be reformed to those things which are contrary to what I have been speaking of—i.e., to humility, sobriety, charity, spiritual occupations; just as Paul wrote to Titus, "Denying ungodliness and worldly lusts, we should live soberly, righteously, and godly in this present world."

But this reformation and restoration in ecclesiastical affairs must needs begin with you, our fathers, and then afterwards descend upon us your priests and the whole clergy. For you are our chiefs—you are our examples of life. To you we look as waymarks for our direction. In you and in your lives we desire to read, as in living books, how we ourselves should live. Wherefore, if you wish to see our motes, first take the beams out of your own eyes; for it is an old proverb, "Physician, heal thyself." Do you, spiritual doctors, first assay that medicine for the purgation of morals, and then you may offer it to us to taste of it also.

The way, moreover, by which the Church is to be reformed and restored to a better condition is not to enact any new laws (for there are laws enough and to spare). As Solomon says, "There is no new thing under the sun." The diseases which are now in the Church were the same in former ages, and there is no evil for which the holy Fathers did not provide excellent remedies; there are no crimes in prohibition of which there are not laws in the body of Canon Law. The need, therefore, is not for the enactment of new laws and constitutions, but for the observance of those already enacted. Wherefore, in this your congregation, let the existing laws be produced and recited which prohibit what is evil, and which enjoin what is right.

First, let those laws be recited which admonish you, fathers, not to lay your hands on any, nor to admit them to Holy Orders, rashly. For here is the source from whence other evils flow, because if the entrance to Holy Orders be thrown open, all who offer themselves are forthwith admitted without hindrance. Hence proceed and emanate those hosts of both unlearned and wicked priests which are in the Church. For it is not, in my judgment, enough that a priest can construe a collect, propound a proposition, or reply to a sophism; but much more needful are a good, pure, and holy life, approved morals, moderate knowledge of the Scriptures, some knowledge of the sacraments, above all fear of God and love of heavenly life.

Let the laws be recited with direct that ecclesiastical benefices should be conferred on the worthy, and promotions in the Church made with just regard to merit; not by carnal affection, nor the acceptation of persons, whereby it comes to pass in these days, that boys instead of old men, fools instead of wise men, wicked instead of good men, reign and rule!

Let the laws be recited against the guilt of simony; which plague, which contagion, which dire pestilence, now creeps like a cancer through the minds of priests, so that most are not ashamed in these days to get for themselves great dignities by petitions and suits at court, rewards and promises.

Let the laws be recited which command the personal residence of curates at their churches: for many evils spring from the custom, in these days, of performing all clerical duties by help of vicars and substitutes; men too without judgment, unfit, and often wicked, who will seek nothing from the people but sordid gain—whence spring scandals, heresies, and bad Christianity among the people.

Let the laws be rehearsed, and the holy rules handed down from our ancestors, concerning the life and character of the clergy, which prohibit any churchman from being a merchant, usurer, or hunter, or common player, or from bearing arms—the laws which prohibit the clergy from frequenting taverns, from having unlawful intercourse with women—the laws which command sobriety and modesty in vestment, and temperance in dress.

Let also the laws be recited concerning monks and religious men, which command that, leaving the broad way of the world, they enter the narrow way which leads to life; which command them not to meddle in business, whether secular or ecclesiastical; which command that they should not engage in suits in civil courts for earthly things. For in the Council of Chalcedon it was decreed that monks should give themselves up entirely to prayer and fasting, the chastisement of their flesh and the observance of their monastic rule.

Above all, let those laws be recited which concern and pertain to you, reverend fathers and lords bishops—laws concerning your just and canonical election, in the chapters of your churches, with the invocation of the Holy Spirit: for because this is not done in these days, and prelates are often chosen more by the favor of men than by the grace of God, so, in consequence, we sometimes certainly have bishops too little spiritual—men more worldly than heavenly, wiser in the spirit of this world than in the spirit of Christ!

Let the laws be rehearsed concerning the residence of bishops in their dioceses, which command that they watch over the salvation of souls, that they disseminate the word of God, that they personally appear in their churches at least on great festivals, that they sacrifice for their people, that they hear the causes of the poor, that they sustain the fatherless and widows, that they exercise themselves always in works of piety.

Let the laws be rehearsed concerning the due distribution of the patrimony of Christ—laws which command that the goods of the Church be spent not in sumptuous buildings, not in magnificence and pomp, not in feasts and banquets, not in luxury and lust, not in enriching kinsfolk or in keeping hounds, but in things useful and needful to the Church. For when he was asked by Augustine, the English bishop, in what way English bishops and prelates should dispose of those goods which were the offerings of the faithful, Pope Gregory replied (and his reply is placed in the *Decretals,* ch. xii q. 2) that the goods of bishops should be divided into four parts, of which one part should go to the bishop and his family, another to his clergy, a third for repairing buildings, a fourth to the poor.

Let the laws be recited, and let them be recited again and again, which abolish the vices and scandals of courts, which take away those daily newly invented arts for getting money, which were designed to extirpate and eradicate that horrible covetousness which is the root and cause of all evils, which is the fountain of all iniquity.

Lastly, let those laws and constitutions be renewed concerning the holding of Councils, which command that Provincial Councils should be held more frequently for the reformation of the Church. For nothing ever happens more detrimental to the Church of Christ than the omission of Councils, both general and provincial.

Having rehearsed these laws and others like them, which pertain to this matter, and have for their object the correction of morals, it remains that with all authority and power their execution should be commanded, so that having a law, we should at length live according to it.

In which matter, with all due reverence, I appeal most strongly to you, fathers! For this execution of laws and observance of constitutions ought to begin with you so that by your living example you may teach us priests to imitate you. Else it will surely be said of you, "They lay heavy burdens on other men's shoulders, but they themselves will not move them even with one of their fingers." But you, if you keep the laws, and first reform your own lives to the law and rules of the Canons, will thereby provide us with a light, in which we shall see what we ought to do—the light, i.e., of your good example. And we, seeing our fathers keep the laws, will gladly follow in the footsteps of our fathers.

The clerical and priestly part of the Church being thus reformed, we can then proceed with better grace to the reformation of the lay part, which indeed it will be very easy to do, if we ourselves have been reformed first. For the body follows the soul, and as the rulers in a State are, so shall the people be. Wherefore, if priests themselves, the rulers of souls, were good, the people in their turn would become good also: for our own goodness would teach others how they may be good more clearly than all other kinds of teaching and preaching. Our goodness would urge them on in the right way far more efficaciously than all your suspensions and excommunications. Wherefore, if you wish the lay people to live according to your will and pleasure, you must first live according to the will of God, and thus (believe me) you will easily attain what you wish in them.

You want obedience from them. And it is right; for in the Epistle to the Hebrews are these words of Paul to the laity: "Be obedient," he says, "to your rulers, and be subject to them." But if you desire this obedience, first give reason and cause of obedience on your part, as the same Paul teaches in the following text, "Watch as those that give an account of their souls," and then they will obey you.

You desire to be honored by the people. It is right; for Paul writes to Timothy, "Priests who rule well are worthy of double honor, chiefly those who labor in word and doctrine." Therefore, desiring honor, first rule well and labor in word and doctrine, and then the people will hold you in all honor.

You desire to reap carnal things, and to collect tithes and offerings without any reluctance on their part. It is right; for Paul, writing to the Romans, says: "They are your debtors, and ought to minister to you in carnal things." But if you wish to reap their carnal things, you must first sow your spiritual things, and then ye shall reap abundantly of their carnal things. For that man is hard and unjust who desires "to reap where he has not sown, and to gather where he has not scattered."

You desire ecclesiastical liberty, and not to be drawn before civil courts. And this, too, is right; for in the Psalms it is said, "Touch not mine anointed." But if ye desire this liberty, loose yourselves first from worldly bondage, and from the cringing service of men, and claim for ourselves that true liberty of Christ, that spiritual liberty through grace from sin, and serve God and reign in Him, and then (believe me) the people will not touch the anointed of the Lord their God!

You desire security, quiet, and peace. And this is fitting. But, desiring peace, return to the God of love and peace; return to Christ, in whom is the true peace of the Spirit which passeth all understanding; return to the true priestly life. And lastly, as Paul commands, "Be ye reformed in the newness of your minds, that ye may know those things which are of God; and the peace of God shall be with you."

These, reverend fathers and most distinguished men, are the things that I thought should be spoken concerning the reformation of the clergy. I trust that, in your clemency, you will take them in good part. If, by chance, I should seem to have gone too far in this sermon—if I have said anything with too much warmth—forgive it me, and pardon a man speaking out of zeal, a man sorrowing for the ruin of the Church; and, passing by any foolishness of mine, consider the thing itself. Consider the miserable state and condition of the Church, and bend your whole minds to its reformation. Suffer not, fathers, suffer not this so illustrious assembly to break up without result. Suffer not this your congregation to slip by for nothing. You indeed have often been assembled. But (if by your leave I may speak the truth) I see not what fruit has as yet resulted, especially to the Church, from assemblies of this kind. Go now, in the Spirit whom you have invoked, that you may be able with His assistance, to devise, to ordain, and to decree those things which may be useful to the Church, and redound to your praise and the honor of God: to whom be all honor and glory, forever and ever, Amen!

CHAPTER IV

Egidio da Viterbo's Address to the Fifth Lateran Council, 1512

Lateran V, "the last attempt at a papal reform of the Church before the break-up of Christian unity," opened in Rome on May 3, 1512, and continued to sit until March, 1517.[1] It had been called by Pope Julius II (1503–13) in July, 1511, in the midst of his war with Louis XII of France and in opposition to the project of the French-sponsored Council at Pisa. In point of origin it was a riposte to an antipapal maneuver by Louis XII and a reaffirmation of papal authority in the face of Gallican conciliarism and potential schism,[2] but the desire and hope of reform were also present, as both the bull of convocation and the opening address of Egidio da Viterbo indicate.[3]

The reform efforts of the Council are touched on in Chapter V, where its reform decree, *Supernae dispositionis arbitrio,* is presented. Here we shall speak only of the man who addressed the initial assembly of the Council and present his opening remarks.[4] When Egidio da Viterbo (1469–1532) delivered this famous sermon—it was given less than two months after Colet's in London— he was General of the Augustinian Order and one of the most renowned scholars and preachers in Italy of his day. Highly lauded by Pontano and

---

[1] The quotation is from Jedin, *A History of the Council of Trent,* I, 128. On the Council, see Philip Hughes, *A History of the Church* (3 vols.; New York, 1935–47), III, 478 ff.; C.-J. Hefele, *Histoire des conciles,* trans. H. Laclercq (8 vols.; Paris, 1907– 21), VIII, pt. I, 339 ff.; and Pastor, *History of the Popes,* VI, 406 ff., VII, 71 ff., VIII, 384 ff. The conciliar acts are in *Sacrorum conciliorum nova et amplissima collectio,* ed. J. D. Mansi (Facsimile reproduction; Paris and Leipzig, 1901), XXXII, 649–1002.

[2] The whole issue of papal vs. conciliar authority at this time is thoroughly discussed in Olivier de la Brosse, *Le pape et le concile* (Paris, 1965). The controversy featured an important defense of papal supremacy by the future Cardinal Cajetan (Thomas de Vio), *De comparatione auctoritatis papae et concilii* (1511), and a reply to him, upholding the conciliar theory, by the Parisian theologian Jacques Almain.

[3] Pastor, VI, 365, 448–49.

[4] On Egidio da Viterbo (Giles of Viterbo), see F. X. Martin, "The Problem of Giles of Viterbo," *Augustiniana,* IX (1959), 357–79, X (1960), 43–60, and "Giles of Viterbo and the Monastery of Lecceto," *Analecta Augustiniana,* XXV (1962), 225–53; G. Signorelli, *Il Cardinale Egidio da Viterbo* (Florence, 1929); E. Massa, "Egidio da Viterbo e la metodologia del sapere nel cinquecento," *Pensée humaniste et tradition chrétienne aux XVe et XVIe siècles,* ed. H. Bédarida (Paris, 1950), pp. 185–239; and, especially pertinent to the address given here, J. W. O'Malley, "Giles of Viterbo: A Reformer's Thought on Renaissance Rome," *Renaissance Quarterly,* XX (1967), 1–11. Father O'Malley has since published a very penetrating study of Egidio's reform thought: *Giles of Viterbo on Church and Reform* (Leiden, 1968).

later Bembo and Sadoleto for his classical style and erudition, he was also a Hebraist, scriptural scholar, and theologian strongly influenced by the Platonism of Marsilio Ficino.[5] As an Augustinian, he had become a member of the reformed congregation of Lecceto near Siena, and after being elected General of the Order in 1507 he vigorously encouraged reform throughout its ranks. "His ideals found practical expression in reform," writes F. X. Martin in his excellent scholarly appraisal of Egidio, "reform which he preached for the daily lives of the people in so many Italian cities, reform of discipline which he formulated when prior general of the Augustinians, reform in theology which was to be presented in Platonic terms, and reform in biblical studies so that the living word of God might be heard in all its keenness."[6] Along with this intellectual, religious, and administrative activity, he undertook many important diplomatic missions in behalf of Julius II and Leo X. Leo X made him a cardinal in July, 1517, together with Cajetan and Adrian of Utrecht, an appointment which led Pastor to comment that "if ever a man deserved the red hat it was this distinguished man."[7] He resigned the Augustinian generalship in February, 1518—at the very time when Luther's protest concerning indulgences was coming to the attention of Rome. He later served as Bishop of Viterbo.

It is an interesting historical coincidence that the man who called the Pope and Fathers of Lateran V to the urgent task of reform was the head of that Order of which Luther was a member in distant Germany. In fact, Luther made his trip to Rome in late 1510 during Egidio's generalship and in connection with Egidio's plan for reform and reorganization in the Saxon province, and he had at least indirect dealings with the Order's head on this occasion.[8] But perhaps more to the point is the sharp contrast the two great Augustinians afford: one the very erudite and devout scholar of the Renaissance, the other the earthy and deeply pious German monk; both sons of Augustine, both students of the Word of God, but representatives of two different worlds of culture and spirituality. A famous sentence from Egidio's sermon also suggests, quite prophetically, the two reformations that were ultimately to diverge and clash: *Homines per sacra immutari fas est, non sacra per homines* (Men must be changed by religion, not religion by men).[9] Egidio sought a renewal in the Church, essentially a reform of its members, a restoration of its discipline and

---

[5] He wrote a commentary on the *Sentences* of Peter Lombard *"ad mentem Platonis."*
[6] *Augustiniana*, X, 60. The first complete Greek Bible to be published—at Venice in 1518—was dedicated to Egidio.
[7] Pastor, VII, 206.
[8] Heinrich Boehmer, *Martin Luther: Road to Reformation*, trans. J. W. Doberstein and T. G. Tappert (New York, 1957), Chap. VIII.
[9] Pastor, VII, 10, sees Egidio's sentence as summing up "the theory of true Catholic reformation." He uses it as a prefatory epigraph to his Volume VII. Jedin, in his *History of the Council of Trent*, I, 169, also alludes to Egidio's dictum and views Luther as in violation of it. A comparable dictum may be found in Egidio's *Historia XX saeculorum: Emendanda non evertenda ecclesia est* (The Church must be corrected not overturned). Signorelli, *op. cit.*, pp. 52, 169. For further comment, see O'Malley, *Giles of Viterbo on Church and Reform*, Chap. V and Conclusion.

4. The Fifth Lateran Council in session.

ideals; Luther preached a new Christianity, faithful according to his insights to the scriptural Word but breaking certainly with the accepted and established tradition.

Egidio delivered his address in the venerable Lateran Basilica on May 3, 1512, in the presence of the Pope, the cardinals, and the nearly one hundred prelates who composed the Council.[10] It was given at a very critical moment in the course of Julius' struggle with France, shortly after the disastrous defeat of the papal forces at Ravenna by the army of Gaston de Foix. Alarm and anxiety gripped Rome, and in a dramatic and moving part of his address Egidio explains this defeat as a providential act, a warning to the Pope and to the Church not to rely on "alien arms" but to regain and renew "the arms of light." His concluding words, which then follow, rehearsing the grave ills and dangers that beset the Christian fold, are a most solemn affirmation of the need for a Council, "the one and only remedy for all evils, the sole port for the ship in distress," and an exhortation to it and to the Pope to reform the stricken Church of Christ.

[10] The Latin text of Egidio's address is in Mansi, XXXII, 669-76. The original publication of it was made in Rome in 1512 and is prefaced by a letter from Sadoleto to Bembo. The English translation here presented, the first to be published, was made by Charles W. Lockyer, Jr., and the editor from the Mansi text.

THERE IS no one here, I believe, who does not wonder, when there are so many men in the city who are famed indeed for their ability to speak with dignity and eloquence, why I, who can in no way be compared with these brilliant men, should be the one to appear before us and should dare to speak on so important a matter and in so great an assembly that the world has none more esteemed or more sacred. I might indeed say that something has intervened, and for this reason I have been preferred over the others, not because of any excellence but because of earlier times and activities. And so for this reason I seem to have been invited as the first to cast a spear in this conflict and to begin the Holy Lateran Council.

For about twenty years ago, as much as I was able and my meager strength allowed, I explained the Gospels to the people, made known the predictions of the prophets, expounded to nearly all of Italy John's Apocalypse concerning the destiny of the Church, and repeatedly asserted that those who were then listening would see great agitation and destruction in the Church and would one day behold its correction.[11] Now it has seemed proper that he who had said these things would happen bears witness that they have happened, and he who had so often cried out, "My eyes will see salutary times," now at last cries out, "My eyes have seen the salutary and holy beginning of the awaited renewal." If only you be present, Renewer of the world, Child of a divine Father, Preserver and Savior of mortal men, you may grant to me the power to speak, to my address the power to persuade, to the Fathers the power to celebrate, not with words but with deeds, a true, holy, and full Council, to root out vice, to arouse virtue, to catch the foxes who in this season swarm to destroy the holy vineyard, and finally to call fallen religion back to its old purity, its ancient brilliance, its original splendor, and its own sources. Thus I shall say of a Council both how useful it is for

---

[11] The time as well as the character of Egidio's prophetic preaching coincide with Savonarola's. See Savonarola's Renovation sermon of January 13, 1495, in Chap. I.

the Church at all times and how necessary it is for our times, with the preface that I would not dare alter the prophetic writings, but would make use of the words and speeches in their entirety, as they are accustomed to be read, not only because men must be changed by religion, not religion by men, but because the language of truth is straightforward. And from the beginning this division came to mind: some things are divine, others celestial, others human.

Divine things certainly do not need correction because they are not subject to motion or change. But celestial and human things, being subject to movement, long for renewal. For when the moon has come into position with the sun and when the sun has descended from the summer solstice to the winter solstice to the great loss, as it were, of men, the loss is completely restored. Nature's law demands that the loss of light be made up for and that whatever was taken away on the wane be restored to men on the ascent. If the paths of the stars in the heavens, even though constant, eternal, and everlasting, nevertheless return and are restored, what then does this third division of things do, since they are changing, transitory, and mortal? Indeed, either they inevitably perish in a quick destruction, or they are restored in a continual renewal. For what food is for bodies that they may live and procreation for species that they may be perpetuated, correction, cultivation, instruction serve as the occasion demands for human souls. And, as no living thing can long survive without nourishment from food, so man's soul and the Church cannot perform well without the attention of Councils. If you should take rain from the meadows, streams from the gardens, tilling from the fields, pruning from the vines, and nourishment from living beings, these would soon dry up and grow wild, and the latter would cease living and die. Such was the case after the time of Constantine when, though much splendor and embellishment were added to religion, the austerity of morals and living was greatly weakened.

As often as the holding of Councils was delayed, we saw the divine Bride forsaken by her Spouse and that message of the Gospel accomplished which was recited yesterday. "A little while and you shall not see me." We saw Christ sleeping in a small boat, we saw the force of the winds, the fury of the heretics, raging against the bright sails of truth. We saw evil's desperate recklessness battering the laws, authority, and majesty of the Church. We saw wicked greed, the cursed thirsting for gold and possessions. We saw, I say, violence, pillage, adultery, incest, in short, the scourge of every crime so confound all that is sacred and profane, and so attack the holy bark, that this bark has been almost swamped by the waves of sin and nearly engulfed and destroyed.

Once again at the prompting of that Spirit to whom public prayers have this day been decreed, the Fathers have had recourse to a Council. As quickly as possible they have corrected and settled all matters. They have exercised their command over the winds and storms, and as though carried to the safest of ports they have compelled might to yield to reason, injustice to justice, vice to virtue, storms and waves to serenity and tranquility. And they have sung a hymn to the Holy Spirit, to the God of fishermen, of the sea, and of waters: "Deep waters cannot quench love," and, "The winter is past, the rains are over and gone. . . . Arise, my beloved."[12] For the Bride lies still, as the leaves of the trees in winter, but with the effort of Councils does she arise and grow strong, as the trees bring forth their leaves in the springtime when the sun returns. With the rays of the returning sun the favoring west wind blows, and the young trees bloom forth in their richness; so with the light of Councils and the Holy Spirit the winds blow and the dead eyes of the Church come to live again and receive the light. And here the other part of the prophecy is fulfilled: "Again a little while and you shall see me." Therefore, she wishes nothing for herself except that the Holy Spirit's light which is extinguished without Councils, like a new fire struck from flint, be again kindled and recovered in the Councils. Paul, the glory of the Apostles, when he declared the source of salvation, said: "Without faith we cannot please God." But without Councils, faith cannot stand firm. Without Councils, therefore, we cannot be saved.

In order to prove from experience what we assert as true by reason, we must consider that there are three fundamental articles of belief from which flows the Church's entire faith. The first is the unity of the divine nature. The second is the most blessed Trinity of parent, child, and love in the same nature. The third is the conception of the divine Child in the womb of the Virgin. On these, as on the highest peaks and most sacred mountains, the remaining nine parts of faith and all piety are founded. "His foundation upon the holy mountains [the Lord loves]." Truly, unity is called the mountain of God because God's essence and nature consist precisely in unity. And in order that we may reflect upon the fact that this unity is not solitary and sterile, but rather endowed with the richest abundance, fertile mountain is added. And when indeed the Word is given body in the Virgin, the prophet describes the mountain as coagulated.[13]

Thus threefold is this vineyard situated on the mountaintops, a vineyard which prophecies have said would be and the Gospels have revealed is here. But now the vineyard had perished, for, as David testified, a wild beast from the woods had ravaged it, that is, the ferment of philosophy had laid it waste. First Arius, who shattered the doctrine of unity, tried to tear down the mountain. Next came Sabellius, who confused the Persons [of the Trinity]. The third was Photius, who overthrew the Virgin Birth with impure recklessness. Like three most base giants, seduced by the desire for glory and the longing for change, they dared to move the mountains from their place, so that they might open a way to attack and pull down heaven. And now their prayers

[12] Song of Solomon 8, 7, and 2, 11-13.
[13] The above references are to Psalm 86 (87), 1-2 ("His foundation . . ."), Isaiah 5, 1 (for fertile mountain), and Psalm 67 (68), 16, in the Vulgate version (for the mountain as coagulated, that is, *mons coagulatus*). In the paragraph that follows in the text David's testimony and prayer concerning the vineyard refers to Psalm 79 (80), the same Psalm quoted in the papal bull *Exsurge Domine* condemning Luther in June, 1520.

were answered, for with arms the princes ordered accepted what these men by philosophy were persuading. Philosophy was pressing us with its arguments, arms with standards gathered attacked. The former by deceit, the latter by force, were trying to overthrow the faith. Philosophy tried to overturn what was believed, force strove to destroy those who believed. The first raged against pious souls, the second against living bodies. What was the divine Bride, now on the very brink of destruction, to do in order to escape? Whose trust, whose strength, whose aid could she beseech? The tempest was raging, the boat was sinking. In short, so as not to delay on many points, no way to flee, no way to escape, was found save only the Council of Nicaea when God appeared to Silvester who sat at the helm, a man already suffering shipwreck, and said: "O you of little faith, why have you doubted?" And immediately by divine power he restored the mountains of faith and destroyed the rash monsters. Whereby the Bride, having been rescued, learned from experience that when she saw any misfortune threatening her she had no defense more effective than a Council, where alone no waters extinguish the fire of charity in the Church and the Holy Spirit makes a resting-place in our souls, even as, according to the testimony of Moses, the only Conqueror of the waves and Ruler of the storms is borne across the waters.

What I have just said about faith, which indeed would not exist without the establishment of a Council, I wish applied to temperance, justice, wisdom, and the other virtues. Certainly we all desire idleness rather than hard work, leisure rather than activity, pleasure rather than deprivation. But whenever we take notice of what is done at Councils, so that an evaluation may be made, the question of morals and living be investigated, and the wicked discovered, judged, and punished, while, on the other hand, the upright are attracted, encouraged, and praised, unbelievable incentives to cultivate virtue are inspired, with the result that men take courage, decide on the better course of action, undertake to give up vice and pursue virtue, and strive after nothing that is not honorable and lofty. It is this which has been the distinguishing characteristic of a Council, from which shone forth, as though from the Trojan horse, the brightest lights of so many minds. This approval of virtue, this condemnation of vice brought forth the Basils, Chrysostoms, Damascenes in Greece, the Jeromes, Ambroses, Augustines, Gregorys in Italy. And what books, writings, and memorials, what a wealth of learning, instruction, and divine wisdom have they not gathered into the Christian treasury?

Since time does not permit, I pass over what should hardly be passed over, namely the question of those in charge of the churches and the shepherds of the people on whom certainly rest the entire Christian faith and salvation. For just as this lower world is ruled by the movement and light of heaven, so the Christian peoples are governed by rulers as though by heavenly shepherds, who, if they are to be good, must teach others while shining themselves with the light of learning, and must lead the way by their own actions, practicing the pious deeds they preach. These are the two things which Christ, the Prince of shepherds, taught, when He ordered them to carry burning lamps in order to teach clearly and to gird themselves in order to live piously.[14] At the same time He himself did this in an extraordinary way, being the Light of the world and the Wisdom of the divine Father, and He was called the Holy of holies, because He excelled all upright men in the holiness of His life. And because of this He said, "I am the good shepherd." The evangelist who writes that He began first to act, then to teach,[15] testifies what He said on both these points. And indeed those twelve leaders who were established as princes over the entire earth were inspired and perfected by the power of the Spirit, and so comprehended the meaning of heaven that they merited the name of heaven, as the very well known prophesy proclaims: "The heavens declare the glory of God." By this we are warned that we should honor the fame of those leaders who imitated and followed the light of heaven by their wisdom and its order by their sanctity. History records how much attention therefore Councils have given to this matter which is by far the most important of all. For those who join a holy rule of life to distinguished learning are sought out from every part of the earth by the Council's Fathers and are raised up and adorned with the highest praise of those selecting them, with the fruits of the churches, and with the favor, the joy, and the applause of the people.

What should I say about that most serious and most dangerous matter of all, which everyone in our days deplores? I mean the wrongs inflicted by princes, the insolence of armies, the threats of armed force. For what can be heard or thought of that is more pitiable than that the queen of heaven and earth, the Church, is forced to be a slave to might, to surrender, or to shudder before the weapons of plunderers? This pestilence today spreads so far, rises to such a height, and gathers so much strength that all the authority of the Church and its freedom conferred by God seem overturned, struck to the ground, and completely destroyed. Therefore, beware, O Julius II, Supreme Pontiff, beware lest you believe that any man has ever conceived a better or more beneficial plan than you have conceived at the prompting of the Holy Spirit in convening a Council, whose decrees certainly no kings, no princes, can despise, nor can they disregard its commands or disparage its authority. For if there are some who by chance have dared to esteem lightly the pope alone, defenseless by himself, they have become accustomed to fear and respect him when he is provided, by the authority of a Council, with the support and devotion of princes and nations.

If we recall the accomplishments of Councils, we realize that there is nothing more effective, greater, or more powerful than these. It was at a Council that Gregory X designated Rudolph Emperor in opposition to John of Spain and Alphonso of Lusitania, at a Council that Martin IV took measures against Pedro of Aragon, at a Council that Boniface VIII decreed against King Philip. It was at a Council that once Gregory and then Eugenius, within the memory

14 Luke 12, 35.
15 Acts 1, 1.

of the Fathers, joined the Greek church to the Latin.[16] It was at a Council that both Innocent IV and Gregory IX took action against the Emperor Frederick. Indeed in this very temple, the foremost of all, ever accustomed to conquer enemies and never to be conquered, it was only at a Council that Innocent II cast down his adversaries, that Alexander III triumphed over [the antipope] Victor and his allies, that Innocent III removed Otto from the Empire, and that Martin V routed the hostile forces of the tyrants. And lest I enumerate every case, whatever measure is worthy of praise, whatever deed is worthy of glory in the Church since the time of Melchiades, either in holding off an enemy or in reconciling a state, in each instance it has had its origin in Councils and therefore should be associated with them.

For what else is a holy Council if not an object of fear for the evil, a hope for the upright, a rejection of errors, a seed-bed and revival of virtues, whereby the deceit of the devil is conquered, the allurements of the senses removed, reason restored to its lost citadel, and justice returned from heaven to earth? Indeed God returns to men. For if He has said: "Where two or three are gathered in my name, I come to them and am in the midst of them,"[17] with what greater joy does He join that gathering, where not only two or three have come, but so many leaders of the Church? If John calls the shepherds of the churches angels, what is there which so great an assembly of angels cannot seek by its petitions or obtain by its prayers from God?[18] Here Eve is called back from exile; here the head of the serpent is crushed by the heel of a more holy maiden. Abraham is led forth from the land of the Chaldeans, Agar the slave-girl submits to her mistress. A covenant with God is again made, and a spiritual circumcision is introduced. Here the father of patriarchs makes firm a ladder and opens an entrance into heaven, and he wrestles with God and receives a name by seeing God. Here the people, as though oppressed by famine in the wilderness, obtain aid from God, receive the bread of heaven and of the angels, and feast at a delectable heavenly banquet. Here, although the hearts of men have turned to stone, as it were, struck by the rod of Moses, they pour forth streams of water. Here the treasure hidden in a field is dug up, the pearl is bought, the lamps are lighted, the seed is sown in good soil, the grain of mustard seed grows up into a tree, and the wild olive is grafted onto the bountiful olive tree. Oh, those blessed times that have brought forth Councils! How foolish are the times that have not recognized their importance! How unhappy those that have not allowed them!

Since we have spoken summarily of the past benefits from Councils, let us now, as briefly as possible, touch upon those from our Council. Therefore I call upon you, Julius II, Supreme Pontiff, and Almighty God calls upon you,

---

[16] I.e., Gregory X at the Second Council of Lyons in 1274 and Eugenius IV at the Council of Florence in 1439. Egidio actually says *Gregorius alter*, but it was the same Gregory X mentioned above who sought to reunite the Greeks.

[17] Matthew 18, 20.

[18] Apocalypse 1–3.

that God who has wished you to act as His vicar on earth, who long ago chose you alone from so great a senate, who has sustained you as bridegroom of His Church into the ninth year, who has given you a good mind for planning and a great facility for acting (to none of your predecessors has He ever given so much) so that you might drive away robbers, clear the highways, put an end to insurrections, and raise the most magnificent temple of the Lord ever seen by man, and so that you might do what no one before has been able to do, make the arms of the Church fearful to great kings that you might extend your rule and recover Rimini, Faenza, Ravenna, and many other places. Even though the enemy can seize these, he cannot prevent you as Pope from accomplishing all this. For the excellence of great princes must be appraised not on the basis of chance or accident, but from plans and actions. Now two things remained for you to do, that you convene a Council and that you declare war on the common enemy of Christians. And what from the beginning you always intended, pledged, and proposed, may you now perform for God, for the Christian flock, and for your own piety and fidelity. Indeed, you should know that you have given great hope to all good men, in as much as you who had been forced to postpone these matters by the injustice of the wars and evil times could not be induced to neglect or renounce them by threats, force, or defeat. Indeed, your soul had been strengthened by that perseverance so that these waves, as numerous as they are, could not extinguish your strong love. And so God also who, besides all these immortal favors which I have mentioned to stir your soul, called you back to life in those earlier years at Bologna and then at Rome, when it was thought even within your own palace that you were dead, and preserved you to accomplish these great deeds, so that God himself by the most evident miracle might restore life to a pope that had expired and the pope by a holy Council might restore life to the Church that had expired, and so that the Church, together with a reviving pope, might restore morals to life, this God, I say, entreats and orders you to consider these two things in your heart, to give attention to them, and to accomplish them. And just as He commands the prophet, He commands you to tear down, root up, and destroy errors, luxury, and vice, and to build, establish, and plant moderation, virtue, and holiness.[19]

Many things, but especially the loss of the army, should prompt us to perform these deeds, for indeed I think that it was an act of divine Providence that relying on arms alien to the Church we suffered defeat, so that returning to our own arms we might become victors.[20] But our weapons, to use the words of the Apostle, are piety, devotion, honesty, prayers, offerings, the shield of faith, and the arms of light.[21] If we return to these with the aid of the Council, just as with arms that were not ours we were inferior to an enemy,

---

[19] Jeremiah 1, 10.
[20] Egidio refers, of course, to the defeat of the Spanish-papal forces by the French at Ravenna on Easter Sunday, April 11, 1512. See Pastor, VI, 398–406.
[21] Ephesians 6, 13–17; Romans 13, 12.

so with our own weapons we shall be superior to every enemy. Call to mind, I beg, the war which Moses waged against King Amalec.[22] You will see that God's chosen people when trusting in the sword were always conquered, but when they offered prayers they were always victorious. Joshua led the army into battle, Aaron with Hur and Moses climbed the mountain. The former with their bodies armed engaged the enemy, the latter with hearts made clean prayed to God; those strove with swords, these with prayers, those fought with iron, these with piety. We see both kinds of arms—of the military and of religion, but with God instructing us let us now learn which are ours. As long as Moses raised his hands, He says, our army gained the mastery, but when he put his hands down the army wavered. And lest we suspect that this happened by chance, at the end of this account it is written that the hand of God and the war is against Amalec, that is against the enemy of the Church from generation to generation. Certainly by these words God warns that both the generation and the Church of Moses and of Christ is conquered by military arms, but conquers by zealous piety, and that by striving with weapons it is overcome, but by doing what is holy it overcomes.

In the beginning relying on its own arms the Church gained Africa, took possession of Europe, occupied Asia. Not by war, not by the sword, but by the deeds of religion and the reputation for sanctity the Church carried the Christian banners throughout the entire world. But when the Bride, who at that time everywhere was called, brought forth, and greatly desired in her golden robes, exchanged the golden cloak of the burning spirit for the iron weapons of a mad Ajax, she lost the power born of the blood of the twelve Apostles, she abandoned Asia and Jerusalem, she was forced to relinquish Africa and Egypt, and she saw a good part of Europe together with the Byzantine Empire and Greece taken from her. It is the voice of God telling us that when Moses' hands grow weary and prayers and offerings cease Joshua is conquered and Amalec triumphs. So we see that when religion exchanges offerings for the sword in virtually the whole world the Church is struck, cast forth, and rejected to the immense profit of Mohammed, who, unless the sword is put down and we return again into the bosom of piety at the altars and the shrines of God, will grow stronger day by day, will subjugate all to his power, and as the wicked avenger of our impiety will take possession of the entire world.

I see, yes, I see that, unless by this Council or by some other means we place a limit on our morals, unless we force our greedy desire for human things, the source of evils, to yield to the love of divine things, it is all over with Christendom, all over with religion, even all over with those very resources which our fathers acquired by their greater service of God, but which we are about to lose because of our neglect. For from extreme poverty these resources became most abundant in such a way that they seem not so long

[22] Exodus 17.

after about to perish, and, unless we sound the signal for retreat, unless we have regard for our interests, this most rich fillet,[23] which had served to decorate the heads of the priests, will be found hardly to cover them. Hear the divine voices everywhere sounding, everywhere demanding a Council, peace, that holy enterprise [against the Moslems]. When has our life been more effeminate? When has ambition been more unrestrained, greed more burning? When has the license to sin been more shameless? When has temerity in speaking, in arguing, in writing against piety been more common or more unafraid? When has there been among the people not only a greater neglect but a greater contempt for the sacred, for the sacraments, for the keys [of forgiveness of sins], and for the holy commandments? When has our religion and faith been more open to the derision even of the lowest classes? When, O sorrow, has there been a more disastrous split in the Church? When has war been more dangerous, the enemy more powerful, armies more cruel? When have the signs, portents, and prodigies both of a threatening heaven and of a terrified earth appeared more numerous or more horrible? When (alas, tears hold me back) has the slaughter and destruction been bloodier than at Brescia or at Ravenna? When, I say, did any day among accursed days dawn with more grief or calamity than that most holy day of the Resurrection?[24]

If we are not without feeling, what, pray, are all these things but words sent from heaven? For, as Proclus says, the words of God are deeds, and the prophecies declare: "He spoke and they were created."[25] In the sacred writings of the Jews, in the ten declarations contained in Genesis,[26] we read that the whole world was created. Therefore, what we are witnessing are words, the words of God warning and instructing you to hold a Council, to reform the Church, to end war between men, to restore peace to your Bride assailed on every side, to avert the sword threatening the throat of the city and of Italy, and to curb our unbridled living which afflicts the heart of the Church with very great wounds.

For it is of no importance how much land we own, but rather how just, how holy, how eager for divine things we are, so that finally after so many evils, so many hardships, and so many calamities, you may hear Christ our Lord making known to Peter and to posterity that the Council is the one and only remedy for all evils, the sole port for the ship in distress, the single means of strengthening the commonweal. He says: "Thou, Peter, being once converted, confirm thy brethren."[27] Do you hear, Peter? do you hear, Paul? Do you hear, O most holy heads, protectors and defenders of the city of Rome? Do you hear into what a mass of evils the Church founded in your blood has been led? Do you see the wretched battle line on both sides? Do you see the

[23] The term fillet is used by extension (and in a classical sense) to signify the wealth and possessions of the Church.
[24] The battle of Ravenna, a most sanguinary one, took place on the Easter Sunday just preceding Egidio's address.
[25] Psalms 148, 5.
[26] I.e., the ten parts beginning "God said" in Genesis 1.
[27] Luke 22, 32.

slaughter? Do you see the destruction? Do you see the battlefield buried under piles of the slain? Do you see that in this year the earth has drunk more gore than water, less rain than blood? Do you see that as much Christian strength lay in the grave as would be enough to wage war against the enemy of the faith and that nothing but ruin and destruction remain for us? Bring us aid, help us, succor us, and, as you, plucked the Church from the jaws of the Jews and the tyrants, raise it up now as it falls under the weight of its own disasters.

The people pray, men, women, every age, both sexes, the entire world. The Fathers ask, the Senate entreats, finally the Pope himself as a suppliant implores you to preserve him, the Church, the city of Rome, these temples, these altars, these your own principal shrines, and to make strong the Lateran Council, proclaimed today in your presence by the Supreme Pontiff Julius II (may it be auspicious, happy and favorable for us, for your Church and for all of Christendom), that it may accomplish under the power of the Holy Spirit the surest salvation of the world. We beg you to see to it that the Christian princes are brought to peace and the arms of our kings turned against Mohammed, the public enemy of Christ, and that the fire of charity of the Church is not only not extinguished by these waves and storms, but that by the merits of the saving Cross and under the guidance of the Holy Spirit, which are jointly commemorated today, it is cleansed from every stain it has received and is restored to its ancient splendor and purity.

CHAPTER V

The Reform Bull
Supernae dispositionis arbitrio,
1514

After its inaugural assembly on May 3, 1512, Lateran V held twelve formal sessions, generally with less than a hundred bishops in attendance, chiefly Italian.[1] In its first period under Julius II there were five sessions, and the attention of the Council centered on the struggle against the French-sponsored *conciliabulum* at Pisa-Milan and on the affirmation of papal authority. After the death of Julius in February, 1513, and the election of Cardinal Giovanni de' Medici as Leo X in March, the Council held seven sessions until its dissolution in March, 1517. In this second period, which witnessed the settlement of the quarrel with France, the question of reform, as well as several other significant matters, was taken up, and the most notable decrees were approved and then promulgated as papal bulls.

The most important and comprehensive of these decrees from the reform standpoint was that approved at the ninth session on May 5, 1514, and published as the bull *Supernae dispositionis arbitrio.*[2] It is the document which is presented here. Several other bulls also dealt with the problem of reform, particularly two from the tenth session on May 4, 1515, and two from the eleventh session on December 19, 1516.[3] The burden of this legislation is (1) to limit exemptions and strengthen the authority of the bishops over their clergy (and, in a brief clause, to stipulate that provincial synods be held every three years); (2) to authorize examination and publication approval for all printed books by the diocesan authorities; (3) to limit unauthorized preaching and to confine preachers to "the truth of the Gospel and the Holy Scriptures in accordance with the teaching, interpretation, and exposition of the doctors of the Church," and (4) to give the bishops greater authority over the regular clergy in their dioceses.[4] Two other bulls issuing from the Council also deserve

[1] On the Council, see the volumes referred to in Chap. IV, n. 1.

[2] The Latin text is in Mansi, XXXII, 874–85, and slightly abridged in *Disciplinary Decrees of the General Councils,* ed. and trans. H. J. Schroeder (St. Louis, 1937), pp. 631–39. Schroeder, pp. 488–98, also gives an English translation, which contains the entire decree minus the opening and closing lines of the bull. This translation, with the permission of the B. Herder Book Co., has been reprinted below. The bull was also printed in Rome in 1514 under the caption *Bulla Reformationis.*

[3] The four bulls specified are *Regimini universalis ecclesiae, Inter solicitudines, Supernae majestatis praesidio,* and *Dum intra mentis arcana.* They may be found in an abridged English translation in Schroeder, *op. cit.,* pp. 500–9.

[4] This last bull involved the old quarrel between the bishops and the mendicants who were exempt from episcopal authority—an issue which produced great friction at the

mention. In *Apostolici regiminis*, perhaps the most famous pronouncement of Lateran V, approved at the eighth session on December 19, 1513, the Fathers declared themselves on a very lively philosophical controversy of the time and condemned the teaching of the Averroists on the mortality of the rational soul.[5] In *Inter multiplices* (tenth session, May 4, 1515) they approved the establishment of charitable pawnshops, known as *montes pietatis*, which loaned money to the poor.

At first glance the legislation of Lateran V seems quite impressive, but unfortunately the reform measures that were taken had very little effect. They "lost much of their value on account of the lack of earnestness and determination of the leading personalities, beginning with the Pope himself."[6] They remained little more than words on paper, ignored by those who had the responsibility of applying them. An opportunity to remedy some of the worst abuses, to begin the reform that was so desperately needed, was missed, and in this failure at this historic moment it is hard not to be struck by the culpability of the Pope and the Curia. In a sense a final warning had been given them. In March, 1517, Gianfrancesco Pico della Mirandola addressed an oration to Leo X and the Lateran Council on the reform of morals in the Church.[7] Condemning the evil lives of priests and prelates and urging the Pope to take action, he uttered these prophetic words:

> These diseases and these wounds must be healed by you, Holy Father; otherwise, if you fail to heal these wounds, I fear that God Himself, whose place on earth you take, will not apply a gentle cure, but with fire and sword will cut off those diseased members and destroy them; and I believe that He has already clearly given signs of his future remedy.

The prompt and conscientious application of the reform bull *Supernae dispositionis arbitrio* that now follows might have begun at least the healing process.

Council. Leo X arranged a compromise that saved the friars. See Hughes, *op. cit.*, III, 482–84.

[5] Schroeder, *op. cit.*, pp. 487–88. On the philosophical controversy, see Eugenio Garin, *Italian Humanism*, trans. Peter Munz (New York, 1965), Chap. V.

[6] Jedin, *op. cit.*, I, 132. See also a comparable judgment in Pastor, VIII, 393, 410–12.

[7] It is not clear whether Pico delivered his oration before a meeting of the Council in the presence of the Pope or whether it was sent to Leo X as a letter. The address is not in Mansi or in the early *Decreta et acta concilii Lateranensis* (Rome, 1521). It appears to have been printed first at Hagenau in 1520 and then at Bologna in 1523.

SINCE THERE is nothing more injurious to the Church of God than the promotion of unworthy prelates to the government of the churches, we ordain and decree that in the future vacant patriarchal, metropolitan, and cathedral churches as well as abbeys be filled in accordance with the requirements of the constitution of Alexander in the Lateran Council,[8] that is, with persons of mature age, good moral character, and the necessary learning, and not at the instance of anyone, nor through *commendam* and administration or any other manner, unless in consideration of the needs of the churches or in consideration of prudence, nobility, uprightness, experience, or time-honored courtesy or common consent (*curialitatis antiquae*) combined with the required learning, it should appear expedient to do otherwise. The same we wish to be observed in regard to the election and postulation of those whose election and postulation the Holy See has been accustomed to accept. Should it happen that vacant bishoprics and abbeys are filled with persons who have not yet attained the thirtieth year of age, dispensations may be granted in the case of the former to those only who have completed their twenty-seventh year, and in the case of abbeys to those only who have completed their twenty-second year.

2. That the promotion of competent persons may be realized, we decree that the cardinal who is commissioned to receive the report of elections, postulations, and provisions of cathedral churches and abbeys, shall, before he presents the result of his examination of the report in consistory, as is customary, make it known in person to the oldest cardinal of each of the three orders in the consistory, or, if on the day on which he received his commission no consistory is held, make it known to them through his secretary or through any one of his *familiares;* these cardinals shall then as soon as possible make it known to the others. The matter of the election, postulation, and promotion is to be summarily examined by the said card-

[8] Alexander III in the Third Lateran Council, canon 3.

inal; opponents, if any, are to be summoned, competent and trustworthy witnesses questioned, and, if deemed expedient, others may be called *ex officio*. A copy of the process, together with the testimony of witnesses, must be laid before the consistory by the cardinal, and he may not confirm the report before the candidate has visited the majority of the cardinals, so that these may, so far as the candidate is concerned, learn through interview (*oculata fide*) and personal contact what will be conveyed to them by the referee colleague. The candidate is bound by an old and laudable custom, which is to be strictly observed, to visit the cardinals in the Curia as soon as possible.

3. That the episcopal dignity may be protected against the machinations of dishonest men and the calumnies of accusers, we decree that no bishop or abbot may be deprived of his dignity at the instance or request of anybody without a complete and legitimate defense; not even in the case of a notorious crime may this be done without an examination of the parties seeking such deprivation and without satisfactory proof. No prelate is to be transferred against his will except for weighty and legitimate reasons, and then in accordance with the form and decree of the Council of Constance.[9]

4. As experience has often taught, monasteries sustain grave losses both in spiritual and temporal affairs through provisional collation and occupation (that is, when given *in commendam*), because, partly through the negligence and partly through the greed and carelessness of those to whom they are entrusted, their buildings fall to ruin, divine worship in them declines day by day, and now and then opportunity is given, especially to laymen, to criticize and speak ill of the practice, not without detracting from the honor of the Apostolic See from which such concessions proceed. Therefore we wish and decree that when in monasteries the office of abbot becomes vacant through the death of the incumbent, these monasteries may not in the future be given *in commendam* to anyone under any agreement, unless, to maintain the authority of the Apostolic See and to meet the malice of the enemies of that see, in consideration of the condition of the times and with the advice of our brethren, it should be deemed expedient to do otherwise. But, in accordance with the above-mentioned constitution, they must be provided with competent persons, so that, as becomes these monasteries, able abbots may preside over them. But those monasteries that will be given *in commendam* are to be given only to cardinals and well-qualified and well-deserving persons, so, however, that the *commendatarii* to whom those monasteries will in the future be given *in commendam*, whatever dignity, honor, or preeminence they may enjoy, including the cardinalitial dignity, if they have a revenue separate from that of the monastery, shall be bound to apply a fourth part of their revenues to the restoration of the buildings or to the purchase and repair of decorations, vestments, and ornamented altar-cloths or to the relief of the poor, as necessity may require; but if the revenue be a common one they shall be bound to apply a third of all the incomes of the monastery given them *in commendam* to the

---

[9] The decree is from the thirty-ninth session (October 9, 1417) and is given in Hefele-Leclercq, *op. cit.*, VII, 465.

above-mentioned purposes and to the support of the monks after all other obligations have been deducted. Documents drawn up in connection with monasteries thus given *in commendam* must be provided with a clause specifically expressing this, otherwise they are to be regarded as null and void. And, since it is only proper that churches of this kind should suffer no diminution of incomes, we decree that no financial burdens of any kind be laid upon the revenues of these churches, except *ex resignationis causa* or for some other reason considered in our secret consistory as just and proper.

5. We decree furthermore that in the future parochial churches, major dignities, and other ecclesiastical benefices with revenues that do not reach annually the sum of 200 ducats according to the common value, as well as hospitals, leper institutions, pilgrim-houses, and the like, which have been established for the poor, whatever their value, may no longer be given *in commendam* to the cardinals of the Roman Church or conferred under any title whatsoever on anybody, unless they have become vacant through the death of their servants (*familiares*), in which case they may be given *in commendam* to the cardinals, who, however, are bound to give them over within six months to persons capable and agreeable to them, without prejudice to their right of regress to these benefices.

6. Branches of churches, monasteries, and military orders are not to be separated from their mother foundations without reasonable and legitimate cause. *Uniones perpetuae* may not be established except in cases permitted by law or without a reasonable cause.

7. Dispensations for more than two incompatible benefices may not be granted except for weighty and urgent reasons to those only who are qualified according to the form of the common law. Those persons, whatever their dignity, who hold more than four parochial churches or their perpetual vicariates and *majores et principales dignitates*, we limit from now on to a period of two years, within which they must resign all but four into the hands of the ordinary, who shall confer them on others, notwithstanding any, even general, reservation or one resulting *ex qualitatibus resignantium personarum*. If at the expiration of this term the required resignations have not been handed in, then all benefices shall be regarded as vacant and be freely bestowed on others, the negligence to resign, however, to be punished in accordance with the constitution *Exsecrabilis* of John XXII. We likewise decree that special reservations of benefices of any and every kind are no more to be granted at the instance or request of anybody.

The second part of this constitution concerns itself with the cardinals.

Since the cardinals are the highest dignitaries in the Church after the pope, it is proper that they should be to all examples of purity of life and of the splendor of virtue. Wherefore, we not only exhort and admonish them but also ordain and decree that they live in accordance with the teaching of the Apostle, soberly, chastely, and piously, abstaining not only from evil but also from every appearance of evil.

1. They are to be vigilant, attentive to the divine offices and the celebration of mass, have their chapels in becoming places, abstain from luxury and pomp in their houses, table, furniture, and servants, have before their eyes priestly moderation, and treat in a friendly manner all who come to the Roman Curia.

2. They shall not have prelates and bishops as servants, lest those by consecration and sacred character superior to others be reduced to a menial ministry and thus bring contempt on the pastoral office. Those whom they now have or will have in the future, let them treat as brothers and in a manner becoming their state.

3. Since they assist the Roman pontiff, the common father of all the faithful, they may not be *personarum acceptores* or advocates. We decree moreover that they harbor no partiality, do not become *defensores* of princes, communities, or others against anyone except in so far as justice and equity demand and their dignity and state require; but, having divested themselves of all prejudice and self-interest, let them strive to end disputes and bring about peace among all. Let them with pious zeal promote the just undertakings of princes and all others but especially those of the poor and the religious and, as becomes their office, let them so far as their resources will permit aid the oppressed and those unjustly burdened.

4. At least once each year they shall, personally if present in the Curia, or, if absent, through a competent vicar, visit the *tituli sui loca*, make inquiry concerning the clergy and people of the churches subject to their title, shall be vigilant regarding divine worship and the properties of those churches, inform themselves about the life and morals of the clerics and people and with paternal affection admonish all to lead upright and virtuous lives.

5. For the increase of divine worship and for the salvation of his soul, each cardinal shall donate to his titular church either during life or by will *in mortis articulo* as much as is necessary for the suitable maintenance of one priest, or, in case the church should need repairs or other aid, let him make his donation for this purpose, according as his conscience may dictate.

6. Although relatives, especially if they are poor and well-deserving, are not to be neglected but are rather to be cared for, nevertheless, they may not be provided with many benefices or so enriched by means of ecclesiastical revenues that others sustain loss through such generosity; a practice that opens the way to scandal. We decree, therefore, that the goods of the churches be not spent thoughtlessly or squandered, but applied to good and pious purposes.

7. We wish also that the cardinals give due attention to the needs of the churches and benefices bestowed on them *in commendam*, and provide worthy and competent auxiliary bishops or vicars for cathedrals with adequate compensation. For other churches and for monasteries given them *in commendam* let them provide a sufficient number of clerics or religious to give praiseworthy service to God. They shall also be solicitous for the preservation of the buildings, possessions, and rights, and dilapidated structures they shall have restored.

8. In regard to the number of servants and horses, the cardinals should act cautiously and with foresight, lest having a greater number than their means, state, and dignity will permit, they can be accused of indulging in luxury and

extravagance; while, on the other hand, they will be considered greedy and niggardly if having an abundance they furnish food to a very few. For the house of a cardinal should be a hospitable one, a harbor and shelter for learned and upright men, for impoverished nobles and persons of high repute and esteem. Let them, therefore, act prudently in this matter, having a knowledge of the character of their servants, lest their wickedness anchor upon them a bad name and thus furnish occasion for gossip and calumny among the common people.

9. Each cardinal should prove himself to be the ruler of his house not only in matters external that are apparent to all but also in matters secreted within; he should be surrounded by virtuous priests and Levites in clerical garb. Let him see to it that no one in his household constituted in sacred orders and having a benefice wears clothes of different colors or clothes out of place in the ecclesiastical order. Those constituted in the order of the priesthood must wear garments of a color not forbidden to clerics by law, and these garments must extend at least to the ankles. Those having dignities in cathedral churches, canons also of cathedrals, and those having the first or chief dignity in collegiate churches, as well as chaplains of cardinals celebrating mass, are bound to wear the capuche in public.

10. The *parafrenarii* whose work is steady and arduous may, even if they are clerics but not constituted in the sacerdotal order, wear shorter and more convenient garments, so however that they are in keeping with propriety.

11. The other clerics shall carry out all things temperately and with discretion; shall not cultivate long hair or a beard; neither shall they have horses and mules with coverings and ornaments made of velvet or silk, but for things of this kind let them use coarse cloth or simply hide or leather.

12. If any of the aforesaid servants act in contravention of these provisions, or after three months from the time of the publication of the present instruction, in spite of a previous admonition, continue to wear the prohibited garments, let them incur the sentence of excommunication. If within three months they do not reform, let them be suspended from the collection of the revenues accruing from their benefices. If for six more months they continue in their obstinacy, let them after a legitimate admonition be deprived of all their benefices, which being then vacant may be freely disposed of by the Apostolic See.

13. All of these provisions are to apply also to the servants of the Roman pontiff, to all *clerici beneficiati*, those constituted in major orders, and to the Curia; by way of a single exception, the servants of the Roman pontiff may in accordance with custom and in consideration of the papal dignity wear garments of red color.

14. And since the *operum optimorum cura* pertains chiefly to the cardinals, these shall endeavor to ascertain what regions are infested with heresies, errors, and superstitions against the true and orthodox faith; where the observance of the divine commandments is neglected; what kings, princes, or people are burdened with war or fear that they will be so burdened. These and similar matters they shall strive to learn and keep the reigning Roman pontiff informed

in regard to them, so that he may seek opportune and salutary measures to remedy such evils.

15. Since it is known from almost daily experience that many evils often come about and not a few scandals arise in provinces and cities, not without detriment to the Apostolic See, on account of the absence of their legates *de latere*, we decree that cardinals who are appointed as legates in provinces and cities, may not entrust their office to representatives or any other officials, but must themselves be present during the greater part of the year and administer it themselves with care and concern. Those cardinals who now hold the title of legate, must within three months if they are in Italy, or if they are outside of Italy, then within five months, from the day of the publication of the present instruction, betake themselves to their provinces and reside there the greater part of the time, unless by our order or by that of our successor they are detained at the Curia on account of some important business or are sent to other localities, as necessity may require. In this case they may have in those provinces and cities vice-legates, auditors, and other customary officials, provided with suitable compensations. He who does not observe each and all of the foregoing provisions, loses all remuneration in connection with the legation. Legations have been established for the benefit of the people, not for the benefit of the legates.

16. Since the chief duties of a cardinal are to assist the pope and to take care of the business of the Apostolic See, we decree further that all cardinals reside at the Roman Curia and that the absentees return, if they are in Italy, within six months, if outside of Italy, within a year, from the day of the publication of this constitution; otherwise they lose the revenues of their benefices and the emoluments of all their offices and shall, moreover, be deprived during their absence of all privileges generally and specially granted to cardinals, those being excepted who by reason of an office bestowed by the Apostolic See, or at the command or with the permission of the Roman pontiff or for some other legitimate cause, such as illness, happen to be absent; those privileges and immunities granted to the cardinals and contained in our bull under date of our coronation, they retain.

17. We decree also that the total funeral expenses of the cardinals must not exceed the sum of 1,500 florins, and only *justis allegatis causis et rationibus* may the executors spend more. The solemn obsequies and the *castrum doloris* take place on the first and ninth day; during the octave the customary masses may be celebrated.

18. Out of reverence for the Apostolic See and for the common honor of the pope and the cardinals; moreover, that occasions for scandal may not be given, that a greater liberty of voting may obtain in the sacred senate (consistory), and that each cardinal may freely and safely express his mind according to his conscience, we decree that no cardinal may under penalty of perjury and disobedience reveal in writing or by word of mouth or in any other way the votes cast in consistory, or anything done or said there that might lead to the hatred, injury, or scandal of another. The silence imposed by the pontiff in reference to certain matters is to be observed, and he who acts contrariwise

incurs besides the ordinary penalties also excommunication *latae sententiae,* from which, except *in extremis,* he can be absolved only by the Roman pontiff.

The third part of the constitution deals with the reform of the Curia and others.

1. Since youth like every age is prone to evil and requires painstaking labor to habituate it to the good, we decree that masters and teachers instruct their pupils not only in grammar, rhetoric, and other subjects of this kind, but impart to them also religious instruction, dealing especially with the commandments, the articles of faith, hymns, psalms, and the lives of the saints. On festival days their instructions ought to be limited to matters pertaining to religion and good morals, urging them to go to church, to attend mass, vespers, and the divine offices, and to listen attentively to the sermons and instructions.

2. To abolish that execrable vice of blasphemy which brings the name of God and things sacred into such contempt, we decree that whoever openly or publicly speaks evilly and dishonorably of God and by offensive and obscene language blasphemes our Lord Jesus Christ or the glorious Virgin Mary, His Mother, shall, if he be a public official, for the first and second offense, lose three months' remuneration attached to that office; for the third offense, let him be regarded as *eo ipso* deprived of that office. If he be a priest or cleric he shall for the first offense be deprived for one year of the revenues of his benefices. For the second offense, if he has only one benefice, he shall be deprived of it; if he has several, he shall lose the one of which his ordinary decides to deprive him. For the third offense, he shall be regarded as *eo ipso* deprived of all his dignities and benefices, and furthermore, rendered unqualified to hold them again, so that they may be freely disposed of. If the offender be a layman of noble extraction, he shall for the first offense pay twenty-five ducats, for the second fifty ducats, which are to be applied to the basilica of the chief of the Apostles, and for the third he shall lose his rank. A layman of the ordinary class shall be punished with imprisonment; if, however, he is guilty of more than two offenses, he shall with the hood of infamy (*mitra infamiae*) on his head stand for one day at the door of the principal church. He who offends repeatedly in this matter is in the discretion of the judge to be condemned to life imprisonment or to the galleys. *In foro conscientiae* no one may absolve a blasphemer without the imposition of the severest penance. He who blasphemes other saints shall be punished more leniently, according to the discretion of the judge and with consideration of the person. We decree also that secular judges who do not proceed against and duly punish blasphemers when they are brought before them, are to be judged guilty of the same offense and punished accordingly. Those, however, who are zealous and strict in punishing those guilty of this vice, gain each time an indulgence of ten years and receive one third of the fines. Whoever hears anyone blaspheming is bound to rebuke him severely if it can be done without danger to himself, or report him within three days to an ecclesiastical or secular judge. If several have heard him at the same time, each is bound to report him unless they agree that one can act for all.

In virtue of holy obedience we exhort and admonish secular rulers and all Christians for the honor of the holy name to enforce and to have these provisions enforced in their dominions and territories, assuring them of a generous heavenly reward for so good and pious a work. For each blasphemer brought to punishment they gain an indulgence of ten years and receive one third of the fines. The same indulgence and financial reward are granted also to those who report blasphemers to the proper authorities. All other penalties directed by ecclesiastical canons against blasphemers remain in force.

3. That clerics especially may live chastely and continently as required by the sacred canons, we decree that those who do the contrary be severely punished. If anyone, cleric or layman, be convicted of the crime on account of which the anger of God came upon the children of unbelief, let him be punished in accordance with the sacred canon or the civil law respectively. *Concubinarii*, whether clerical or lay, shall be punished in accordance with the same canons. Toleration by superiors, contrary custom, or any other subterfuge cannot be accepted as justifiable excuses; these must be corrected and those who tolerate them punished in accordance with the law.

4. For the peace and benefit of the cities and of all localities subject to the Roman Church, we hereby renew the *Constitutiones Aegidii olim episcopi Sabinensis* (1356)[10] and prescribe their strict observance.

5. That that nefarious pest known as simony be forever banished from the Roman Curia and from all Christendom, we hereby renew the constitutions published by our predecessors against it, decreeing their strict observance and the imposition of the penalties prescribed therein on delinquents.

6. We decree also that anyone who has a benefice, with or without the *cura animarum,* and after six months from the time that he obtained it has not said the divine office (Breviary), though every reasonable impediment has ceased to exist, may not make the revenues of the benefice his own in proportion to the time of the omission, but is bound to apply them as unjustly obtained to the church building or use them to supply the needs of the poor. If he continues this neglect, he shall, after having been warned beforehand, be deprived of the benefice, for it is *propter officium* that the benefice is conferred. He who does not recite the divine office at least twice in fifteen days is punishable in this way, that he has placed himself in a position to be deprived of his benefice; in addition he will have to give an answer to God for this neglect. In the case of those who have several benefices, the punishment is reiterative as often as they are convicted of acting in contravention of this provision.

7. Since the plenary disposition and administration of the revenues of cathedral and metropolitan churches, of monasteries, and all other ecclesiastical benefices belong solely to the Roman pontiff and to those who canonically hold them, and secular princes may not intrude themselves and interfere in matters belonging to said churches, monasteries, and benefices, we decree that the incomes and revenues of churches, monasteries, and benefices may not be

---

[10] Cardinal Albornoz, *Liber constitutionum* (Jesi, 1475).

sequestrated, seized, or in any manner held, nor, if held under some fancied pretext, may the respective ecclesiastical administrators be hindered in their free disposition of them by secular princes, not even by the emperor or kings or their officials and judges, nor by any other person whether public or private. What has been sequestrated or seized must be restored freely and integrally, without exception and delay, to the prelates to whom they *de jure* belong. If anything has been dissipated or squandered, those who are responsible for the sequestrations and seizures must make full satisfaction to the prelates under penalty of excommunication or interdict. Those who act contrary to these provisions shall be punished with ecclesiastical censures, with the deprivation of the fiefs and privileges that they have received from the Church, and with the punitive measures prescribed by the canons, all of which we hereby renew.

8. Since human and divine law give laymen no authority over ecclesiastical persons, we renew the constitutions *Felicis* of Boniface VIII and *Si quis suadente* of Clement V, and also all other Apostolic decrees issued in defense of ecclesiastical liberty and against those who seek to destroy it, the penalties contained in the bull *In Coena Domini*[11] against the latter to remain in force. The decisions of earlier general councils forbidding, under penalty of excommunication, the imposition of tithes and other burdens on ecclesiastical persons, or even their acceptance when freely given, are hereby renewed. Those who give aid or advice in the matter or in any manner abet transgressors, incur excommunication *latae sententiae*. Cities and communities are subject to interdict. Prelates submitting to such impositions or consenting to them without the express permission of the Roman pontiff incur *ipso facto* excommunication and deposition.

9. Since sortileges through the invocation of demons, incantations, divinations, and other species of superstition are forbidden by the civil and canon law, we decree that clerics who are found guilty of such practices be punished in accordance with the judgment of superiors; in case of obstinacy they are to be deposed and confined temporarily in a monastery. Laymen of both sexes are subject to excommunication and other penalties of the law, both civil and canonical.

10. That all false and fictitious Christians of whatever race or nation, especially those tainted with heresy, and Judaizers may be completely driven out of Christian communities and especially out of the Roman Curia and duly punished, we decree that careful investigation be made everywhere and above all in the said Curia, and action taken against them by judges appointed by us. If convicted, let them be duly punished; in case of relapse, let them be banished from the Church without hope of pardon.

11. These decrees and ordinations concern life, morals, and ecclesiastical discipline. They are binding on all, including our officials, whether they reside at the Roman Curia or elsewhere, and we wish and decree that they be inviolably observed. We decree further that they become effective two months from the time of their publication.

[11] This bull is so called because from 1364 to 1770 it was published annually at Rome, and since 1567 elsewhere, on Holy Thursday, i.e., *on the Lord's Supper.*

CHAPTER VI

Erasmus' Sileni Alcibiadis, 1515

The influence and importance of Erasmus, the great Christian humanist, in the early sixteenth century can hardly be overestimated.[1] He was the foremost scholar of his day, and his scholarly achievement, reinforced by the wit and grace of his style and the thrust of his purpose, won wide acclaim. It is this union of attributes that is most interesting in Erasmus and that accounts for the fame and stature he attained. In the essay *Sileni Alcibiadis* presented here, this characteristic Erasmian combination will be seen, but it is the purpose of the scholar that chiefly concerns us. Erasmus was above all a reformer—a reformer of theology, a reformer of morals, a reformer of Christian society—and the essential aim of his life's work was to lead men back to the honesty and simplicity of the Gospel pattern. He sought to accomplish this by bringing humanist scholarship to bear on the scriptural and patristic sources of Europe's faith and by reopening them thereby for the religious enlightenment and moral guidance of the men of his day. If he is the humanist in the classical sense, his classicism is nevertheless subordinate to his religious purpose and to the propagation of what he came to call "the philosophy of Christ."[2] His scholarly and

---

[1] The literature on Erasmus is vast, and the interpretation of him and his work is marked by a variety of views and judgments. Two excellent introductions are Margaret Mann Phillips, *Erasmus and the Northern Renaissance* (London, 1949), and J.-C. Margolin, *Erasme par lui-même* (Paris, 1965). A standard biography is J. Huizinga, *Erasmus of Rotterdam*, trans. F. Hopman (New York, 1952). See also introduction, "Erasmus and Reform," in *Christian Humanism and the Reformation: Selected Writings of Erasmus*, ed. John C. Olin (New York, 1965), and the bibliography appended.

Erasmus' own works in recent translation are: Margaret Mann Phillips, *The 'Adages' of Erasmus* (Cambridge, 1964), a study together with translations of some of the most important Adages; *The Enchiridion of Erasmus*, trans. Raymond Himelick (Bloomington, Ind., 1963); *The Praise of Folly*, trans. Hoyt Hudson (Princeton, 1941); *The Colloquies of Erasmus*, trans. Craig R. Thompson (Chicago, 1965); and the selections in *Christian Humanism and the Reformation*.

The standard *Opera* is that edited in ten volumes by Johannes Clericus (Leiden, 1703-6). A new one under the patronage of the Union académique internationale is now in progress. Erasmus' huge correspondence has been edited in the *Opus epistolarum Des. Erasmi Roterdami*, eds. P. S. Allen, H. M. Allen, and H. W. Garrod (12 vols.; Oxford, 1906–58)—a magnificent work, indispensable for the serious student of Erasmus and his age.

[2] This significant Erasmian phrase is first used in 1516 in the *Paraclesis*, Erasmus' preface to his Greek and Latin New Testament. It comprehends nothing more than the teaching of Christ as revealed in the Gospel, which Erasmus sees as capable of effecting a transformation, in fact "a rebirth . . . the restoration of human nature originally well formed." *Christian Humanism and the Reformation*, p. 100. The phrase is previously suggested in the *Sileni Alcibiadis*. See also Margaret Mann Phillips, "La

5. Erasmus of Rotterdam. Copy of Quentin Metsys' portrait of Erasmus by Cornelis Visscher.

literary endeavors, often pursued with a biting criticism of the ways of the world about him and with an irony peculiar to his mind, can only be understood in the light of this broad reform goal.

He was born, out of wedlock, in Rotterdam, probably in the year 1466, and as a boy attended a famous school in Deventer staffed by the Brothers of the Common Life. There he came into close contact with the *Devotio moderna* and was introduced to the new humanism then making its appearance in northern Europe. (His thought is frequently said to embody the fusion of these two currents.) He entered the monastery of the Augustinian canons at Steyn around 1487 and was ordained a priest there in 1492. He left his monastery shortly after that, taking a post as secretary to the Bishop of Cambrai and later proceeding to Paris to study theology. His career as humanist and scholar now begins to unfold, but most important, even decisive, in the story of this development was a visit he made to England in 1499. There he met John Colet, then lecturing at Oxford on St. Paul's Epistles, and several other notable English scholars, including the young Thomas More. The example and friendship of these men, above all of Colet, helped Erasmus set the goal which would henceforth give direction to his life's work.[3]

The following year, after his return to Paris, his first book appeared, the *Adagia,* a collection of some eight hundred Latin proverbs drawn from the major classical authors.[4] This small volume launched his public career, which was to continue with unusual dedication and untiring energy down to his death in 1536 and was to carry him to a pinnacle of influence attained by few other writers or scholars in European history. His life was restless and marked by frequent travel and change of residence—Louvain, Venice, Cambridge, Basel, and Freiburg became his temporary home—but his books and editions poured forth, his renown grew, and he continued to serve the cause of Christian learning and renewal with remarkable constancy of purpose to the end of his days. The titles of only a few of his most significant works can be mentioned: the *Enchiridion,* or *Handbook of the Christian Soldier* (1503), *The Praise of Folly* (1511), the Greek and Latin New Testament (1516), the edition of St. Jerome (1516), *The Education of a Christian Prince* (1516), the *Colloquies* (1522).[5]

'Philosophia Christi' reflétée dans les 'Adages' d'Erasme," *Courants religieux et humanisme à la fin du XVe et au début du XVIe siècle* (Paris, 1959), pp. 53–71.

[3] On Colet, see Chap. III. On Colet's influence and on the community of ideas he, Erasmus, and More shared, see especially Frederic Seebohm, *The Oxford Reformers* (2d ed.; London, 1869), and E. E. Reynolds, *Thomas More and Erasmus* (New York, 1965).

[4] The *Adagia* went through many editions and enlargements during Erasmus' lifetime and came to contain more than four thousand adages, some of them, like the *Sileni Alcibiadis,* major essays. Notable are the edition of the Aldine Press in Venice in 1508, the *Adagiorum Chiliades,* and Froben's edition at Basel in 1515. See Phillips, *The 'Adages' of Erasmus.*

[5] The dates in parentheses indicate the original year of publication. Most of Erasmus' principal works saw numerous editions, reprints, and revisions during his lifetime. There are, for example, well over one hundred such printings of his very popular *Colloquies.* The titles given are those of his best-known works, though they by no means exhaust

The cataclysm of the Protestant Reformation swept across the course of Erasmus' active life, and his relationship to its coming and progress has been the subject of much discussion and analysis. We cannot hope to treat this thorny question here, but we may say that though there is some resemblance (and even in instances connections) between Erasmian reform and Protestantism on certain points of criticism and on certain theological tendencies, Erasmus was and remained a Catholic reformer, faithful to the authority and tradition of the Church, to her doctrine, to her unity.[6] He sought basically the renewal of Christian life and society within the traditional frame of Christendom, and the schism that did come was for him and his cause a "tragedy." Though he continued to be the critic of those ills and abuses within the Church he had so long attacked, he nevertheless repudiated the extreme measures, the unsound doctrine, and the disruptive action of the Protestant reformers, and it was the Catholic Church whose reformation he labored to achieve. It has not always been easy to acertain and appraise Erasmus' role in the midst of the great religious crisis, but the ecumenism and spirit of renewal in our own day, it would seem, can help us approach Erasmus' position in his tumultuous time with greater understanding and appreciation.

The essay of Erasmus that·follows is certainly one of his most explicit and pointed statements on the general problem of Church reform.[7] It first appeared

---

the list of his important and widely circulated publications. For a complete listing, see F. Vander Haeghen, *Bibliotheca Erasmiana* (Ghent, 1893; repr. Nieuwkoop, 1961). For a concise and representative statement of Erasmus' Christian humanism, I should like to call attention to his *Paraclesis* and his Letter to Paul Volz, prefacing the 1518 edition of the *Enchiridion*, both of which are published in English translation in *Christian Humanism and the Reformation*, pp. 92–133. And for a most significant treatise on his theological method and approach, I point out his *Ratio verae theologiae* (1518), the Latin text of which may be found in *Erasmus: Ausgewählte Werke*, ed. Hajo Holborn (Munich, 1933), pp. 177–305, and in the Leiden *Opera omnia*, V, 75–138.

[6] My summary judgment on this important question is not universally shared, though it is in line with a good deal of recent study and evaluation. Huizinga, for example, in his biography of Erasmus (pp. 102, 136, 168, *et al.*) expounds the view that Erasmus' conception of the Church and his creed were "no longer purely Catholic," and the reader will find a bewildering variety of shading, defining, categorizing, and appraising in all that may be read on this subject. *Quot homines, tot sententiae!* In further confirmation of my view, see Louis Bouyer, *Erasmus and His Times*, trans. F. X. Murphy (Westminster, Md., 1959), Chaps. VIII–XIII, and Myron Gilmore, *Humanists and Jurists* (Cambridge, Mass., 1963), Chap. V. For a more critical appraisal from a Catholic standpoint, see Jedin, *op. cit.*, I, 156–62, 358–60. Finally, I should like to call attention to the superb analysis of Erasmus' religious orientation and purpose, upholding his orthodoxy and affirming his fidelity to the patristic tradition, in Henri de Lubac, S.J., *Exégèse médiévale*, Second Part, II (Paris, 1964), 427–82.

[7] The English translation is that of Margaret Mann Phillips, reprinted with her kind permission from her book *The 'Adages' of Erasmus* (The Cambridge University Press, 1964), pp. 269–96. Passages between minute strokes are later additions to the 1515 text, and the dates of editions where they first appear are indicated by Mrs. Phillips in the footnotes. The last and longest of these passages, at the end of the essay, added in 1528, is especially noteworthy. The Latin text may be found in the Leiden *Opera omnia*, II, 770–82. An early English translation was also published—by John Goughe, London, c. 1540. On the early publication of Erasmus in English and the use of these versions at the time of the English Reformation, see E. J. Devereux, "English Translators of

in the revised edition of the *Adagia* which John Froben published in Basel in 1515, and it was subsequently published as a separate work by Froben in 1517. The reader will find a similiarity of theme with Colet's Convocation Sermon, though the conflict between conforming to the world and fidelity to the Christian standard is handled more imaginatively in the *Sileni Alcibiadis* and with characteristic Erasmian style. The whole play with the reversal of values, with the choice of the mask for the truth, recalling *The Praise of Folly,* particularly reflects the sense of irony and paradox so congenial to his mind.

Erasmus, 1522–1557," *Editing Sixteenth Century Texts,* ed. R. J. Schoeck (Toronto, 1966), and J. K. McConica, *English Humanists and Reformation Politics under Henry VIII and Edward VI* (Oxford, 1965).

6. Title page of Froben's 1518 edition of Erasmus' *Adagiorum Chiliades*.

THE SILENI OF ALCIBIADES (Σειληνοὶ ’Αλκιβιάδου), seem to have become proverbial among the learned, at any rate they are quoted as a proverb in the Greek collections; used either with reference to a thing which in appearance (at first blush, as they say) seems ridiculous and contemptible, but on closer and deeper examination proves to be admirable, or else with reference to a person whose looks and dress do not correspond at all to what he conceals in his soul. For it seems that the Sileni were small images divided in half, and so constructed that they could be opened out and displayed; when closed they represented some ridiculous, ugly flute-player, but when opened they suddenly revealed the figure of a god, so that the amusing deception would show off the art of the carver. The subject of these statuettes is taken from that ridiculous old Silenus, the schoolmaster of Bacchus, whom the poets call the jester of the gods (they have their buffoons like the princes of our time). Thus 'in Athenaeus, book v, the youth Critobulus jeers at the old misshapen Socrates, calling him *more deformed than Silenus*—the place is to be found in Xenophon, the *Banquet*.

Socrates: You boast as if you were the more beautiful.
Critobulus: Yes, by Jupiter! otherwise I should be the ugliest of all Sileni among the Satyrs.[8]

And' in the *Symposium* of Plato, Alcibiades starts his speech in praise of Socrates by drawing a comparison between him and the Sileni, because he looked quite different to the eye of an intent observer from what he had seemed at first appearance. Anyone who took him at his face value, as they say, would not have offered a farthing for him. He had a yokel's face, with a bovine look about it, and a snub nose always running; you would have thought him some stupid, thick-headed clown. He took no care of his appearance, and his language was plain, unvarnished, and unpretentious, as befits a man who was always talking about charioteers, workmen,

[8] 1528.

fullers, and blacksmiths. For it was usually from these that he took the terms
with which he pressed his arguments home. His wealth was small, and his wife
was such as the lowest collier would refuse to put up with. He seemed to admire the beauty of youth, he seemed to know love and jealousy, though even
Alcibiades learnt how far Socrates was from these emotions. In short his
eternal jesting gave him the air of a clown. In those days it was all the rage,
among stupid people, to want to appear clever, and Gorgias was not the only
one to declare there was nothing he did not know; fusspots of that kind have
always abounded! Socrates alone said that he was sure of one thing only, that
he knew nothing. He was apparently unfitted for any public office, so much
so that one day when he stood up to do something or other in public he was
booed out.

But once you have opened out this Silenus, absurd as it is, you find a god
rather than a man, a great, lofty and truly philosophic soul, despising all those
things for which other mortals jostle and steer, sweat and dispute and struggle—
one who rose above all insults, over whom fortune had no power, and who
feared nothing, so that he treated lightly even death, which all men fear;
drinking the hemlock with as cheerful a face as he wore when drinking wine,
and joking with his friend Phaedo even as he lay dying. 'You had better sacrifice
a cock to Aesculapius to liberate yourself from your vow,' he said, 'since when
I have drunk this medicine I shall feel the benefit of true health'—leaving the
body, from which arise all the many maladies of the soul. So it was not
unjust that in a time when philosophers abounded, this jester alone should have
been declared by the oracle to be wise, and to know more—he who said he knew
nothing—than those who prided themselves on knowing everything. In fact
that was the very reason for his being judged to know more than the others,
because he alone of them all knew nothing whatever.

Another Silenus of this kind was Antisthenes, grander with his stick, his
wallet and his cloak than all the riches of the greatest kings. Another Silenus
was Diogenes, whom the mob considered a dog. But it was about this 'dog'[9]
that a divine observation was made by Alexander the Great, the fine flower of
princes, it seems, when in his admiration for so great a soul he said 'If I were
not Alexander, I would wish to be Diogenes'; though he ought all the more
to have wished for the soul of Diogenes, for the very reason that he was
Alexander.

Epictetus was another of these Sileni, a slave, and poor, and crippled, as
his epitaph tells; but, greatest fortune of all, he was dear to the gods, something
which can only be attained by purity of life combined with wisdom. Indeed,
this is the nature of truly noble things; what is most valuable in them is hidden
away in secret, what is worthless is exposed to view, and they hide their
treasure under a miserable covering rather than show it to profane eyes. But
the commonplace and the trivial have a very different approach: they please

[9] 1526.

at the outset and put all their finest wares in the shop-window, but if you examine more deeply, you find they are anything but what their style and
appearance led you to expect.

But is not Christ the most extraordinary Silenus of all? If it is permissible to
speak of him in this way—and I cannot see why all who rejoice in the name of
Christians should not do their best to imitate it. If you look on the face only
of the Silenus-image, what could be lower or more contemptible, measured by
popular standards? Obscure and poverty-stricken parents, a humble home; poor
himself, he has a few poor men for disciples, chosen 'not from kings' palaces,
not from the learned seats of the Pharisees or the schools of the Philosophers,
but'[10] from the customs-house and the fisherman's nets. Then think of his life,
how far removed from any pleasure, the life in which he came through hunger
and weariness, accusation and mockery to the cross. The mystic prophet was
contemplating him from this angle when he wrote, 'He hath no form nor
comeliness; and when we shall see him, there is no beauty that we should
desire him. He is despised and rejected of men', and much more in this vein.[11]
But if one may attain to a closer look at this Silenus-image, that is if he deigns
to show himself to the purified eyes of the soul, what unspeakable riches you
will find there: in such service to mankind, there is a pearl of great price, in
such humility, what grandeur! in such poverty, what riches! in such weakness
what immeasurable strength! in such shame, what glory! in such labours, what
utter peace! And lastly in that bitter death, there is the source of everlasting
life. Why do the very people who boast of his name shrink from this picture?
Of course, it would have been easy for Christ to have set up his throne over
all the earth, and to possess it, as the old rulers of Rome vainly claimed to do;
to surround himself with more troops than Xerxes, to surpass the riches of
Croesus, to impose silence on all the philosophers and overthrow the emptiness
of the Sophists. But this was the only pattern that pleased him, and which he
set before the eyes of his disciples and friends—that is to say, Christians. He
chose that philosophy in particular, which is utterly different from the rules
of the philosophers and from the doctrine of the world; that philosophy which
alone of all others really does bring what everyone is trying to get, in some
way or another—happiness.

The prophets were Sileni of this kind in old time, exiles, wandering in the
wilderness, dwelling with the wild beasts, living on wretched herbs, clothed
in the skins of sheep and goats. But one had looked right into these Silenus-
images when he said, *Of whom the world was not worthy*.[12] Such a Silenus
was John the Baptist, who with his robe of camel-hair and his belt of hide
outshone all the purple and jewels of kings, and with his dinner of locusts sur-
passed all the dainties of princes. Indeed, one perceived the treasure hidden
beneath the rough cloak when he summed up all his praises in that wonderful

[10] 1523.
[11] Isa. liii. 2–3.
[12] Heb. xi. 38.

testimony, saying, *Among them that are born of women there hath not arisen a greater than John the Baptist.*[13] Such Sileni were the Apostles, poor, unschooled, unlettered, base-born, powerless, lowest of the low—the objects of everyone's scorn, ridiculed, hated, accused—in fact the public laughing-stock and abomination of the world. But just open the Silenus-image, and what tyrant could possibly claim to equal the power of these men who commanded demons, quieted the raging sea with a nod, brought back the dead to life with a word? What Croesus would not seem poor beside them, as the mere falling of their shadow gives health to the sick, and the touch of their hands imparts the Holy Spirit? What Aristotle would not seem stupid, ignorant, trivial, compared to them, who draw from the very spring that heavenly wisdom beside which all human wisdom is mere stupidity? 'No offence is meant to those who think that it is a shocking and criminal thing to detract in any way from the authority of Aristotle.'[14] 'I grant that he was a man of most consummate learning, but what light is so bright that it is not dimmed by being compared with Christ?'[15] The kingdom of heaven has as its symbol a grain of mustard seed, small and contemptible in appearance, mighty in power; and diametrically opposite to this, as I have said, is the reckoning of the world.

Such a Silenus, scorned and ridiculed, was the great 'Bishop'[16] Martin, and such were those bishops of old, sublime in their humility, rich in their poverty, glorious in their forgetfulness of glory. There are still today some hidden good Sileni, but alas, how few! The greater part of mankind are like Sileni inside out. Anyone who looks closely at the inward nature and essence will find that nobody is further from true wisdom than those people with their grand titles, learned bonnets, splendid sashes and bejewelled rings, who profess to be wisdom's peak. In fact you may often find more true authentic wisdom in one obscure individual, generally thought simple-minded and half-crazy, whose mind has not been taught by a Scotus (the subtle as they say) but by the heavenly spirit of Christ, than in many strutting characters acting the theologian, three or four times Doctor So-and-so, blown up with their Aristotle and stuffed full of learned definitions, conclusions, and propositions. 'I would not say this of all, but alas, of how many!'[17] In the same way you would find in no one less real nobility than in those Thrasos with their long pedigrees and collars of gold and grand titles, who brag of their noble blood; and no one is further from true courage than those who pass for valiant and invincible just because they are rash and quarrelsome. There is no one more abject and enslaved than those who think themselves next to the gods, as they say, and masters of all. None are in such trouble as those who think themselves most fortunate; the world grovels before some men because they are rich, but they are really the poorest of the poor. No one is less bishop-like than those who

[13] Matt. xi. 11.
[14] 1520.
[15] 1528.
[16] 1523.
[17] 1533.

hold first rank among bishops. 'Again and again I beg you, reader, not to think that I mean this as an insult to any particular person: I am talking of the thing itself, not the people. Let us hope there are none whom the cap fits! And if there are none now—which the Lord grant—there have been such in the past, and there will be in the future.'[18] I wish it were also not true, that those who are furthest from true religion are just the people who claim to be the most religious—in name, in costume, and in external appearance of sanctity. And so it is always the same: what is excellent in any way is always the least showy.

In trees, it is the flowers and leaves which are beautiful to the eye; their spreading bulk is visible far and wide. But the seed, in which lies the power of it all, how tiny a thing it is! how secret, how far from flattering the sight or showing itself off! Gold and gems are hidden by nature in the deepest recesses of the earth. Among what they call the elements, the most important are those furthest removed from the senses, like air and fire. In living things, what is best and most vital is secreted in the inward parts. In man, what is most divine and immortal is what cannot be seen. In every kind of thing, the material of which it is made is the baser part, most apparent to the senses, and the essence and value of it is felt through its usefulness, and yet that is far from sense-impressions. So in the organisation of the body, phlegm and blood are familiar and palpable to the senses, but the most important thing for life—breath—is least observable. Lastly, in the universe, the greatest things are those not seen, like substances, which are called separate. And at the highest point of these there stands what is furthest removed from the senses, namely God, further than our understanding or our knowing, the single source of all things. Indeed one may find some similarity with the Sileni in the Sacraments of the Church. 'Let no one be offended by this.'[19] You see the water, the salt and the oil, you hear the spoken words, these are like the face of the Silenus; you cannot hear or see the power of God, without which all these things would be but mockeries.

The very Scriptures themselves have their own Sileni. If you remain on the surface, a thing may sometimes appear absurd; if you pierce through to the spiritual meaning, you will adore the divine wisdom. Speaking of the Old Testament, for instance, if you look at nothing but the story, and you hear of Adam being made from mud, his little wife being abstracted secretly from his flank as he slept, the serpent enticing the woman with the bait of an apple, God walking in the cool of the day, the sword set at the gates of Paradise lest the exiles should return—would you not think all this a fable from Homer's workshop? If you read of the incest of Lot, the whole story of Samson (which Saint Jerome judging by the externals calls a fable), the adultery of David and the girl lying in the old man's arms to warm him, the meretricious marriage of Hosea—would not anyone with chaste ears turn away as from

[18] 1528.
[19] 1528.

an immoral story? And yet under these veils, great heaven! what wonderful wisdom lies hidden! The parables of the Gospel, if you take them at face value—who would not think that they came from a simple ignorant man? And yet if you crack the nut, you find inside that profound wisdom, truly divine, a touch of something which is clearly like Christ himself. It would be too discursive to go on piling up examples; suffice it to say that in both the domains of nature and faith, you will find the most excellent things are the deepest hidden, and the furthest removed from profane eyes. In the same way, when it is a matter of knowledge, the real truth always lies deeply hidden, not to be understood easily or by many people. The stupid generality of men often blunder into wrong judgements, because they judge everything from the evidence of the bodily senses, and they are deceived by false imitations of the good and the evil; it is the inside-out Sileni which they marvel at and admire. I would speak here of the bad, I would not insult the good—nor the bad either for that matter. After all, a general discussion about moral faults does not lead to the injury of any individual—and would that there were fewer to whom these words could apply. When you see the sceptre, the badges of rank, the bodyguards, and when you hear those titles—'Your Serene Highness, Most Clement, Most Illustrious'—do you not revere the prince like a god on earth, and think you are looking at something more than human? But open the reversed Silenus, and you find a tyrant, sometimes the enemy of his people, 'a hater of public peace, a sower of discord, an oppressor of the good, a curse to the judicial system, an overturner of cities, a plunderer of the Church,'[20] given to robbery, sacrilege, incest, gambling—in short, as the Greek proverb has it, an Iliad of evils. There are those who in name and appearance impose themselves as magistrates and guardians of the common weal, when in reality they are wolves and prey upon the state. There are those whom you would venerate as priests if you only looked at their tonsure, but if you look into the Silenus, you will find them more than laymen. Perhaps you will find some bishops too in the same case—if you watch that solemn consecration of theirs, if you contemplate them in their new robes, the mitre gleaming with jewels and gold, the crozier likewise encrusted with gems, the whole mystic panoply which clothes them from head to foot, you would take them to be divine beings, something more than human. But open the Silenus, and you find nothing but a soldier, a trader, or finally a despot, and you will decide that all those splendid insignia were pure comedy. There are those—and I wish they were not to be met with so frequently—who, judging by their flowing beards, pale faces, hoods, bowed heads, girdles, and proud truculent expressions, might be taken for Serapio and St Paul; but open them up, and you find mere buffoons, gluttons, vagabonds, libertines, nay, robbers and oppressors, but in another way, I dare say more poisonous because it is more concealed— in fact, as they say, *the treasure turns out to be a lump of coal*. Again I must warn you that no one need be offended by these remarks, since no one is

---

[20] 1520.

alluded to by name. Anyone who is not like this may consider it has nothing to do with him; anyone who recognises his own weakness, may take the admonition to himself. Let the first congratulate himself, and the second give me thanks.

Among all kinds of men, there are those everywhere to be found whose physical appearance would make you think they were not only men, but noble examples of mankind: but if you open up the Silenus, you will perhaps find a pig, or a lion, or a bear, or an ass. Something has happened to them which is different from what the poets' fables tell of Circe and her magic potions. In her house they had the shape of beasts and the minds of men; but these people look like men, and inside are worse than beasts. On the other hand, there are those who on the face of it, as they say, hardly resemble men, and yet in the depths of their heart they hide an angel.

Here then lies the difference between the follower of the world and the follower of Christ: the first admires and chases after the worthless things which strike the eye at once, while the second strives only for the things which are least obvious at a glance, and furthest from the physical world—and the rest he passes over altogether, or holds them lightly, judging everything by its inner value. Among the 'good things' (as Aristotle calls them) which are not a natural property of man, come first and foremost riches. But with the common people, nay, with almost everyone, the man who has got hold of them by hook or by crook is regarded most highly. The whole world hunts for them over hill and dale. The thing next in order of importance is noble birth— though if nothing else goes with it, it is simply laughable, an empty name. Is it sensible to half-worship a man who can trace his descent from Codrus King of Athens, or from the Trojan Brutus (was he ever born, I wonder?) or from the Hercules of legend, and call the man obscure who has won fame by his learning and his merit? Is one man to be illustrious because his great-grandfather made a great slaughter in war, and another common, with no statues erected to his name, when he benefited the whole world with the riches of his soul? In the third place come the gifts of the body; anyone who happens to be tall, hardy, handsome, and powerful is included among the number of the lucky ones, but all the same riches come first and birth second —the last thing to be thought of is the mind. If you divide man according to St Paul into three parts, body, soul, and spirit (I am using his very words),[21] it is true that the common people value highest what is most obvious—the lowest part, condemned by the Apostle. The middle term, which he considers good if it joins forces with the spirit, is approved of by many also. But the spirit, the best part of ourselves, from which springs as from a fountain all our happiness—the spirit, by which we are joined to God—they are so far from thinking it precious that they never even ask whether it exists or what it is, although Paul mentions it so often in his teaching. And so we get this utterly reversed estimate of things; what we should particularly honour passes with-

21 Thess. v. 23.

out a word and what we should strive for with all our might is regarded with contempt. Hence gold is more valued than learning, ancient lineage more than virtue, the gifts of the body more than the endowments of the mind, ceremonies are put before true piety, the rules of men before the teaching of Christ, the mask is preferred to the truth, the shadow to the reality, the counterfeit to the genuine, the fleeting to the substantial, the momentary to the eternal.

The reversing of values brings about a reversed use of words. What is sublime they call humble; what is bitter they call sweet; the precious is called vile, and life, death. To give one or two instances in passing: can those people be said to *love* who ruin others by indulgence, or who have designs on their modesty and fair fame? when no enemy could do worse? They call it justice, when evil is conquered by evil and crime by crime, and when the injury received is paid back with high interest. It is supposed to be unfair to marriage to expect it to be untainted, as near as possible to virginity and as far as possible from the brothel. A man is called traitor and enemy of his prince, because he wishes that prince not to be free to act outside the law and against the right—because, in fact, he wants him to act like a true prince, and to be as far as possible from the portrait of the tyrant, the most hideous of wild beasts. The man who is called the supporter, the friend, the partisan of princes, is he who corrupts them by wrong education, instils into them worthless opinions, cheats them by flattery, makes them an object of popular hatred by his evil counsels, involves them in wars and crazy disturbancies of the peace. They say it increases the dignity of a prince to have a touch of the tyrant—that is, a large share of the worst of evils. They call anyone who wishes to cut down enforced taxation an embezzler of public money. But since the chief attributes of the prince, by which he represents God, the only true king, are these three, goodness, wisdom, and power, is it really being a friend to the prince to rob him of his two most important possessions, goodness and wisdom, and leave him with only power, and that not only false, but not even his own? For power, unless it is allied to wisdom and goodness, is tyranny and not power, and as it has been conferred by popular consent, so it can be taken away; but even if a prince loses his throne, if he possesses goodness and wisdom they are his own, and go with him. It is a capital offence to desecrate the royal standard; but a reward is given to those who vitiate the mind of the prince, and turn him from a good one to a cruel one, make him crafty instead of wise and a tyrant instead of a ruler. One death is too mild a punishment for the attempt to poison the prince's cup; is a prize to be offered for corrupting and poisoning his mind with unwholesome ideas, as it were tainting the very fount and source of the common weal, to the detriment of the whole world? The office of a prince is called dominion, when in reality to fulfil the role of a prince is simply to administer what belongs to all. The marriage alliances of kings, and their treaties continually being renewed, are supposed to be the cement of Christian peace— when it is from these sources that nearly all wars and most disturbances in human affairs arise. It is called a just war, when princes act in collusion to exhaust and oppress the state; they call it peace, when they plot together for the same purpose. They say it is an extension of empire, when the name of one town or another is added to the domains of the prince, although it may be bought by pillaging the citizens and shedding much blood, by making so many women widows and so many children fatherless.

In the same way they call the priests, bishops and Popes 'the Church', when in reality they are only the servants of the Church. The Church is the whole Christian people, and Christ himself says it is too great to lie down before the bishops who serve it—they would have less obsequious treatment, but be more truly great, if they were to follow Christ in his life and actions as they are his successors in their office—if they were to do as he did, who although he was prince and lord of all, took upon himself the part of a servant and not of a master. The whole force of the thunder-bolt is hurled against those who defraud the priests' collecting-bag of a few coins—they are called enemies of the Church, and very nearly heretics. Now I am not on the side of the defrauder, let no one think it; but pray tell me, if there is any pleasure in hating the enemy of the Church, could there be any enemy more pernicious, more deadly than a wicked Pope? If there is any diminution of the landed property or income of the priests, a general protest arises that the Christian church is being oppressed. When the world is being incited to war— when the evil-living of the priests is the means of bringing so many souls to ruin—no one mourns for the sad fate of the Church, although this is when the Church is really being hurt. They say that the Church is being honoured and adorned, not when piety is growing among the people, when vices are diminishing and good behaviour increasing, when sacred learning is in full bloom, but when the altars glitter with jewels and gold; nay, even when the altars themselves are neglected, and the accumulation of property, troops of servants, luxury, mules and horses, expensive erection of houses or rather palaces, and all the rest of the racket of life, make the priests no better than satraps. 'And all this seems right and proper, so much so that in the very papal documents themselves we find this kind of clause: 'Since such-and-such a cardinal, keeping up an establishment of so many horses and so many officials, does great honour to the Church of God, we grant him the fourth part of the dignity of a bishop.' And for the ornament of the Church, the bishops, priests and clergy are ordered to wear silk and purple. O marvellous dignity of the Church! What is there left, when we have lost even the name of honour?'[22] There are those—I have no wish to mention them—who spend the wealth of the Church on wicked purposes, to the great offence of the people. When they have made a gain, we congratulate them and say the Church of Christ has been added to; whereas the Church has one kind of true wealth and one only—the advance of the Christian life. They call it blasphemy, if anyone speaks without due reverence of Christopher or George, or does not put every

[22] 1528.

fable from every source on the level of the Gospel. But to Paul, it is blasphemy whenever the evil ways of Christians bring shame upon the name of Christ before the eyes of the heathen. What are the enemies of Christ likely to say, when they see Christ in the Gospel calling men to despise riches, renounce the pursuit of pleasure and abandon pride, and they observe exactly the opposite going on among the chief of those who profess themselves Christians, but live so as to out-heathen the heathens in their passion for heaping up wealth, their love of pleasure, their sumptuous living, their savagery in war, and almost all other vices? The wise reader will understand what I am passing over in silence here, out of respect for the name of Christian, and what I am privately sighing for. 'How much they must laugh, don't you think, when they see that Christ in the Gospel did not want his followers to be marked out by their dress, or by ceremonies or by particular foods, but wished Christians to be known by this mark, that they should be united in their love for one another—and then they look round and see us so far from being united, that no breed of men were ever in such shameful and deadly turmoil. Prince makes war on prince, state fights with state, there is no agreement between one school and another, or one religion (as they say now) and another; brawls, factions, litigation abound among us. This is the real blasphemy, and the authors of it are those who provide its just cause.'[23] They call it heresy, to say or write anything which differs in any way from the petty propositions of the Masters of Theology, or even to disagree on matters of grammar; but it is not heresy, to proclaim the chief part of human felicity to lie in precisely the very thing which Christ always teaches us to set aside; it is not heresy, to encourage a mode of life quite unlike the teachings of the Gospel and the ordinances of the Apostles; or to run counter to the meaning of Christ, who sent his Apostles out to teach the Gospel armed with the sword of the spirit, which alone makes it possible (earthly passions having been cut away) to do without the sword—to run counter to this, I say, by arming them with steel to defend themselves from persecution? (There is no doubt that under the name of the sword he would include the ballista, the bombard and the machine, and all the rest of the apparatus of war. In the same way the burdensomeness of the wallet in which they carried their money for everyday necessities, may be taken to apply to everything which makes provision for this life.) 'But he who teaches these things is counted among the great theologians.'[24] It is an unforgivable sacrilege to take anything from a church; and is it to be held a light offence to plunder and defraud and grind down the poor and the widow, the living temple of God? 'Yet this is done everywhere by the

[23] 1520.
[24] These lines were substituted in 1523 for the following: 'For thus far the words of Luke are distorted by that great Lyranus, who is to be set far above all the Jeromes, and yet he is counted among the great theologians.' The medieval theologian Nicolaus of Lyra (c. 1265–1349) to whom Erasmus alludes ironically here, was the author of two commentaries on the whole Bible, Postilla litteralis and Postilla mystica. (Brackets in the text have been added by the translator.)

princes and the nobles (sometimes by bishops and abbots).'[25] It is wicked profanity to pollute the sacred building by fighting or by seminal fluid, and yet we do not execrate the man who profanes that temple of the holy spirit, a pure and chaste maiden, who violates and corrupts her by means of endearments and gifts and promises and enticement? 'But the man who does this is popularly called a merry, fashionable fellow.'[26] I am not defending ill-doing, as I have said before, I am pointing out that the mass of the people have far more esteem for what they can see with their eyes, than for the things which are all the truer for being less easy to discern. You see the consecration of the stones of the temple, but because you cannot see the dedication of the spirit, you think it unimportant. You fight for the preservation of its ornaments, but when it comes to protecting uprightness of life no one seizes that Gospel sword of which Christ said 'let him sell his garment and buy one.'[27] It is called the height of piety, to take up arms for the defence or the increasing of the authority and wealth of the priesthood, and throw sacred and profane together into the confusion of war. But while the priests' money, a paltry thing in itself, is being championed, what a tremendous desolation of all religious life is incurred by allowing war? For what evil is there which war does not bring about?

Perhaps here the reader's unspoken thought shouts at me, asking 'What are all these disgusting remarks leading up to? Do you want a prince to be like Plato makes the guardians of his republic? Do you want to rob the priests of their power, dignity, glory and riches, and recall them to the wallet and staff of the Apostles?' Careful with your words, please. I am not robbing them, but enriching them with greater possessions than these, I am not turning them out of their domain but calling them to better things. I ask you, which of us has the more splendid ideal of the greatness of a king, you or I? You want him to be able to do whatever he likes, to be a tyrant and not a prince; you glut him with pleasures, hand him over to luxury, make him the slave and captive of all his desires, you want him to be no wiser than the man in the street, you load him down with the things which even among the pagans it was fine to despise. I want him to be as near as possible to the likeness of God, whose image he represents, I want him to excel others in wisdom, the true glory of kings, and to be far from all low passions, the diseases of the soul, by which the stupid and common vulgar herd is carried away. I want him not to admire anything mean, to rise above wealth, in short to be to the state what the soul is to the body, what God is to the universe.

Which of us two estimates more truly the dignity of a bishop? You weigh him down with earthly riches, entangle him in sordid and vulgar cares, involve him with the storms of war. I want him, as the vicar of Christ and the guardian of the sacred spouse, to be free from all earthly contagion, and to

[25] 1528.
[26] 1520.
[27] Luke xxii. 36.

resemble as closely as possible the one whose place and office he fills. The Stoics say that to be a good man is only possible if one is free from the maladies of the soul. By the maladies of the soul they mean the desires or affections. Much more then should Christians be free from these things, but especially the prince. And still more especially the prince and father of the Church, a prince belonging to heaven and ruling over the people of heaven. I want the priest to reign, but I consider mere earthly power too unimportant for this man of heaven to be burdened with it. I want to see the Pontiff ride in triumph, not in the bloodthirsty triumphs of a wicked Marius or a conscienceless Julius, so empty as to be the butt of the Satirists (if old Democritus were to see them I think he would die of laughing), but truly magnificent and Apostolic, such as Paul (a warrior himself and a much finer general than Alexander the Great) describes with a great flourish, as it were blowing his own trumpet:

> In labours more abundant, in stripes above measure, in prisons more frequent, in deaths oft. Of the Jews five times received I forty stripes save one. Thrice was I beaten with rods, once was I stoned, thrice I suffered shipwreck, a night and a day have I been in the deep; in journeyings often, in perils of waters, in perils of robbers, in perils by mine own countrymen, in perils by the heathen, in perils in the city, in perils in the wilderness, in perils in the sea, in perils among false brethren; in weariness and painfulness, in watchings often, in hunger and thirst, in fastings often, in cold and nakedness. Besides those things that are without, that which cometh upon me daily, the care of all the churches. Who is weak, and I am not weak? Who is offended, and I burn not?[28]

And a little before this:

> In all things approving ourselves the ministers of God in much patience, in afflictions, in necessities, in distresses, in stripes, in imprisonments, in tumults, in labours, in watchings, in fastings; by pureness, by knowledge, by long-suffering, by kindness, by the Holy Ghost, by love unfeigned, by the word of truth, by the power of God, by the armour of righteousness on the right hand and on the left, by honour and dishonour, by evil report and good report; as deceivers, and yet true; as unknown, and yet well known; as dying, and behold, we live; as chastened, and not killed; as sorrowful, yet always rejoicing; as poor, yet making many rich; as having nothing, and yet possessing all things.[29]

Do you see the trophies of war, the victory, the Apostolic triumph? This is that famous glory, by which Paul sometimes swears, as by something sacred. These are the high deeds for which he believed there was laid up for him an immortal crown.[30] Those who claim to stand in the place and wield the authority of the Apostles, will not be reluctant to follow in the Apostles' footsteps.

---

[28] 2 Cor. xi. 23–9.
[29] 2 Cor. vi. 4–10.
[30] 2 Tim. iv. 8.

I wish the Popes to have the greatest riches—but let it be the pearl of the Gospel, the heavenly treasure, which abounds to them all the more, the more they lavish it on others; for there will be no danger of kindness perishing through kindness. I wish them to be fully armed, but with the arms of the Apostle: that is, with the shield of faith, the breastplate of righteousness, the sword of salvation, which is the word of God.[31] I wish them to be fierce warriors, but against the real enemies of the Church, simony, pride, lust, ambition, anger, irreligion. Christians must always be watching out for, and attacking, Turks such as these. It is in this sort of war that the bishop should be general and exhort his troops. I want the priests to be acknowledged among the first of the land, but not for their noisy domineering, rather for the excellence of their holy learning, for their outstanding virtues. I want them to be revered, but for their upright and ascetic lives, not only for their titles or dramatic garb. I want them to be feared, but as fathers, not as tyrants. I want them to be feared, but only by evil-doers, nay, I want them to be such as strike awe, not terror or hate, into the hearts of the wicked. Finally, I wish them abundant delights, but delights of a rarity and sweetness far beyond what the common herd can know.

Do you want to hear what are the true riches of a Pope? Listen next to the prince of Popes: 'Silver and gold have I none, but such as I have give I thee: in the name of Jesus arise and walk.'[32] Do you want to hear the grandeur of the name of an Apostle—surpassing all titles, all arches and statues? Listen to Paul, the truly illustrious: 'For we are to God a sweet savour of Christ in every place.'[33] Do you want to hear of power more than kingly? 'I can do all things,' he says, 'through Christ who strengtheneth me.'[34] Do you want to hear of glory? 'You are my joy and crown in the Lord.'[35] Do you want to hear the titles worthy of a bishop, the ornaments of a real pontiff? Paul points them for you, 'sober, blameless, prudent, given to hospitality, apt to teach; not given to wine, no striker, but patient, not a brawler, not greedy of filthy lucre, not a novice; moreover he must have a good report of them that are without, lest he fall into reproach and the snare of the devil.'[36] Look upon the ornaments which grace Aaron the priest of Moses, the riches which adorn him, the many-hued embroideries, the starry shining of varied gems about him, the gleam of gold. What all these signify you may find out from the interpretations of Origen and Jerome, and you will understand what the trappings are which should be furnished to bishops 'who are truly great.'[37]

Who should the pontiffs portray in their lives, if not those whom they portray on their seals, whose titles they bear, whose places they occupy? Which models are more suitable for imitation by the vicar of Christ—the Juliuses,

[31] Ephes. vi. 14–17.
[32] Acts iii. 6.
[33] 2 Cor. ii. 15.
[34] Phil. iv. 13.
[35] Phil. iv. 1.
[36] 1 Tim. iii. 2–7.
[37] 1520.

Alexanders, Croesus, and Xerxes, nothing but robbers on the grand scale, or Christ himself, 'the only leader and emperor of the Church?'[38] Whom could the successors of the Apostles more properly strive to copy, than the prince of the Apostles? Christ openly declared that his kingdom was not of this world, and yet you think it right that Christ's successor should not only accept worldly power, but canvass for it, and leave no stone unturned, as they say, to get it? In this world there are two worlds, at variance with each other in every way: the one gross and material, the other celestial, having its thoughts centered even now, as far as may be, on that which is to come hereafter. In the first of these the chief place goes to him who is least endowed with true possessions, and most weighed down with false ones. The pagan king, for instance, surpasses everyone in lust, luxury, violence, pomp, pride, riches, and greed, and he comes first just because the major portion of this flood of sewage has come his way, and the least share of wisdom, self-control, moderation and justice, and the rest of the things which are truly valuable. In the second, on the other hand, the highest is the man who is least besmirched with those gross and vulgar gifts, and richest in the true wealth of heaven. Now why should you wish a Christian prince to be just what the philosophers, even pagan ones, condemned and scorned? Why should you consider his greatness things which would be unbecoming to an ordinary good man? Why should you load the Angel of God (for so is the bishop called in holy writ) with those things which would be unbecoming to an ordinary good man? Why should you estimate him according to the wealth which makes robbers rich, and tyrants terrifying?

A priest is something celestial, he is more than man. Nothing is worthy of his lofty station, except what is heavenly. Why do you dishonour his dignity with commonplace things? Why do you taint his purity with the squalor of the world? Why do you not let him wield his own kind of power? Why may he not be illustrious with his own kind of glory, revered for his own majesty, rich with his own wealth? This man was chosen for the highest ends from the divine body, which is the Church, by the divine spirit. Why do you force him to take part in the wild commotions of the despots? Paul prides himself on having been set apart: why do you plunge my churchman into the slime of the dregs of the people? Why drive him to be worried by money-lenders? Why drag this man of God into business scarcely fitting for men at all? Why measure the blessedness of Christian priests by those things which were a laughing-stock for Democritus and a cause for sorrow to Heraclitus, which Diogenes rejected as trivial, which Crates put aside as burdensome, which all the saints fled from as pestilential? Why evaluate the successor of St Peter on those very riches which Peter himself gloried in not possessing? Why think the Apostolic rulers should give an impression of greatness, by those very trappings which the Apostles themselves trampled underfoot, and thereby were great? Why call 'Peter's patrimony' a thing which Peter himself was

[38] 1528.

proud not to have? why think the vicars of Christ should be ensnared by riches, when Christ himself called them thorns? The true, the chief duty of such a man is to sow the seed of the Word of God, so why overwhelm him with wealth, which chokes the seed when it is sown? He is the expert, the judge, of equity; why do you want him to serve the mammon of unrighteousness? It is for him to dispense the holy sacraments, why do you make him the overseer of the vilest things? The Christian world looks to him for the nourishment of sound doctrine, it expects him to supply wholesome advice, fatherly consolation, a pattern of life. Why should a man destined and devoted to such high things be reduced to the treadmill of vulgar cares? This both robs the bishop of his own dignity and deprives the people of their bishop. Christ has his own kingdom, of such rare excellence that it should never be polluted by heathen rule, or rather tyranny; he has his own magnificence, his own riches, his own delights. Why do we mix up together things which are so conflicting? Earthly and heavenly, highest and lowest, heathen and Christian, profane and sacred—why do we confuse them all? So many and so great are the gifts of the Spirit, in the generous overflowing of its wealth— gifts of tongues, gifts of prophecy, gifts of healing, gifts of knowledge, gifts of wisdom, gifts of learning, the discerning of spirits, the gift of exhortation, the power to console.[39] These are sacred offerings, how can you put them on the same plane as the unhallowed gifts of the world? (Not to say put them out.) Why try to combine Christ and Mammon, and Belial with the spirit of Christ? What has the mitre to do with the helmet, holy vestments with warlike armour, blessings with bombards, the merciful shepherd with the armed robbers—what has the priesthood to do with war? Is the same man to demolish towns with machines and hold the keys of the kingdom of heaven? Is it right that the maker of war should be the one who greets the world with the solemn word of peace? Can he have the face to teach the Christian populace that riches are to be despised, when money is the be-all and the end-all of his life? How can he have the impudence to teach what Christ taught both by precept and example, what the Apostles are always impressing on us— that we must offer no resistance to evil, but overcome evil with good, pay back an injury with a kindness, overwhelm an enemy with good deeds—when for the sake of possessing one little town or levying a tax on salt he throws the whole world into the storms and tumults of war? How can he be a leader in the kingdom of heaven, for so Christ calls his Church, who is entirely immersed in the kingdom of this world? But you are excessively pious, you want the Church to be adorned with this kind of riches too. I would agree, if the thing did not carry with it, for the sake of a little benefit, such a number of evils. Once you have granted imperial rule, you have granted at the same time the business of collecting money, the retinue of a tyrant, armed forces, spies, horses, mules, trumpets, war, carnage, triumphs, insurrections, treaties, battles, in short everything without which it is not possible to manage the

[39] 1 Cor. xii. 4–10.

affairs of empire. Even if the wish is there, when will there be the leisure to carry out the duties of an Apostle, for one who is torn asunder by so many thousand cares? While the lists of the levied troops are being made out, while treaties are being made or annulled, while force is applied to those who refuse to obey authority, and those who have revolutionary ideas are persuaded to remain loyal, while enemies are being crushed and citadels fortified, while plans are being considered and secular embassies handled, while the captains are being received at banquets and friends promoted to honour, and those driven away who must give place to the more fortunate—and many other things, which are beyond remembering, and yet must be done! Does it seem to you to argue a real understanding of the high distinction of a Pope and cardinals, to think they should be dragged away to these squalid matters of business—from prayer, in which they speak with God, from holy contempla-tion, by which they live with the angels, from the verdant meadows of Holy Scripture, where they walk in bliss, from the Apostolic office of spreading the Gospel, in which they are most like Christ? Is it truly wishing them well to want to force them into this storm of affairs, these toilsome distresses, from so great a felicity and tranquillity of life, which they were enjoying? The fact is, not only that political power carries with it infinite hardships, but also it is much less successful in the hands of the priesthood than in those of laymen. And that for two reasons, partly because the rank and file of men are more willing to give this kind of obedience to laymen than to ecclesiastics, partly because the former, intending to leave the kingdom to their children, do their best to make it as flourishing as possible. The latter, on the other hand, since they come to power later in life and often as old men, and rule for themselves, not for their heirs, are more given to plunder than to embellish, precisely as if they were offered a prey rather than a province. Add to this that when a secular ruler takes possession, he may have to fight once for his kingdom, and once for all those favoured by the prince are raised and enriched. When it is otherwise, the contention is always being renewed, and those thrown out of power whom the previous ruler had raised up; over and over again there are new men to be enriched at the expense of the people. It is not unimportant too, that a people will more easily bear the rule of one to whom it is accustomed, even if his rule is severe; and if he should die, he yet seems to be living in his son and heir, and the populace fancies that it has not changed one prince for another, but has the same one renewed. Children are liable to resemble their parents in their ways, especially when they have been educated by them. But when sovereignty is vested in men dedicated to God, there is suddenly a com-plete change all round. Add to all this that the secular ruler comes to the man-agement of power after much study, educated to it from his cradle. But in the other case it often happens that the highest position of all is allotted with-out warning, so that he who was by nature born to the oar, is lifted to sovereign power by the whim of fortune.

Finally, it is hardly possible for one man to be equal to two difficult forms of administration, like Hercules with his two monsters. It is the most difficult of things to fulfil the duties of a good prince. And yet it is much finer, but also much more difficult, to act as a good priest. Pray, why both? 'Is it not inevitable that when they take both offices upon themselves, they must discharge neither well?'[40] Hence it results, I think, that while we see cities ruled by temporal kings flourishing more and more—this is clear from their wealth, their buildings, their men—the towns ruled by priests are lifeless and falling to ruin. Whatever was the need to add one thing to another like this, when they are accompanied by so many disadvantages? Are you afraid that Christ will not be powerful enough through his own wealth, unless a lay tyrant contributes a little of his power? Do you think Christ is too unadorned unless an ungodly soldier makes him an allowance of gold, a Phrygian embroiderer, a few white horses, and a retinue, that is, spatters him with a little of his pomp? Does he seem to you not magnificent enough, unless he may use those insignia which that most ambitious Julius refused, for fear of envy? Do you judge him insignificant unless burdened with worldly kingship, which means tyranny if it is used selfishly and press of business if one uses it for the common good? Leave worldly things to the world; in a bishop, what is lowliest surpasses all the pride of empire. The more you add in the way of worldly goods, the less will Christ bestow of his own; the purer the man is from the former, the more will the latter be lavished upon him. You see now, I think, how everything comes out differently if you turn the Silenus inside out. Those people who seemed the heartiest supporters of the Christian prince—you can see now that they are the greatest traitors and enemies he can have. You would have said that some people were defending the dignity of the Pope, and you understand now that they besmirch him. Now I am not saying this because I think everything the priests happen to have should be taken away from them, whether power or wealth: 'for no religious man should favour civil strife:'[41] but I wish them to remember and be aware of their own greatness, so that they may either cast away altogether these common, not to say heathen, things, and leave them to the lowest of men, or else at least hold them contemptuously, and as Paul says, have them as if they did not have them at all. Finally, I want them to be so adorned with the riches of Christ, that everything which may come to them from the glory of this world may either be outshone by the light of better things, or seem sordid by comparison. And so it shall be, that what they possess, they may possess in joy, and all the more for being free from care; for when there is an increase they are not in fear lest anyone break through and steal, and if there is any falling-off they will not struggle so furiously to retain base and passing things. Finally, they will not be in the position of losing their true possessions while they exult over riches that are not for them. They will not lose the pearl of the Gospel as they strive for the sham jewels of the world. In saying this I am leaving out of account that these very things, which we think should be despised, are all the more likely to be added to those who despise them, and they will follow those who flee

---

[40] 1520.
[41] 1528.

from them, much more creditably than if they are chased and snatched at. From whence did the Church get its wealth, unless from the contempt of wealth? from whence its glory, unless from putting glory aside? Laymen will be readier to give their worldly wealth away, if they see that it is rejected by those whom they believe to be wiser. Evil princes must perhaps sometimes be tolerated, some respect must be paid to the memory of those whose place they apparently occupy, something is due to their title. It would be as well not to try to find a remedy, because I dare say if the attempt were made without success the result would be even worse disaster. But human affairs are really in a bad way, if those whose life should be a kind of miracle are the sort of people who provoke cheers from the worst of men and sighs and groans from the good, and whose entire prestige depends on the support of villains, or on the moderation of the ordinary people, or the inexperience of the artless, or the tolerance of the good; 'or should even be those who shelter behind public dissensions, who become great through nothing else than civil strife, whose good fortune is fed by the misfortune of the public.'[42]

'If the priests had a true estimate of the matter, the truth is that the acquisition of secular wealth brings so much trouble with it that it would be better to refuse it even when voluntarily offered. They become slaves of the princes and the court, they are at the mercy of rebellion, they are involved in wars, in the midst of which they die; in short, even if we suppose that their servitude to the monarch is an honourable estate, what becomes of the fathers of the Christian people in the meantime? where are the shepherds? What sort of arrangement is it, that bishops and abbots should buy titles of that sort at a high price from the monarchs? An abbot seems to lack honour if he is not a count as well. It is an ornament to the priesthood to buy the title of duke. A fine coupling of words, to be sure—abbot and despot, bishop and fighting-man. But what is much more absurd is that in these capacities they act the part of strong men, but in the function which should really have been their own, they are mere shadows. They have hands and swords, with which they kill the body—and that is justice, if you like; but the same people have no tongue to heal the soul. The abbot has learnt how to draw up a line of battle, but he does not know how to lead people to religion. The bishop is well versed in methods of warfare with arms and bombards, but he is dumb when it comes to teaching, exhorting, consoling. He is well armed with javelins and missiles, but absolutely unarmed with Holy Scripture. And meanwhile they exact every farthing from their people which would be owed to devout abbots and good bishops; in fact often it is not the sum due, but any sum they like. The Lord will give his blessing to the people for their patience, which endures such men for the sake of peace; but I fear they will find God a severer judge than their people. What else does this general turmoil tell us, but that God is angry with us all? What else is left for us to do, but for us all, great and small alike, churchmen and laymen, with humble hearts, to fly for refuge to the mercy

---

[42] 1520.

of God? How much wiser that would be, than for each to refuse to acknowledge his fault and blame it on the other, thus provoking still more the divine
wrath, and making more deadly wounds by biting each other, instead of
healing ourselves. The people murmur against the princes, the princes spare
neither sacred nor secular, the populace insults the priesthood. It certainly
often happens that God, displeased by the evil-doing of the people, sends
them the rulers they deserve.

Nothing has been gained so far, from complaints, harshness, quarrels, and
turmoil. There is one way left—let us all make a joint confession together, that
the mercy of God may be ready for us all.'[43]

But where is my flow of words carrying me—professing to be a proverb-
writer, I am turning into a preacher? To be sure, it was the drunken Alcibiades
with his Sileni which drew us into this very sober discussion. However, I
should not have too many regrets for having strayed if what did not pertain
to relating proverbs turned out to pertain to amendment of life, and what
made no contribution to learning did conduce to piety; and if what seemed
subordinate or unrelated to the plan of this work, could be adapted to a plan
for living.

[43] 1528.

CHAPTER VII

Contarini's *De officio episcopi*, 1516

In his excellent study of Reginald Pole, Wilhelm Schenk speaking of Gasparo Contarini remarks that "his zeal for Church reform went back to a time before the beginning of Luther's public career," and he points to Contarini's 1516 treatise on the duties of a bishop, *De officio episcopi*, as bearing out this observation.[1] The untenable view that Catholic reform was simply a response to the Protestant revolt hardly needs to be challenged at this point in our study, but it is important to note that the man who perhaps more than any other came to exemplify and lead the movement for reform in the Church during the pontificate of Paul III expressed the highest and most ardent reform ideals prior to the Lutheran controversy. In his person the continuity between a scholarly and devout Christian humanism and the actual task of reforming the institutional Church finds its most striking embodiment. The author of *De officio episcopi* was to be elevated to the cardinalate in 1535 and to become Paul III's right-hand man in his reform endeavors.

Long before this Contarini had had an active and distinguished career in the service of his native Venice, and his life in many respects—his learning, his political service, his nobility of character—calls to mind that of his great English contemporary, Thomas More.[2] Born in 1483 (a few weeks before Luther), he was a member of one of the oldest and most prominent Venetian families. He studied at the University of Padua, where he received a thorough grounding in the classics as well as in philosophy and theology. Aristotle became his master in the former science, St. Thomas Aquinas his preceptor in the other. After leaving Padua in 1509 he took his seat on the Great Council

---

[1] W. Schenk, *Reginald Pole, Cardinal of England* (London, 1950), p. 53.

[2] There is unfortunately no adequate work on Contarini available in English. On him, see *ibid.*, pp. 49–54 *et passim*, and Pastor, XI, 144–48 *et passim*. Two unpublished Ph.D. dissertations are very useful and relevant: George E. Tiffany, "The Philosophical Thought of Cardinal Gasparo Contarini" (Harvard University, 1953), and Elisabeth G. Gleason, "Cardinal Gasparo Contarini (1483–1542) and the Beginning of Catholic Reform" (The University of California, Berkeley, 1963). The basic modern monograph is F. Dittrich, *Gasparo Contarini* (Braunsberg, 1885). *Opera omnia* were published in Paris, 1571, and in Venice, 1578 and 1589. Four theological treatises are in Contarini, *Gegenreformatorische Schriften*, ed. F. Hünermann (Vol. VII of *Corpus Catholicorum*; Münster i. W., 1923). Letters are in F. Dittrich, *Regesten und Briefe des Cardinals Gasparo Contarini* (Braunsberg, 1881).

In addition to *De officio episcopi* Contarini's earliest works are *De immortalitate animae* (c. 1516), a treatise defending philosophically the immortality of the soul and taking issue with the views of his former teacher Pomponazzi, and a political treatise, *De magistratibus et republica Venetorum* (c. 1524?).

of Venice, though in 1511 the entry of his close friends Tommaso Giustiniani and Vincenzo Quirini into the Camaldolese Order and their effort to persuade Contarini to join them coincided with a personal religious crisis in his life and occasioned great soul-searching on his part.[3] Like More, however, he declined the cloister and followed a lay vocation. He served as ambassador to the court of Emperor Charles V from 1521 to 1525 and subsequently, 1528 to 1530, as ambassador to the papal court. Thereafter and until the call to Rome in 1535 he resided in Venice, active in the civic administration and a member of a zealous religious reform group which included the Theatine leader, Gian Pietro Carafa, the Abbot of San Giorgio Maggiore, Gregorio Cortese, and latterly the young English noble and scholar Reginald Pole.

Contarini's appointment as cardinal in 1535 opens a new and most significant phase in his career and is briefly discussed in Chapter XIII. Here we wish only to speak of the background of this outstanding man whose "great characteristics and virtues," as Pastor declares, "were consecrated by his profoundly Christian and genuinely Catholic convictions,"[4] and to introduce his treatise on the office of a bishop. This latter work was composed in 1516 for a friend, Pietro Lippomano, who had just been appointed to the see of Bergamo. The model for it is the exemplary prelate, Pietro Barozzi, Bishop of Belluno and Padua (d. 1507), whom Contarini had known in his student days, though as Jedin points out, it is inspired by ideals that go back to the patristic age.[5] The treatise is divided into two parts or books: the first is general and explains the virtues, natural and supernatural, the good bishop must have; the second is more specific and shows how the bishop should conduct himself and carry out his duties as shepherd of a Christian flock. The importance of this theme in the history of the Catholic Reformation cannot be exaggerated. The restoration and renewal of the bishop's office was one of the greatest needs, and as Evennett points out, "the strengthening of the

---

[3] Hubert Jedin, "Ein 'Turmerlebnis' des jungen Contarini," *Historisches Jahrbuch*, LXX (1951), 115–30, and "Contarini und Camaldoli," *Archivio italiano per la storia della pietà*, II (1960), 51–117. Giustiniani (1476–1528) and Quirini (1479–1514) were Venetians of patrician background and scholarly achievement like Contarini. Shortly after joining the Order of hermit monks at Camaldoli, they drafted the remarkable *Libellus ad Leonem X*, a lengthy reform memorandum which they presented to the newly elected Pope Leo X. The text may be found in *Annales Camaldulenses*, eds. J. B. Mittarelli and A. Costadoni (9 vols.; Venice, 1755–73), IX, 612–719. Though Contarini did not join his friends in the contemplative religious life or share in the drafting of the *Libellus*, it is certainly not amiss to link him with the concerns and aims of their reform program. Quirini died in 1514, but Giustiniani went on to inaugurate the reformed Camaldolese congregation of Monte Corona and to write extensively on the spiritual and eremitical life. On him, see Dom Jean Leclercq, *Un humaniste ermite: Le bienheureux Paul Giustiniani* (Rome, 1951).

[4] Pastor, XI, 146.

[5] Jedin, *A History of the Council of Trent*, I, 148, 163. See also Paul Broutin, *L'évêque dans la tradition pastorale du XVIe siècle* (adaptation of *Bischofsideal der Katholischen Reformation* by Hubert Jedin; Bruges, 1953), Chap. III, and Silvio Tramontin, "Il 'De officio episcopi' di Gasparo Contarini," *Studia Patavina*, XII (1965), 292–303, where the community of ideas with the reform *Libellus* of Giustiniani and Quirini is stressed.

episcopate in every respect, as the nodal point of every aspect of reform, may be regarded as a corner-stone of the counter-reformation Church."[6] The translation that now follows presents about half the treatise and includes two excerpts from Book I—on the role of the bishop and on the duty of residence—and the major part of Book II.[7]

[6] H. O. Evennett, *The Spirit of the Counter-Reformation* (Cambridge, 1968), p. 96.

[7] The treatise was first published in Contarini, *Opera* (Paris, 1571), pp. 401–31. The translation was made from this text, collated with that in the Venetian *Opera* of 1589, by John Monfasani and the editor. The selections presented here are on pp. 402–3, 412–13, and 416–26 of both *Opera*.

THE BISHOP, however, has a higher goal prescribed [than the temporal good for which the secular ruler aims]. For he undertakes to instruct the city entrusted to his care in Christian principles and divine laws and to maintain it in its duty. And he directs his ward by every effort to that supreme happiness which it is foolish and at the same time wicked to hope for without Christian piety and instruction. For this reason the Bishop ought to be regarded as endowed with a far greater dignity than the civil ruler of the city.

Now the civil ruler has the care of human happiness which is a certain ordering toward the Christian virtues and that supreme happiness, of which, as we have said, the Bishop is the guide and teacher. Thus each of them should be of lofty spirit and adorned with all the virtues. First, because nature has ordained that every efficient cause brings forth an effect similar to itself. For the form and nature proper to that which acts is the principle of its activity. Whence it follows that as a governor and prince are so do they have effect on the city. Therefore that governor by no means will render a city good and blessed unless he himself also will have been endowed with such a disposition.

Add to this the fact that in the sphere of conduct everyone follows the deeds rather than the words of the instructor and believes the words truly given him by the instructor if the latter lives accordingly and teaches others that they must live in like manner. Lastly, as Plato observes, the governor of a city so orders the Republic of the city as he has in the first place managed the Republic of his soul. For in every man there is formed, as it were, a Republic out of the irascible and concupiscible as well as the rational parts of the soul. Therefore, if anyone so lives that his appetites do not turn away from the virtues, but follow in every action the lead of reason alone, he has established in his soul the best form of the Republic and that form which in a city leads to the rule of an aristocracy or of an upright prince. But if the irascible power of the soul influenced by ambition or some similar disease exercises control in our soul, and everything else in a man yields to it, he immediately brings forth a vain and warlike form of government over the people and city subject to him. If, however, inordinate desire or avarice or the other ills and pestilences of the concupiscible part outstrip everything else, thereupon a popular and finally a tyrannical city is produced to the greatest detriment of all citizens. Wherefore it especially befits the civil ruler of a city and the pastor of a Christian flock to form within themselves the best possible Republic of the soul, if they are to administer the city properly and lead it to the best of their abilities to the desired blessedness.

A far greater perfection of soul however is required of the Bishop than of the prince, both because he must guide the people of whom he has care toward the highest end and according to the most excellent Christian virtues, and because, since no one is equal to bearing so great a burden by himself, he who girds himself for such a great task must have a most purified soul and one worthy to receive divine illuminations. For although the Supreme Artificer rules this universe with an extraordinary and wonderful order and leads lower beings toward their own and natural ends by means of higher ones, as by certain instruments, yet He especially manifests this order in guiding mankind toward eternal happiness. Wherefore He uses angels as ministers for purifying and illuminating the minds of men. He manifests this more obscurely, however, in the case of those who are subject to the rule and guidance of others, but with the greatest clarity and light in the case of those who have the charge of caring for others, provided that these men themselves do not fall short and mankind itself wishes to be the source to some extent of that highest beatitude.

The Bishop moreover stands between the divine spirits and mankind. Whence it is clear that the Bishop must share in a certain sense both in the angelic nature and in human nature. Since no one can announce this about himself, even though he is adorned with every virtue, a man cannot seek the episcopacy therefore without the reproach of arrogance or avarice or ambition. Nevertheless, without any reproach one can desire that by divine providence that excellence of soul be granted him, so that he can be worthy to hold the episcopal office. Yet by no means should anyone approach that dignity unless called by God and chosen by the Supreme Pontiff without any striving on his own part, just as we read that Aaron was called to the priesthood by his brother Moses.[8] In the light of this therefore no one, however dull of mind, can fail to perceive how great a perfection and excellence of soul he should have who, we have said, must be raised above the human rank to a participation in the angelic nature.

At this point I cannot fail to deplore with all my heart the calamity of our age, when you will find very few guardians of the Christian people who spend their time in the cities entrusted to their care. In truth they think they have

[8] Lev. 8, 1–12.

done enough with respect to their duty if they have handed over the administration of the city to a deputy, though they themselves obtain the revenues. And indeed they join the retinue of some great personage in the Roman Curia and busy themselves with the affairs of kingdoms and of wars. But concerning the people over whom they are placed, they do not even receive news as to whether they are making progress in the Christian religion or whether they are forsaking it, and they completely neglect and disregard the poor of their flock. Is this the conduct of a Bishop? Is this the imitation of the disciples of Christ? Is this the observance of the Gospel precepts? The good Bishop therefore will do his best not to hand over the care of his flock to another, but will be away from the sheepfold as short a time as possible, unless for some reason the Pope summons him to serve in some capacity, since the Pope has the welfare of all Christendom in mind. But let the Bishop not desire that this occasion be given him, nor seek out any such post; rather let him accept a burden of this kind with the greatest reluctance. And after he has been released from it, let him not look for another, but let him return to his flock as quickly as possible.

Book II

We have in the first book instructed the Bishop both in human and in divine virtues. Now we shall seek to explain to the best of our ability how a Bishop, so instructed and adorned by these virtues, should conduct himself and with what duties he should be occupied. And since actions have to do with specific cases, we shall also be more specific than we were in the first book in proposing precepts. In this regard we shall appear to imitate the ingenuity of the painters who first form and express the whole figure by certain lines and afterwards fashion the individual parts with the suitable and proper delineations and colors. In the same way we also shall have sketched the Bishop by means of all the virtues, as if they were the basic lines, and we now begin to explain how he can properly carry out every virtue pertaining to his office. At the outset, since charity is the chief of all the virtues, if we run through the specific duties of charity, we shall rightly seem to have omitted nothing which bears on this question. First, therefore, lest the discussion depart from the right order as from the road, we must set forth the duties which pertain to divine worship. Next are those which should be exercised in the government and care of the Christian flock in accord with the life and example of Christ. After these come the duties of beneficence and the generosity which it becomes the Bishop to practice in relieving and assisting the needs of the poor. Lastly, we shall discuss how the revenues of the Bishop ought to be both exacted and expended. When these have been explained (I believe) all the duties of the Bishop will have been treated properly and diligently enough.

Divine worship, in addition to the interior disposition of the soul about which we have said much above, first requires of the Bishop, as of any priest, that he say daily the divine praises and prayers contained in the ecclesiastical

Office with a great lifting up of the soul to God (I am using moreover the customary name of Office which has indeed been derived from that task of saying daily those divine praises, because it is the special duty [*officium*] of the priest). And it requires that no other mind distract him when he sings the divine praises, but that he endeavor with every effort both to understand what his words express and to approach them, if possible, with a certain relish of soul. The power of an exertion of that sort is certainly astonishing, if we believe upright and pious men, and it is a power which no one will believe in unless he experiences it. And he will attain to this more easily if he says the divine Office not all at one time but in parts at the appropriate hours of the day, so that at each division of the day those portions of the Office are recited which have been adapted to these times by a certain holy custom. For the mind affected by the tedium of a lengthy reading is generally burdened and oppressed by aversion rather than carried to loftier heights. Aside from this the Prophet himself in the Psalms indicates that the divine praises ought to be said thus in parts. For he says, "Seven times in the day I have given praise to you," and the prayers and hymns adapted for each division of the day clearly explain this.[9]

For that reason I would wish (as I begin at last to conduct the Bishop from the beginning to the end of the day) that the Bishop residing in the city entrusted to his care (for we have said above that he must do this) rise up from bed before day-break and sing the early morning lauds, for these morning hymns and prayers have been adapted to this time of day. The Prophet also says, "At midnight I arose to acknowledge you." That time happens to be very opportune for this, and that silence for the contemplation of divine things. And that early morning vigil is wonderfully advantageous to the good health of the body, if we believe what Aristotle says in *Oeconomicus*. After the early morning lauds when dawn draws nigh and the hour hovers between day and night I would especially desire that, when the body has been completely released from sleep and the mind elevated by saying the divine praises, some time be devoted to prayer customarily offered to God without the din of any voice and only by the lifting up of the mind and by meditation. In no way can a greater flame be added to the mind than by this awakening of the soul. Of this experience men noted for sanctity and religion say that occasionally there floods into the heart so great and clear an understanding of divine things that God is felt to be present to the mind no longer by the usual way of understanding but by some way foreign to man, and they say that such a great ardor of divine love is enkindled in the soul that the mind thus affected can think of nothing save God, nor be aware even of itself, not to mention other things, while it is aware of God. It cannot be sufficiently explained by words how much light and how much strength and force of mind come to the understanding from this illumination of the divine ray. A

[9] The reference is to Psalm 118 (119), 164, and to the seven canonical hours of the day that made up the divine Office, *viz.*, lauds, prime, tierce, sext, none, vespers, and compline.

mind touched by such a flash of lightning is able to understand the most secret things and to be equal to any task however arduous. But may it preserve the humble and submissive soul in its duty and not encourage it to pursue by intelligence that divine secret most remote from all the mind of man can grasp. For, as it is written in Holy Scripture, he who searches out majesty is crushed by the glory.

I would not wish the Bishop to linger to satiety in that kind of contemplation, from which aversion and dullness of soul are commonly wont to arise. On that account, if at any time he feels himself not having the proper disposition for that prayer, I would not want him to undertake anything with Minerva being unwilling (as they say), that is, with an opposed nature. But for that period of time let him devote himself to studies, either of Holy Scripture or of something else pertaining to sacred literature. For let him not only consider certain unchaste studies and some superstitious sciences like magic and the knowledge of prophesying from the stars or from something of that sort alien and opposed to the interests and duties of the Bishop, but let him also strive with all his strength to banish them entirely from the city over which he presides.

When the day will have become truly light and the cover of darkness will have been driven back by the sun's rays, then at the first hour of the day let him sing praises to God, and, if he should wish to join the praises of the third hour to these, I believe he does nothing reprehensible. Immediately after this let him either celebrate himself the sacred rites of the Eucharist or at least each day be present at their celebration by another priest. Still I hink that he should frequently, if not daily, celebrate the sacred rites of the Mass and consecrate and consume the most holy sacrament of the Eucharist. For when it is the duty of any priest to do this, lest he show too little thanks to God for the dignity of the priesthood, and lest he cease by the neglect of so great an oblation to relieve the souls of the living and the dead, or lest he cherish the memory of the Lord's death with a reluctant spirit, then especially does it seem to be the duty of the Bishop, who since he is a priest ought certainly to be of the most purified spirit and open in every way to divine illumination. And he will attain to this above all by the frequent offering and use of that sacrament. Thus it is that I think the practice of certain Bishops who rarely come and partake of the heavenly banquet must be reproved. I myself have seen Pietro Barozzi, Bishop of Padua, a man who never can be praised enough for his merits, celebrating daily at dawn the solemn rites of the Mass in a private chapel with an extraordinary sanctity and dedication to God. It has also been recorded that most good Bishops have done the same, and from the frequent practice of this sacrament they have gained the most suitable and penetrating power for understanding all of the most difficult passages of Scripture and the ability by effective and rigorous preaching to incite everyone most skillfully to adopt a Christian life and Christian morals. For, as the Prophet says in the Psalm, "they will declare the memory of your sweetness."

After finishing these tasks which are done both for the worship of God and for the elevation of the soul, promptly at the third hour of the day our Bishop will devote himself to receiving and hearing those who will approach him as a judge or as a counselor or as a helper; and to these let him show himself open and benign, yet in such a way that he does not depart from dignity. Let him settle immediately what he can, let him judge rightly and fairly, let him give sure counsel to those asking advice, and let him give assistance to those he can. And let him not cease from this task until he will have heard all. For this duty I think must take precedence before any other. Let him indeed dismiss, as far as possible, everyone glad, no one grieving. But if this is not possible, let him try at least to mitigate their grief and disturbance of soul by humane and gentle speech. Nevertheless, I believe that he should also check occasionally with severe and harsh words the insolence of wicked and obstinate men whom you make more savage the more gently you treat them. Indeed parents are accustomed now and then to use such words with the sons they especially love. He will certainly perform all these duties as well as possible, if he is endowed with genuine, not feigned, charity and if he loves those committed to his care as sons. For that virtue will give him excellent instruction in all these duties.

I am not unaware that most Bishops delegate these tasks to a vicar. They do this (I think) from a certain weakness of soul, that is, lest they be disturbed by the burden of these matters and be not able in spirit to render service. May I never praise this withdrawal and this management of affairs through a vicar, unless the Bishop, impeded either by ill health or by involvement in some other duty which he cannot neglect without reproach, cannot himself discharge his responsibility. I do not, however, think it wrong that a Bishop have some learned and upright man as a vicar whose service he makes use of in the majority of cases. For, if weighed down by a multitude of business he himself should not be equal to the task of settling every case, or if he must visit remote places, to which he himself cannot conveniently go, it is fitting and practically necessary to make use of the services of a vicar in duties of this kind.

After concluding these affairs let him again return to the divine praises and say the sixth and ninth hours. For those hours of the waning day are appropriate for these praises. After that, if he wishes, let him attend to luncheon. In this matter I praise not sordid frugality, but indeed I censure very much magnificent pomp and lavishness and excessive elegance in the food and its service. For, by heaven, what can be seen more alien to the nature of things than to behold the shepherd of a Christian flock, for whom the life of Christ has been set up as the model, given over to feasts and doing those very things which he himself from the start ought to be censuring and correcting in others? Furthermore, what is more unseemly than to have the revenues of the Bishop, which good men had formerly bequeathed to advance the worship of God and to alleviate the needs of the poor, squandered on the magnificence of great dinners and on gluttonous feasting? The meal of the Bishop then will not be niggardly but it will be sparing, a matter more of the necessity of nature than of the pleasures of the table. But lest even then they be completely absorbed by the enjoyment of the food, I have a great deal of praise for the custom of certain Bishops who always have some spiritual reading at the luncheon or dinner. From this custom they derive, I believe, a twofold benefit. For first, as I was saying, the soul is elevated and is not weighed down by the enjoyment of food, and at the same time provision is made against a lapse into the ludicrous jesting which sometimes occurs during meals. For all these reasons I think it the wisest plan to add spiritual reading, if not for the entire luncheon or dinner, then for most of it. After luncheon a little jesting with friends who are present may be permissible, provided that it does not become insulting to anyone or obscene. But buffoonery ought very much to be avoided, and dignity should be preserved in pleasantry of speech as much as possible, and unrestrained laughter should be repressed.

Nor shall I reprove some kind of music, for I am of the opinion that the most noble relaxation comes to the soul from music. But, since the soul is very much affected by harmony, and the latter is able both to soothe and to excite the emotions, as well as to set right the disposition of the soul, I consider that the warning which even among the pagans Aristotle, the prince of philosophers, gave in the *Politics* and Plato issued in many places must be observed most diligently, so that the ears of the Bishop and through them his soul may not be accustomed to certain soft harmonies of song and sound which can weaken and dull the vigor of the most robust soul and arouse lustful desires. Nor on the other hand should that Phrygian type of harmony be allowed, whereby the minds of men are often driven into a frenzy. This fault is more rarely committed in our age, but it was indeed most frequent in former times. Yet strong and steady music should be permitted, which delights the soul of a noble and upright man, provided that the entire day is not whiled away in such delight.

Humor and relaxation should have a place with the day's affairs and activities so that the soul actually made more cheerful by humor can better engage in the performance of every duty. Thus, after what would seem to be enough time for the relaxation of the soul and the good health of the body has been spent on jesting, the Bishop should immediately return to serious things, and, if any affairs press heavily, he should do his best to take care of them. But indeed if any time remains, it should all be spent either in the company of friends or in literary pursuits, though conversation with friends ought in no way to be at variance with the course of the Bishop's life. Therefore, let the talk be about Christian matters or about something which pertains to good morals or to the study of letters. And indeed this kind of intercourse with learned and upright man sometimes takes the place of and is preferable to a great deal of study. For generally we take much from friends, as if from living books, and it often happens that this cleaves more to the soul than what we learn from the reading of books. Still, I would not want anyone to suppose for that reason that we are praising a certain morose and weighty kind of conversation; on the contrary, we believe that affability and pleasantness ought to be present as much as possible.

But when the day moves toward sunset, we should return to the divine praises, lest our routine seem to miscarry, as it were, in the final hour of the day. Therefore, vespers should be said and the mind directed toward God. If the Bishop joins compline, that is, the last part of the Office, to this, I do not think it wrong. But if he says this last part after supper, when he is making ready to retire, I am of the opinion that he does so at the proper time. The rest of the time extending from vespers to supper I might wish to be spent, if nothing else intervenes, on reading and study, on the nature of which enough has been said by us above. At supper let him observe the same practice which he followed at luncheon, that the meal may be frugal and spiritual reading accompany it and good humor and music, if it be pleasing, bring it to a close. Nevertheless, temperance in eating will be very beneficial, if he enjoys a larger meal at supper than at luncheon, for he will have a lighter sleep, and he will be more prompt for the early morning vigil. In both cases a stomach burdened with too much food is a hindrance.

We believe that this schedule should in general be observed by the Bishop. I would want no one, however, on that account to think that we have so established this program for daily living that we consider it must be kept by all and in every situation. Rather we are of the opinion that it is impossible for human activity in any sphere to be bound by some fixed rule, and we believe that a Lesbian rule ought to be employed with regard to human actions, that is, a rule made of lead, flexible and not rigid, so that it can be bent and adjusted according to the circumstances of the time and the persons involved.[10] Therefore, in this matter also this rule prescribed by us can be bent and applied in keeping with the time and the circumstances and conforming to the natural inclination of individual persons. For nothing prevents the Bishop, if ever he leaves the city for the countryside in order to devote himself for several days to some suitable exercise for the sake of refreshing his spirit, from observing another way of life. Yet, if either the opportunity of completing some business or the arrival of a friend intervenes, he certainly ought not to neglect the Office nor abandon the prescribed pattern of living.

The Bishop indeed will be able to remain faithful to such duties with difficulty, unless he has provided himself with a household which is distinguished for uprightness of life and does not spurn good habits—a situation, I think, which also contributes very greatly to the reputation of the Bishop. For a member of a household who has bad morals both greatly disturbs the entire household and in most cases brings the greatest shame on it outside. Hence, great care should be exercised by the Bishop lest he admit anyone into his household who is not noteworthy for being upright. And thereby the Bishop will preserve the peaceful life of the household and at the same time will not hear

10 Aristotle, *Eth. Nic.* 5.10.7.

ill of it abroad. He must especially take heed regarding this not only for his own sake but also lest by the bad example he does harm to his fellow citizens. For nature has ordained that other men think that anything whatsoever is permissible for them by reason of the imitation of those in command. And also he must take care that he does not admit anyone into his household who may indeed not have bad morals, but who can nevertheless justly bring suspicion of bad conduct on himself or on the head of the house or on another member. In this matter let him follow, by Hercules, the very beautiful maxim certainly worthy of Caesar, who said when he dismissed his wife because of a suspicion only of unchastity with Claudius: "The wife of Caesar must be free not only from unchastity but also from the suspicion of unchastity." Thus the Bishop, and all the more so because his life has been set before others as an example, ought to be free not only from stain but also from every, even the slightest, suspicion of stain.

He must also take pains to keep the virtuous household he has selected to their duty and to promote to a higher level of dignity everyone according to merit and virtue. By the same token let him look to the nourishment and clothing of his servants, so that neither the dignity of the Episcopacy is neglected, nor any pomp or luxury entertained. Let him care for the members of his household when they are ill, and let him provide for their welfare in a way that takes account neither of expense nor of any inconvenience. I remember when I was living at Padua that Pietro Barozzi, a remarkable Bishop, of whom I have spoken above, most faithfully observed—besides supplying everything necessary for those who were ill in his household—that a doctor never visited a sick member of the household without himself being present. He himself took a part in the consultations of the doctors. Indeed he did this in every case, so that he neglected neither the last nor the lowliest. A charity that must be highly praised, and an action truly worthy of a Bishop! Moreover, let the Bishop's relationship with the members of his household be founded both on dignity and on affability, lest it become a matter of either contempt or hostility. And there must be a certain skillfulness, so that the Bishop is respected and loved by his household.

Enough has been said, I believe, in the short space of our little work concerning the duties of the Bishop whereby he must maintain divine worship and keep himself and his household faithful in the performance of virtuous acts. I now propose in the second place to explain those duties a Bishop should fulfill in governing the flock entrusted to his care, in so far as this pertains to virtue and the Christian life.

The entire population of a city, first of all, is divided between males and females. Further, some of the males are priests or have been consecrated to religion; others are laymen. Likewise, certain of the women have vowed virginity to Christ and live in convents. The rest have chosen another kind of life. The Bishop's first care should be for the men rather than for the women, both because men surpass women by nature and also because the governance of a city proceeds with a certain order. Women by nature are subject to men and ought to wait upon their command. Wherefore it seems proper that the Bishop's rule be brought to the women by the men as mediators or instruments, so to speak. And since some of the men observe a common way of Christian life, in fact have been consecrated to religion, by the same token clerics first come under the care of the Bishop. For it is fitting that he uses them as helpers in directing the rest of the flock. And among the clergy those who are called secular should be given preference over those who are commonly called religious and who are subject to their own superiors and seem to be apart from the flock of the city. The secular clerics therefore are admitted into ecclesiastical Orders by the Bishop, and they should be kept in their duty by him. Accordingly, at the very start it is necessary to make a careful inquiry and to use excellent judgment in advancing clerics to ecclesiastical Orders.

In this matter at this time nearly all, it seems to me, sin most grievously, for without discrimination the most wicked men, as well as men ignorant of every good art, are admitted to a sharing in the divine power which belongs to priests. Afterwards these with polluted hands and the most contaminated minds daily touch the ineffable sacrament of the Body of Christ, most worthy of all veneration. Moreover, observed in their villainous deeds they cause the greatest harm to the Christian community. And at length the people think that a license for perpetrating any crime whatever has been given them by the example of these authorities. Thus I believe that great diligence should be exercised lest any monster of this kind be admitted to ecclesiastical Orders with the approval of the Bishop we are instructing. Rather let men graced by good morals and outstanding for learning be chosen so that qualified assistants can be available to the Bishop in teaching the city the Christian religion and in cultivating good morals.

At this point incidentally it comes to mind to warn lest the Bishop in any way admit to the ecclesiastical order those who seek to be consecrated to religion so that they might have immunity from punishment for their crimes, rather than because they wish to be clerics. Among these the majority are men who are noble by class but servile by nature, men who take refuge in religion and Holy Orders as if it were the asylum for scoundrels which they conceive it to be. These must be completely rejected from sharing in this sacrament. And if it ever happens that any one of these detected in a crime seeks to ward off paying the penalty owed by seeking the aid of a Bishop because of Holy Orders, let the Bishop in no way be guilty, with my approval, of wishing religion and Orders to be a protection for criminals and an obstacle to justice. But, unless such a man has observed all things which one consecrated to religion should observe in his way of life, in worship, and even in his physical appearance, let the Bishop hand him over to the secular ruler for punishment. But if there is some reason for not handing him over to the judge and the civil laws, then let the Bishop himself as judge pass the severest sentence lest he seem to make the Church of Christ a place of refuge.

But let the discussion return from where it digressed. There will indeed be little work left for the Bishop in governing the clergy, if he has not erred in choosing his clerics. For he will easily keep in their duty those who ever since their youth have been instructed in good qualities and upright ways. Therefore, he will see to it that the young are educated not in the classics or studies of that kind, except in so far as may be sufficient, but in Christian learning, in theology I mean, 'and not in that contentious and headstrong variety, as I call it, which swells the mind with vanity and hinders more than it serves, but in the teachings of the old theologians and in pontifical law which is in accord with that theology. For this contentious law which revolves about the rights and legal suits of priests and has been ingeniously devised in the majority of cases by those who fawn on clerics (let me speak freely as the matter demands) and by which permission is granted to do safely anything whatever—I shall say nothing further—this law I firmly believe should not be regarded highly, and indeed wherever the lawyers of our age are out of step with the ancient theologians it must be completely rejected.'[11] Nevertheless, the study of Holy Scripture which at length brings to perfection all the studies of the cleric should be preferred before all. These books ought always to be at hand, so that we might say of the sacred texts what Horace says of the Greek authors: "O ye priests, day and night study the sacred books."[12] And let all lewd poets and the superstitious arts be kept far away from the cleric.

Indeed the effort and industry of the Bishop will accomplish all these things well, if he knows everyone of the clergy and summons them often to appear before him, and if he questions them to see how far each has progressed. And if any one has not advanced because of some natural incapacity, the Bishop at least will see to it that he does not fall back. And he will instruct the young men that he will confer honors on each one in consideration of their progress. Indeed, he will inquire whether the older clerics are wanting in their duty, and he will handle roughly those who have been. But those who have been conducting themselves well he will praise and reward, if the opportunity is given.

He will also most diligently protect the rights of these men lest the ministers of religion be treated with derision and be unable to uphold the honor and majesty of the priestly dignity. It is necessary, however, that he give more attention to caring for those priests to whom the responsibility of ruling others has been entrusted and by whom in the sacrament of Penance the sins of the people are wont to be washed away and purged as by a medicine. He will attend to this not only in the city but also in the towns and villages, granted that neither the learning nor the course of study which are required of a city priest shall also be required of a country priest. Yet I would not want the country priest to be completely ignorant of letters, but rather to be as proficient in letters as is necessary for instructing the country-folk in what every

---

[11] This passage which has been placed within minute strokes was expurgated in the 1589 edition.

[12] Horace in *Ars Poetica*, 269, writes: *"vos examplaria Graeca/nocturna versate manu, versate diurna."*

Christian ought to know. Nevertheless, I especially call to mind that good morals and a blameless life should be required of these priests. For nothing is more harmful for the Christian flock than a wicked and shameful priest.

Up to this point we have been speaking about clerics bound to no particular Order. But those who serve in some Order or community are accustomed by a certain privilege of the Roman Pontiff not to be under the care of the Bishop; rather they have other superiors under whom they perform their duties. Yet I do not believe on that account that the Bishop ought to refrain from exhorting those in charge of convents to maintain the monasteries in their religious obligations. And if, by chance, any of these men commit some deed which can result in injury to others, let the Bishop, as far as he can, see to it that the culprit is expelled from the city entrusted to his care, if he has no other way of curbing this evil influence.

But these matters are what I might call the duties relating to individuals which the Bishop should carry out with regard to the clergy. Now let us discuss what may be called the Bishop's public duties toward all of the people. On solemn feast days, most of which occur once a year, the Bishop should celebrate the holy sacrifice of the Mass before the entire people. He should also be present at vespers as the leader of the choir. Robed in the sacred vestments he himself should consecrate the oil of the chrism, and he should deem it his obligation to perform the other rites rather than entrusting them to others. For, as Paul says, whoever desires the Episcopacy desires work and not a quiet and idle life.[13] It will indeed not be amiss for me to warn the Bishops of our time not to neglect altogether a very ancient custom most faithfully observed by our fathers. These illustrious men were wont on feast days and sometimes daily to preach to all the people during Mass, whereby they both instructed those ignorant of Christian doctrine and exhorted all marvelously to an upright life. There are extant very many excellent sermons given to the people not only by Bishops but also by the Supreme Pontiffs. The religious have assumed this duty in our age because of the slothfulness of the Bishops, nevertheless this task, nay, this honor, of instructing the people belongs especially to the Bishop. Would that this custom, if not entirely, at least in some way, be revived and restored to its former state by that guardian whom we are instructing. For on every feast day and on days marked by some special occasion I would recommend that the Bishop preach and either proclaim the Gospel or develop some theme from Holy Scripture or moral philosophy for the public good. If this is not done before all the people, it should at least be done with the clergy present and attending, for it is likely that through the clergy this sermon will be carried to all. By no means should the good Bishop, in my opinion, fail to observe this obligation, unless he thinks that he is completely unsuited for performing it. In this case let him trust the judgment of others rather than his own.

His next duty after this is to keep the whole populace on the right religious

13 1 Tim. 3, 1.

path not by warnings and exhortation alone but by decrees and the sanction of the laws. This, in fact, will be most easily achieved if he avoids by what I might call a middle course two opposite vices which are frequently wont to appear among men. One of these we shall call irreligion or impiety, the other superstition. The first vice arises for the most part from certain studies and arts hostile to religion which display the name of wisdom, although they are, however, the enemies of true wisdom. The arts of this kind are the several sciences of predicting, such as magic and astrology, all of which can be recognized as a form of idolatry by those who should know that these arts attribute to stars and demons what belongs to the divine nature alone. Not less discordant with religion and entirely at logger-heads with it is a certain kind of philosophizing which nowadays has sprung up in the schools. Inexperienced youths are led astray, who though they know nothing reach a high opinion of their knowledge—on the basis of what fictions I know not—to the extent that they think nothing of others compared to themselves and consider them ignorant of the nature of things and call them only a rabble. All these most pernicious arts let the Bishop to the best of his ability drive far away from his flock. Let him order under pain of punishment that all such arts hostile to religion must be shunned and rejected by all. And to accomplish this let him zealously take the necessary steps with sanctions, as I have said, and with sermons and exhortations. The Bishop should also exercise the greatest diligence lest heresy creep in or the books of heretics be secretly introduced into his diocese. For there is no deadlier disease nor anything which more easily opens the window to atheism than heresy which, when it destroys the foundations of faith, also suddenly overturns all public order.

The other sin contrary to the above is superstition which is what I might call an exaggeration [excessus] of religion, just as the former vice is what may be called a lack [defectus] of religion. Therefore let all superstition be diligently destroyed, so that when the saints dwelling in heaven are invoked or their relics are venerated or likenesses of the Lord, the Most Blessed Virgin, and other saints are depicted in the churches everything be done with the greatest propriety and in good order. Such practices ought to lead the people to the worship of the one God as if they were leading them step by step by hand, so to speak. But if any abuse in these matters does creep in, it will be well for the prudent Bishop and ecclesiastic to do away with it gradually, lest, if we are carried along hastily or without consideration, we destroy the very worship of God, faith in the sacraments, and also the hierarchical order of the Church as heretics have done. Consequently, let the people often be taught that in all things God must be loved and worshipped; also, that all exists because of God without whom nothing has been made; and that the saints themselves are nothing. Thus, let every action and thought proceed from Him and to Him finally return, as the Alpha and Omega. If men have recourse to the saints, let them know why they are doing it and in addition what has been most wisely decreed and explained by the Councils. But if anyone, either because of avarice or for some other reason, should make wrong use of relics or sacred images, let such plagues at once be kept far from the Church of God and let a heavy penalty be imposed, lest Christian purity be corrupted by these perversions.

When the error of superstition and the sin of impiety have been avoided, the people can be easily kept in the right religious path. Nevertheless, let the Bishop take care that everyone frequent the sacraments of Penance and the Eucharist at least at the proper times, and let him inquire about this of the priests in charge of the districts of the city and the villages. If anyone fails in this obligation, let the Bishop first endeavor, having summoned the offender before him, to call him back to his duty and the right path of piety by persuasion and gentle rebuking. But if he observes that anyone obstinately persists in his wrongdoing and refuses to be corrected, then let him judge him guilty before others and subject to the ecclesiastical fines and censures, lest others also be infected by contact with the evil of that man.

Further, let the Bishop attend to the education of the young people, and let him not allow, as far as he is able, the souls of boys from their youth to be corrupted by the licentiousness of poets and other authors of this kind. If the young drink in such wantonness in their childhood years, it will be almost impossible to summon them again at a maturer age to greater virtue. In this matter, as I have said in the first book, our age sins greatly. Aristotle in the *Ethics* very clearly and fully explains how one becomes accustomed to things from youth. On that account also the divine Plato in the books of the *Republic* by the best of rights is seen to curse the poets and to expel them from that city which he himself established as the best. Yet, I would not want anyone to think therefore that we consider all poets to be in the same category and that we do not realize that a divine inspiration, so to speak, influences poets. We are not so ignorant or so slow of wit as not to be aware of that. But we think that integrity of spirit and modesty should be placed far ahead of the pleasure and titillation which is wont to be taken from reading poets of the kind we have mentioned. For gradually corruption bathed in sweet song and concealed by the divine breath of the poet creeps into the soul and deeply engages it, so that afterwards it can scarcely ever be cleansed. Young people should abstain from studying poets of this kind. But if any poet, such as Virgil among the Latins, either seeks to restore good morals—the best of goals—or sings of wars and misfortunes, I do not say that he should not be read; nay, rather I praise anyone who so reads that he not only finds enjoyment, but also is benefited by it. Meanwhile it would be a wonderful achievement indeed if school boys had to study some Christian reading together with the profane authors. For, to tell the truth, it is most shameful for those professing devotion to Christ to know the deeds of the Romans and their sacred ceremonies and rites but to be completely ignorant of the Christian religion. Would that at the instigation of our Bishop the practice would grow that boys right from infancy were accustomed to Christian reading! For Latin authors are plentiful enough among us so that anyone need not fear that Latin eloquence would be corrupted by the study of sacred literature.

CHAPTER VIII

Lefèvre's Preface to His Commentaries on the Four Gospels, 1521

Jacques Lefèvre d'Étaples, or Faber Stapulensis, to give his name in its Latin version, was "the greatest French representative of Christian humanism."[1] Born about 1455 in Picardy and dying in 1536 in Navarre, his career is contemporary with Colet's and Erasmus', and his aims and life's work are comparable to those of the great English and Dutch scholars. Like them he was profoundly influenced by the humanism of Italy; like them he came to focus on the study of scripture and the early Fathers; like them he saw reform as flowing from a return to the Gospel, from a rediscovery of the Word of God and the purer faith of the primitive Church. *Evangélisme* is a term that has been applied to this broad intellectual and religious movement that swept Europe in Lefèvre's day, and his own role in its propagation and development is of the utmost significance.[2]

Lefèvre attended the University of Paris, where he received his master of arts and where he subsequently taught philosophy in the College of Cardinal Lemoine. In 1491–92 he visited Italy and made close contact with both the

[1] P. Imbart de la Tour, *Les Origines de la Réforme* (4 vols.; Paris, 1905–35; 2d ed., rev., of Vols. I and II, Melun, 1944–48), II², 383. On Lèfevre, see *ibid.*, II², 383 ff., and III, 109 ff.; A. Renaudet, *Préréforme et humanisme à Paris pendant les premières guerres d'Italie (1494–1517)* (Paris, 1916); Margaret Mann, *Erasme et les débuts de la réforme française (1517–1536)* (Paris, 1934); and the following recent articles: J. W. Brush, "Lefèvre d'Étaples: Three Phases of His Life and Work," *Reformation Studies*, ed. F. H. Littell (Richmond, 1962), 117–28; E. F. Rice, "The Humanist Idea of Christian Antiquity: Lefèvre d'Étaples and His Circle," *Studies in the Renaissance*, IX (1962), 126–41 and appendices; J. Dagens, "Humanisme et évangélisme chez Lefèvre d'Étaples," *Courants religieux et humanisme à la fin du XVe et au début du XVIe siècle* (Paris, 1959), pp. 121–34; and A. Renaudet, *Humanisme et Renaissance* (Geneva, 1958), Chap. XIII: "Un problème historique: la pensée religieuse de J. Lefèvre d'Étaples."
There are no modern editions of Lèfevre's own works and editions, with the exception of a facsimile reproduction of his *Epistres et Evangiles pour les cinquante & deux sepmaines de l'an* (1525?) with introduction and notes by M. A. Screech (Geneva, 1964). English translations of Lefèvre's prefaces to his *Quincuplex Psalterium* (1509) and his *Sancti Pauli Epistolae* (1512) may be found in *Forerunners of the Reformation*, ed. H. A. Oberman, trans. P. L. Nyhus (New York, 1966), pp. 297–305.
[2] The term is originally that of Imbart de la Tour, who uses it as the title of Volume III of *Les Origines de la Réforme* (Paris, 1914). Carrying overtones of a deeply pious and even mystical character, it seems particularly applicable in the case of Lefèvre. For a discussion of the movement, though limited mainly to Italy, see Eva-Maria Jung, "On the Nature of Evangelism in Sixteenth-Century Italy," *Journal of the History of Ideas*, XIV (1953), 511–27.

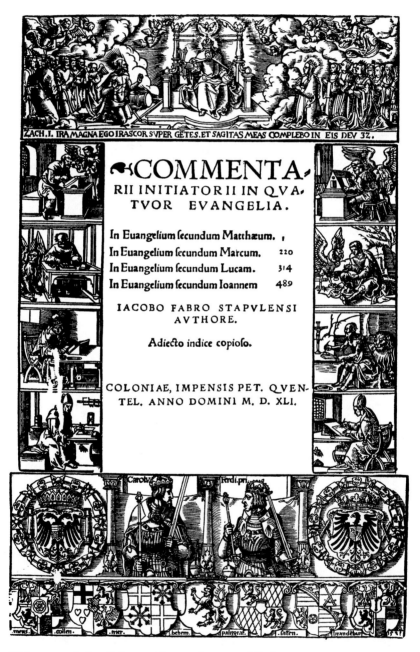

ZACH.I. IRA MAGNA EGO IRASCOR SVPER GETES. ET SAGITAS MEAS COMPLEBO IN EIS DEV 32.

◄COMMENTA-
RII INITIATORII IN QVA-
TVOR EVANGELIA.

In Euangelium secundum Matthæum. 1
In Euangelium secundum Marcum. 220
In Euangelium secundum Lucam. 314
In Euangelium secundum Ioannem 489

IACOBO FABRO STAPVLENSI
AVTHORE.

Adiecto indice copioso.

COLONIAE, IMPENSIS PET. QVEN-
TEL. ANNO DOMINI M. D. XLI.

7. Title page of the Cologne edition of 1541 of Lefèvre's *Commentaries on the Four Gospels.*

Aristotelianism of Ermolao Barbaro and the Platonism of Marsilio Ficino and Pico della Mirandola. After his return to Paris he began to edit and publish the texts of Aristotle (beginning with a paraphrase of the *Physics* in 1492)—an enterprise which inaugurates the first phase of his scholarly work.[3] Many varied influences, however, bore on the thought and scholarship of Lefèvre, and the works of other important authors also appeared under his auspices: Dionysius the Areopagite (1499), Raymond Lull (1499 and 1505), St. John of Damascus (1507), Nicholas of Cusa (1514). But it was Holy Scripture that came to occupy the center of his attention and to be his chief object of study and the very heart and soul of his reform program. This "phase"—the most important and consequential of his career—was announced by the appearance of his *Quincuplex Psalter* in 1509 and his edition of St. Paul's Epistles in 1512. Both publications embody a new textual and exegetical approach, emphasizing (1) the critical and philological analysis of the early texts and (2) the understanding or interpretation of scripture in the "spiritual" sense, and they are landmarks in the progress of biblical humanism comparable to Colet's Oxford lectures or Erasmus' Greek and Latin New Testament.[4]

In 1508 Lefèvre had joined his friend and patron, Guillaume Briçonnet, who had recently been made abbot of Saint-Germain-des-Prés, at that ancient monastery, and in 1521 he followed Briçonnet to Meaux (some twenty miles east of Paris) after the latter took up residence in that diocese which had been entrusted to his care. The period which then began and extended to 1525 when Lefèvre left Meaux is one of the most interesting and active in Lefèvre's long career. It is marked by the attempt to inaugurate practical religious reform under the auspices of Bishop Briçonnet, by Lefèvre's own participation in this endeavor and in actual diocesan administration (he became Briçonnet's vicar general in 1523), and by the creation of the so-called "Meaux circle" of humanists whose leader and inspiration Lefèvre unquestionably was.[5] It was also during these years that he published two of his masterworks—his *Commentaries on the Four Gospels* in 1522 and his French translation of the New Testament in 1523. It is the preface to the former work, which Imbart de la Tour identifies (along with two *épistres exhortatoires* in the French New

---

[3] A full bibliography of Lefèvre's editions to 1517 may be found in Renaudet, *Préréforme et humanisme*, pp. xxxviii–xli. For an attempt to order and analyze the pattern of Lefèvre's thought and work, see Brush, *op. cit.*, where three successive phases are observed: the Aristotelian, the mystical, and the biblical.

[4] Renaudet, *Préréforme et humanisme*, pp. 514–17, 622–34. Luther used both of Lefèvre's editions in the preparation of his lectures on the Psalms and on Romans at Wittenberg in the years 1513–16, and there is little doubt that Lefèvre's exegesis had considerable influence on him. On this, see W. Schwarz, *Principles and Problems of Biblical Translation* (Cambridge, 1955), pp. 172 ff. This latter book, although it does not deal extensively with Lefèvre, is an excellent introduction to the humanist biblical method and to the whole subject of biblical study and exegesis in the fifteenth and sixteenth centuries.

[5] Imbart de la Tour, *op. cit.*, III, 110 ff. On Meaux, see also René-Jacques Levy, *Les origines de la réforme française: Meaux, 1518–1546* (Paris, 1959), and M. Mousseaux, *Aux sources françaises de la réforme: La Brie protestante* (Paris, n. d.), Chaps. I–III.

Testament) as a manifesto of the Lefèvre school of reform, that is presented here.[6]

The Protestant Revolt seriously compromised the *évangélisme* of Lefèvre, and like Erasmus he was accused of sowing the seeds of the Lutheran schism. It was such suspicions and accusations that led to the disruption of the "Meaux circle" in 1525 and to Lefèvre's taking temporary refuge in Strasbourg and Basel. He soon returned to France, however, at the behest of the king, became a royal tutor and librarian at Blois, saw his complete French Bible—the first printed in that language—published at Antwerp in 1530, and spent the later years of his very long life at the court of Francis I's sister, Queen Marguerite of Navarre. He died at Nérac in March, 1536, preceding in death by four months his great contemporary, Erasmus.

As for his affinity to Protestantism, the question has divided historians, but François Wendel's judgment seems particularly incisive and authoritative. His view is that "after an impartial examination of Lefèvre's writings, whatever has been advanced to show that Lefèvre ever really adhered to the Reform or to its theological principles can be cast into the limbo of tendentious legend."[7] In brief, the thought and spirituality of Lefèvre, influenced by the medieval mystical tradition and by Nicholas of Cusa, are fully Catholic, and though—like Erasmus—he may have been a cause for anger and alarm on the part of those who opposed the scriptural emphasis and exegesis of the humanists, he wished only to see the Catholic Church renewed and reformed by a spiritual revival. The following statement reveals something of the nature and ardor of his aspiration.

[6] III, 123–28. It was written at Meaux in 1521 (or is so dated). The *Commentaries on the Four Gospels*, or *Commentarii initiatorii in IV Evangelia*, was published in Meaux in June, 1522, in Cologne later that year, and in Basel in 1523. The translation herewith published has been made from the Basel edition by Charles W. Lockyer, Jr., and the editor.

[7] François Wendel, *Calvin*, trans. Philip Mairet (New York, 1963), p. 42, and also p. 130. See also Imbart de la Tour's appraisal, especially III, 139–53, which, however, is challenged by M. A. Screech in his introduction to Lefèvre's *Epistres et Evangiles pour les cinquante & deux sepmaines de l'an*. Screech, like Renaudet in *Humanisme et Renaissance*, sees Lefèvre as in accord with Luther on the major problems of justification and the Bible. I should like also to call attention to Henri de Lubac's judgment in "Les humanistes chrétiens du XV–XVI siècle et l'herméneutique traditionelle," *Ermeneutica e tradizione* (Padua, 1963), pp. 203–29, where Lefèvre (like Erasmus) is viewed as returning to the exegesis of the early Fathers.

THE PREFACE of Jacques Lefèvre d'Etaples to Christian Readers:

O you who are truly chosen by God and especially dear to me in Christ! Whoever loves Our Lord Jesus Christ and His Word in perfect purity, these alone are truly Christian, a name holy and venerable, about which Ignatius said to the Magnesians: Whoever is called by any other name than this is not of God. For the Word of Christ is the Word of God, the Gospel of peace, liberty, and joy, the Gospel of salvation, redemption, and life—the Gospel of peace, I say, after perpetual war, of liberty after a most harsh slavery, of joy after incessant grief, of salvation after the greatest ruin, of redemption after a most wretched captivity, and finally of life after endless death. And hence it is called the Gospel, which means the herald of good tidings and of the infinite blessings awaiting us in heaven. But whoever does not cherish Christ and His Word in this way, how are they Christian? Everything touches them in quite a different way. I wish that no one be among this group, but that all be among the former. Nor is this an empty wish indeed, for God himself wills that all men be saved and come to a knowledge of the truth and thus to a love of the Gospel's light.

Bishops should have the first and highest roles in this, and above all he who is declared the first, highest, and greatest of those in visibly carrying out the sacred offices. For a person can only be designated such by virtue of that immortal, incorrupt, and spiritual love of Christ and the Gospel. Then may kings, princes, and all important personages, and thereupon the peoples of all nations, reflect on nothing else, embrace nothing so much, manifest nothing to the same extent as Christ, the vivifying Word of God, and His holy Gospel. And may this be the only striving, comfort, and desire of all, to know the Gospel, to follow the Gospel, everywhere to advance the Gospel. And may all hold most firmly to what our ancestors and what the early Church, red with the blood of martyrs, perceived, that to know nothing except the Gospel is to know all things. By the study of this alone Hungary, Italy, Germany, France, Spain, England, yes, all of Europe, Asia, Africa, can be blessed.

And certainly every bishop ought to be like that angel whom John in the sacred Apocalypse saw flying in mid-heaven, having an everlasting Gospel, crying out above every nation and tribe and tongue and people: Fear the Lord, and give Him honor.[8] For because the angel must announce only what God commands, because in flight he must continually attend with a keen mind to what is on high, because having an everlasting Gospel he must not trouble himself with what is outside the boundaries of the Gospel—since it is everlasting, what else but immortality can he promise?—and finally because crying in a loud voice to every nation, tribe, tongue, and people he must never cease to proclaim and summon to the true worship of God, he strives for one thing only (Fear the Lord, he says, and give Him honor, and he adds: Worship Him who made the heaven and the earth, the sea and fountains of waters), and he excludes everything which is not in accord and agreement with this one most true and simple purpose. Since it is one thing only, it has power, and all else is destitute of power except insofar as it draws it from that one alone. And therefore the many should not be reckoned with the one, nor impotence with power, nor nothingness with being, nor the finite with the infinite. The worship of Him alone is pure, the worship of others can not be pure. The angel of the sacred Apocalypse (as we have already said) declared this crying out in a loud voice: Fear the Lord, and give Him honor. Fear signifies a holy reverence, and honor that pure and sincere worship which is owed to God alone, indivisibly (as I shall say) to Father, Son, and Holy Spirit. Therefore the effort, vigor, and all the strength not only of bishops but also of kings and all rulers should be exerted to intensify this worship where it exists and to restore it where it has been destroyed. For in this alone the hope of gaining eternal life has been left to us.

Act, therefore, bishops, act, kings, act, generous hearts! Awaken the nations everywhere to the light of the Gospel, to the true light of God! Restore to life and cast out whatever does not aid or whatever impedes this pure worship! Pay no attention to what the flesh says or does, but to what God says and commands! Diligently bear in mind that maxim of Paul: Do not touch, nor taste, nor handle things that must all perish in their very use, following the precepts and doctrines of men, which, to be sure, have a show of wisdom in superstition and self-abasement![9] The Word of God suffices. This alone is enough to effect life everlasting. This rule alone is the guide to eternal life. All else, on which the Word of God does not shine, is as unnecessary as it is undoubtedly superfluous. Nor should such be reckoned with the Gospel as far as the purity of pious worship and the integrity of faith are concerned, for it is not the creation of God.

---

[8] Apoc. 14, 6–7.
[9] Col. 2, 21–23. Lefèvre's use of this maxim is somewhat curious. Actually St. Paul does not enjoin this rule, but is questioning the giving of such an injunction by those who were teaching a false asceticism.

But someone may say: "Consequently I desire to understand the Gospel so that I may believe in the Gospel and come near to the pure worship of God." Christ, the guide and giver of eternal life, does not propose that the Gospel be understood, but that it be believed, since it contains very many things, not just a few, which transcend the capacity of our intelligence and of every creature (I think) who has not been united hypostatically with God. Believe in the Gospel, He says. But first He commanded that we have a change of heart, when He said: Μετανοεῖτε, Repent.[10] And rightly so indeed. For all savor the flesh before they savor the spirit, and they embrace the things of men more eagerly than the things of God. Nor perhaps is this without cause, since the latter are above man and the former are close to man. Therefore, there must be a change of heart with respect to the former, and the flesh and the things of men must be rejected so that we can believe in the Gospel. Thus let the divine conquer and the human, which does not possess the light of the Gospel, although it may manifest wisdom and piety, depart. For this discourse treats of the Word of God, of faith, and of the pure worship of God, and in it certainly the truth alone, which is the Word of God, brings salvation, but what is not the truth brings ruin. The one thing [i.e., the Word of God] binds together, all else scatters.

And would that the model of faith [credendi forma] be sought in that early Church which consecrated so many martyrs to Christ, which knew no rule save the Gospel, which had in short no goal save Christ, and which gave worship to no one save the Triune God. Truly, if we lived in this fashion, the everlasting Gospel of Christ would flourish now as it flourished then. They depended entirely on Christ; let us also depend entirely on Him. All their faith, all their trust, all their love were gathered in Him; let ours also be gathered in Him. No one lived by his own spirit, but by the spirit of Christ; let us live in this way. And thus at last we shall go from this life to Him, as those for whom Christ was all have gone before us. All these we love and praise because of Christ, and so with them we give all worship and glory to God alone.

And why may we not desire that our age be restored to the likeness of that primitive Church? Then Christ was worshipped more purely, and His name shone forth more widely, because then Persians, Medes, Elamites, Mesopotamians, Armenians, Phrygians, Cappadocians, men of Pontus, Asia, Pomphylia, Egypt, Carthage, Cyrenaica, Rome, Jerusalem, India, and Ethiopia, Moors, Spaniards, Gauls, Britons, Sarmatians, Dacians, Germans, Scythians, and islands of unknown nations believed in Christ, worshipped Christ, adored Christ (not a few testify to this, including Tertullian, a man of that time, in his book against the Jews).[11] The kingdom of Christ and His name (he says) extends everywhere, is believed everywhere, is worshipped by nations without number, reigns everywhere, is adored everywhere, is given equally to all everywhere.

[10] Mark 1, 15.
[11] Lefèvre's list is very similar to that in Acts 2, 9–11.

With Him the influence of a king is not greater, nor is the joy of any imperious barbarian less, nor is the importance of the honors or birth of anyone taken into account. He is the same to all, king to all, judge to all, God and Lord to all. From the faith in Christ of that time these sentiments spread far and wide. With the returning light of the Gospel may He who is blessed above all grant also to us this fullness of faith, thus purity of worship.

I say, with the returning light of the Gospel, which at last in this age is again penetrating the world, and by which divine light a great number have been enlightened, so much so that, besides many other changes, since the days of Constantine, when the primitive Church, which gradually declined, disappeared, there has not been a greater knowledge of languages, a greater exploration of the globe, or the propagation of the name of Christ to more distant corners of the earth than in these times. For the knowledge of languages, and especially of Latin and Greek (John Reuchlin afterwards renewed the study of Hebrew letters), began to return about the time Constantinople was taken by the enemies of Christ, when a few Greeks, notably Bessarion, Theodore of Gaza, George of Trebizond, and Emmanuel Chrysoloras, took refuge in Italy. Soon afterwards the Portuguese discovered lands and thereupon propagated the name of Christ in the east, as did the Spaniards (under the leadership of a Genoese) in the southwest and the French in the northwest. Would that in all these places the name of Christ might have been proclaimed purely and sincerely and henceforth may be so proclaimed, so that soon these words may be fulfilled: Let all the earth adore Thee, O God. And of course may this be a sincere and evangelical worship in spirit and in truth. Above all this must be desired.

But come, since the Lord commands, as has been said, to believe in the Gospel, not to understand it, should one not aspire to understand it? Why not? But only to the extent that believing holds first place and understanding second, for he who believes only what he understands does not yet believe in a proper and sufficient manner. For there are in the Gospel (as has already been said) not a few things which can be believed by men, but can not be understood. No one ought to aspire to an understanding of these, since it is enough that Christ and the spirit which is in the believer understand these things. And also the immensity and majesty of the faith overwhelms the human mind, as the source of the sun's light overwhelms the eye of the senses, so that it understands nothing, just as the eye sees nothing. Nevertheless, the eye believes, and without a doubt, in that source of light, even if it can not see it in its source. And so the mind ought to believe, even though it can not understand. But as the eye's credulity is something greater than its vision, since the latter pertains to what is small and the former to what is great, so also the credulity of the mind is something greater than its capacity to understand, for the latter's object is finite and the former's is infinite.

However, in order to lead us forward to an understanding of the Gospels, many of our forefathers, certainly famous men, either in homilies or in commentaries enlightened their times, and others tried other forms of writing in explaining these texts. I esteem most highly the attempts of all these men and especially of those who undertook their task at the prompting of the Spirit. But yet, as the light of the sun cannot be explained by the innumerable stars shining in the night, so the light of the Gospels cannot be explained by the lamplights of innumerable writers (even though they treat these Gospels divinely). Likewise, as a newly risen star obstructs nothing, but renders brighter the night, although the radiance of the sun has not yet dawned, so we have concluded that new commentaries on the Gospels, if any are being prepared, commentaries which may indeed enlighten our mind, do not obstruct anything.

But these commentaries which we have written on the Gospels first for the glory of God, then for a knowledge of the Gospel truth, and finally for the profit of all, we in no way claim are of this kind, but are in the category of those which dispel the darkness of the mind and in some way effect that breakthrough of light. For, as the night is not illuminated by the light of the stars unless first the atmospheric mist has been dispelled and the air cleansed, so ignorance is not illuminated by the light of commentaries unless first the mind's darkness has been removed and the mind cleansed. For that reason by preparing new commentaries on the Gospels we have sought to dispel the darkness of the mind and work, as it were, a certain cleansing in it. We have followed only that grace which we desired from God, save if anywhere we have been left to our own devices and have added something of our own. This we acknowledge as our own, and in no way must it be magnified, but what is not our own we set down as coming from God. Nor have we borrowed from the work of others, so that, impoverished as we are, we might depend more on God. And indeed it is no secret to me that diligence which aids in study and in reading books cannot give an understanding of these sacred texts, but that this understanding must be sought through the gift and grace of God which is wont to be granted not according to the merits of anyone, but according to the pure generosity of Him who gives.

We wish therefore that these commentaries be compared not indeed to a star shining in the night, but rather to a cleansing of the air. For there are three things which our forefathers have set down: purgation, illumination, and perfection, whereby what is lower leads to what is higher. Among these perfection holds the highest place, illumination the middle, purgation the lowest. We place our commentaries, such as they are, in the latter category, and we therefore call them purgative, that is, introductory [initiatorios]. May God grant that there may be those who will add commentaries of illumination and (as He wills) of perfection, for it is His alone to bestow every divine gift and especially what achieves perfection. Moreover Paul says this of purgation: He has effected man's purgation from sin.[12] He says this of illumination: Lest they should see the light of the Gospel of the glory of Christ.[13] And he says this of

---

[12] Heb. 1, 3. Lefèvre quotes this passage, as well as the two that follow it, in Greek.
[13] II Cor. 4, 4.

perfection: Therefore, leaving the elementary teaching concerning Christ, let us pass on to things more perfect.[14]

Besides, when we say these commentaries on the Gospels are purgative, let no one think that the Gospels are in need of purgation. For they do not require it, nor do they need illumination or perfection, since they are in themselves most pure, most enlightened, and most perfect. But let him understand that this purgation, of which we speak here, pertains to dispelling the darkness of minds, especially of those who, still untrained, approach the innermost recesses of the sacred Gospels, the secret mysteries of the Word of God, so that they can admit within themselves the pure and holy rays and the inviolable sacrament of the Eternal Light, while now the night of ignorance departs and the light of the Gospel rises in their hearts. For unless this darkness is dispelled, such minds will often grope about the letter itself [of the Gospel]. Commentaries are usually a guarantee against this occurrence. But however remarkable they may be, they can add no light to the Gospels (for this cannot happen, since no light can be added to the visible sun), but on the contrary the Gospels can add light to the commentaries. If the latter were not the case, commentaries would be nothing else than hues in the darkness and a variety of vapors before the mind.

Moreover, lest it be obscure to you in what way these commentaries are purgative, I shall in conclusion briefly advise you of their arrangement. First the old text [of the Gospel] appears. Then come brief annotations, some of which throw light on obscurities in the old text, some correct what has been corrupted, some indicate by an asterisk placed before what is somewhat more full among the Greeks [i.e., in the Greek texts], some mark by an obelisk what is not found among them, and some give reference to other passages which are more easily understood by those who have been given some little clarification. All these notes effect a purgation not only of minds, but also of the old text. Thirdly the commentary follows, accomplishing more precisely the same thing, that is, a purgation sometimes of the old text, sometimes of minds, sometimes of both, and clearing away the errors in the one and the darkness in the other. Also two sets of numbers appear in the old text: those which have been placed in the outside margin correspond with the numbers of the commentary, those in the text itself correspond with the numbers of the brief annotations. And before we go on to the work proper we prefix a concordance of the four evangelists, in which two dots signify that less is found there, three dots in the form of a triangle more, four dots in the form of a quadrangle a similar version, two dots placed before a triangle first less and then more, and the contrary when this order is reversed. But these perhaps are too insignificant to require an explanation.

Take counsel therefore, good Christians and pious readers, and beseech the Lord of the Word, who is the Lord Christ, that His Word does not fall without fruit, but that throughout the world it bears fruit unto life everlasting,

[14] Heb. 6, 1.

and that He himself, who is Lord of the harvest, sends new and eager workers to the new harvest. Farewell in the same Christ Jesus Our Lord who for us by God became wisdom, justice, sanctification, and redemption, and himself Christ Jesus in the glory of the Father and the charity of the Holy Spirit. May He be all things to you, as He will be all in all to those who will enjoy eternal life in blessedness.

Meaux, in the year 1521.

CHAPTER IX

Adrian VI's Instruction to Chieregati, 1522

The short pontificate of Adrian VI, lasting from January, 1522, to September, 1523, broke the disastrous pattern of the Renaissance Papacy and showed at a most critical time the possibility and promise of the highest authority in the Church espousing the cause of renewal and reform.[1] Circumstances surrounding the tenure of this last non-Italian Pope, especially the brevity of his term, did not allow effective action, but a new attitude was announced and the lines of a serious and constructive policy in the face of the Lutheran challenge and the needs of the age were declared. "The significance of his career," says Pastor, "lay not in his achievements, but in his aims."[2] In this sense the Counter-Reformation begins—or at least is foreshadowed by the outlook and intentions of the Dutch theologian who now occupied the Chair of Peter.

Adrian Florenszoon, or Adrian of Utrecht, as he came to be known, was born in Utrecht in 1459 of humble parents. He attended the school of the Brothers of the Common Life at Zwolle and in 1476 entered the University of Louvain, where for the next thirty years his career as student, doctor of theology (in 1491), professor, and scholar unfolded. In 1507 the Emperor Maximilian appointed him tutor for his grandson, young Archduke Charles, the future Emperor Charles V. Broader responsibilities and higher honors soon were thrust upon him. He was sent to Spain in 1515 to represent the interests of the young Habsburg prince who the following year succeeded his grandfather Ferdinand as king there, and he was subsequently associated with the great Cardinal Ximenes in the regency. He was made Bishop of Tortosa in 1516, and Leo X elevated him to the cardinalate in 1517. When Charles left Spain in May, 1520, to assume the imperial crown, he designated Adrian

---

[1] The fullest account of Adrian's pontificate is given in Pastor, IX, 1–230. A far more critical appraisal may be found in Mandell Creighton, *A History of the Papacy during the Period of the Reformation* (5 vols.; London, 1882–94), V, 184–235. It is interesting to compare the two. Cardinal van Roey *et al.*, *Adrien VI, le premier pape de la Contre-Réforme* (*Bibliotheca Ephemeridum Theologicarum Lovaniensium*, Vol. XIV; Gembloux, 1959), contains several excellent articles on Adrian, including L.-E. Halkin, "Adrien VI et la réforme de l'église," and a bibliography. Also notable is J. Coppens, "Adrien VI, pape de l'union," in *Union et désunion des chrétiens* (Bruges, 1963), pp. 57–78. The basic collection of early lives, letters, and documents is C. Burmannus, *Hadrianus VI sive analecta historica de Hadriano Sexto* (Utrecht, 1727).

[2] Pastor, IX, 125.

his Viceroy, and it was at that post that the news came to him of his election as Pope in January, 1522. He arrived in Rome in August and died there in September the following year.

The problems that faced the new pontiff, a stranger to Rome and curial practice, were grave indeed. War continued between Charles V and Francis I of France (the Papacy had been allied with Charles); the menace of the Turks in the East was most serious; the revolt of Luther, already condemned by Church and Empire, agitated Germany and gained wide support. Basically Adrian's response, at least in purpose, was simple and direct: he sought peace among the Christian princes, aid for those threatened by the Turks, action to repress Luther and his adherents, and reform in the Church. This latter aim, as his Instruction to Chieregati clearly shows, was closely related to the restoration of religious peace and the Church's authority in Germany, and its realization was intended to remove the cause of the infection and disorder. Yet it was not simply a device, a reaction to the Lutheran revolt alone. The background, life, character, and piety of this scholarly Pope bespeak an austere morality and place him in the ranks of those serious churchmen who sought the correction and reform of the Church of Christ because of what it was and what it must be. This too is evidenced in the Instruction to Chieregati.

During his short reign Adrian was the butt of the ridicule and contempt of the Roman *literati* and the papal bureaucracy, yet from the start there were earnest men who set high hopes on him as a reformer and who gave him expert instruction and advice. Two of the most eminent of these were the Swiss Cardinal Schinner and Cardinal Lorenzo Campeggio.[3] Both laid bare the ills that beset the Church, particularly at Rome, and stressed the urgent need of curial reform. Their advice had the merit of being informed and practical, and there is every reason to believe that it was guidance Adrian highly valued and took to heart. Cardinal Carvajal also urged the new pontiff to undertake reform, as did the learned Cardinal Cajetan.[4] And the injunction *Purga Romam, purgatur mundus* (Cleanse Rome and the world will be cleansed), addressed to the Pope by Zaccaria Ferreri, an Italian bishop and the former secretary of the *conciliabulum* of Pisa, may be said to have summed up the thought of many who hoped that now the hour of regeneration had arrived.[5]

The document that follows incorporates the principle *Purga Romam, purgatur mundus*, in a striking way. Drafted by the Pope himself for the papal nuncio Francesco Chieregati, whom Adrian had dispatched to the imperial Diet of Nuremberg in September, 1522, it is a document, in the words of Pastor, "unique

---

[3] The Latin abstract of Cardinal Schinner's memorial is in Pastor, IX, 472–75. The text of Cardinal Campeggio's is in *Concilium Tridentinum*, XII, 5–17. They and other similar proposals are discussed in Pastor, IX, Chap. III.

[4] Cardinal Carvajal was dean of the Sacred College, and his exhortation was his address of welcome when Adrian arrived in Rome. It is in *Concilium Tridentinum*, XII, 18–21. Cardinal Cajetan spoke at Adrian's first consistory, September 1, 1522, and also submitted a reform memorial. The text of both is in *ibid.*, XII, 31–39.

[5] *Ibid.*, XII, 27. The full text of Ferreri's memorial, *De reformatione ecclesiae suasoria*, which was published in Venice in 1523, is in *ibid.*, XII, 21–30.

8. Tomb of Pope Adrian VI.

in the history of the papacy."[6] This uniqueness lies primarily in the public admission of guilt which Adrian makes and in his excoriation of Rome as the fountainhead of the evil and corruption that had come. Chieregati read the Instruction before the Diet on January 3, 1523, along with a papal Brief to the German princes urging them to take action against the Turks and to enforce the Edict of Worms against Luther. The Diet's reply was equivocal, to say the least. Unwilling to meet the Pope's demands, its members asked for "a free Christian Council" on German soil and renewed their list of grievances against the Holy See.[7]

[6] Pastor, IX, 132. Chieregati's mission as well as the Instruction are discussed in Pastor, IX, Chap. IV, and Creighton, *op. cit.*, V, 217–25. See also Kidd, *Documents Illustrative of the Continental Reformation*, pp. 105–21. The full text of the Instruction is in *Deutsche Reichstagsakten*, new series, ed. Historische Kommission, Munich (Gotha, 1893 ff.), III, 390–99. The translation here presented was made by John Marrone and the editor from the *Reichstagsakten*.

[7] On the Diet's reply, see the comments in Jedin, *A History of the Council of Trent*, I, 211–13; and also Pastor, IX, 138–42.

YOUR INSTRUCTION, Francesco Chieregati, concerning certain matters which you can state in your own words, when and where you judge it opportune, to the prelates, princes, and representatives of the German cities.

You will especially make clear to them the very great sorrow which afflicts us because of the progress of the Lutheran sect, above all because we see countless souls who have been redeemed by the blood of Christ and entrusted to our pastoral care being turned away from the true faith and religion and going to perdition. This occurs in the nation where we were born, which, from the beginning of its conversion to Christ down to these recent years, has always remained most faithful and religious. Therefore, you will declare that we most strongly desire that this pestilence be more quickly countered before it infects Germany itself, as it once infected Bohemia. You will declare that we are most prepared to do everything that can be expected of us to this effect, that we ardently desire that each one of them also strives to do the same to the best of his ability, and that, as far as we can, we exhort and call on each one of them to do this. Moreover, the following should spur them to this task:

First, and above all, the honor of God, which is seriously offended by these heresies and whose customary worship is not only diminished but also totally corrupted, must come before all else. Likewise, charity toward neighbor must take precedence. In this each one should strive to the best of his ability to recall straying neighbors from error. Unless this is done, God will hold him accountable for those who perish because of their own negligence.

Second, the dishonor of their own nation should move them. Although it was always considered most Christian in comparison with other nations, now it is regarded most unfavorably by all because of those who follow the Lutheran sect.

Third, let regard for their own honor move them—an honor greatly damaged, if these men who hold authority and power in Germany do not strive with all their energy to expel those heresies, first, because they will degenerate from their own ancestors, most Christian men, who played a major role in the condemnation of John Hus and the other heretics at the Council of Constance, some of whom are said to have led John Hus himself to the fire by their own hands, and second, because these men, or the majority of them, have approved the imperial edict drawn up for the execution of the apostolic sentence against Martin Luther and his followers and have used their authority for this purpose. Therefore, unless they carry that out to the best of their ability, they will either be judged inconstant or even be considered to favor Luther, since it is clear they can easily outlaw him when they effectively wish to do so.

Fourth, let the injury inflicted by Luther upon them and their parents and ancestors move them. Since their own parents, ancestors, and they themselves have always held to the faith which the Roman and Catholic Church affirms, and since Luther and his followers hold a far different faith, asserting that many things are not *de fide* which those men have nevertheless held to be *de fide*, obviously those persons are condemned by Luther as infidels and heretics. Consequently, according to Luther, all of their ancestors who have died in our faith are in hell, since error in faith makes men liable to damnation.

Fifth, let them look to the end toward which the Lutherans go: namely, that under the guise of evangelical liberty which they proclaim to men every source of authority is destroyed. Although they boasted from the outset that they wished to annihilate or curb ecclesiastical power, as if it has been seized tyrannically and contrary to the Gospel, yet since their basic principle, namely, the liberty which they preach, is equally or even more opposed to secular power, since that power cannot oblige men to obey under pain of mortal sin any laws, no matter how just and reasonable they are, it is clear that these men also wish to weaken secular power, albeit they cleverly pose as saving it. The intention is that, while the secular princes believe that this stratagem is not directed against themselves, but only against the clergy (to whom the laity generally are hostile), and therefore in part have been drawn to their side and in part overlook or do not contradict their teaching, they themselves [the Lutherans] might more easily overthrow the clergy. After that it is certain that the people will attempt the same thing against those very secular princes.

Sixth, let the enormous scandals, disturbances, plundering of goods, homicides, quarrels, and dissensions, which this most mischievous sect has stirred up and daily stirs up throughout all Germany, move them. Similarly, let the blasphemies, curses, gibes, and bitterness, which are always on their lips, move them. Unless these men take care to hold their tongue, we fear that the wrath and desolation of God may come upon a Germany so internally divided, or rather upon those very princes who, although they received power and the sword from the Lord for the punishment of evil, permit such things to occur among their subjects. Cursed be he, says the prophet, who does the Lord's work remissly and holds back his sword from the blood of the wicked.[8]

[8] Jer. 48, 10.

Seventh, let them consider the fact that Luther employs almost the same method in seducing the Christian people as that most detestable Mohammed used in deceiving so many thousands of souls, namely, by permitting those things toward which carnal men are inclined and thereupon freeing them from those things which seem very important in our law, except that Luther seems to act with a little more restraint in order to deceive more effectively. Mohammed granted permission for having several wives, for spurning them at will, and for taking others. Luther, in order to win for himself the favor of monks and virgins consecrated to God and of priests lusting for the delights of the flesh, proclaims that vows of perpetual chastity are illicit, to say nothing of not being binding, and therefore that those persons may marry because of evangelical liberty. He is unmindful of the words of the Apostle when he says concerning younger widows that when they have wantonly turned away from Christ they wish to marry and are to be condemned because they have broken their first troth.[9]

After you have explained these and several other matters, which you will be able to gather in part from the examples in our letters on this subject and in part contrive from your own knowledge, you will urge in our name the said princes, prelates, and people to rouse themselves at long last and rise up to meet such a great injury as the Lutherans are known to inflict upon God and His holy religion, and especially the dishonor they inflict upon your whole German nation and those princes themselves, and the very great disgrace and insult they inflict upon their ancestors whom (as we have said) they condemn in effect to hell; and you will urge them to proceed to the execution of the apostolic sentence and the said imperial edict in their entirety. Let pardon be granted to those who will have wished to come to their senses and to abjure their errors. Let them be always more inclined to pity than to punish, in imitation of our God who does not wish the death of sinners but rather that they might be converted and live. But let those who remain steadfast in error be punished with the rod of destruction according to the decrees of the sacred canons and the laws, so that by their example others might continue in the right faith or having lapsed might return to the right path.

But if perchance anyone might say that Luther had been condemned by the Apostolic See without a hearing and a defense, and therefore that he should certainly be heard and should not be condemned before he has been convicted, you will reply: Those matters which are part of the faith must be believed because of divine authority and are not to be proved. Away with proofs, says Ambrose. When faith is sought, credence is to be given to the fishermen, not to the dialecticians. And certainly we admit that we should not deny him a defense in questions of fact, that is, whether or not he has said certain things, whether or not he has preached or written them, and so forth. But indeed concerning divine law and the subject of the sacraments the authority of the saints and of the Church must prevail. Add the fact

[9] I Tim. 5, 11–12.

that almost all the matters in which Luther dissents from others have previously been condemned by various Councils. Moreover, it should not be called into doubt that what the General Councils and the universal Church affirm has been established as belonging to the faith. For he does injury to the Council of the Church who seeks to call into doubt matters once rightly disposed. For what can ever be certain among men or what will be the end of controversies and strife, if there will be liberty or license for every presumptuous and perverse man to renounce those doctrines which have been definitively ordained, not by the consent of one man or a few men, but by the consent of so many centuries and of so many of the wisest men and by the Catholic Church (whom God never permits to err in matters of faith)? Furthermore every community may require its own laws to be observed inviolably. How will there not be complete disorder, scandal, and confusion, unless those laws, which have once been established, and indeed more often following mature deliberation, are strictly observed by everyone? Since therefore Luther and his followers condemn the Councils of the holy fathers, burn the sacred canons, throw everything into confusion as they will, and disturb the whole world, it is clear that they must be outlawed as enemies and disturbers of the public peace by all who love that peace.

You will also say that we frankly confess that God permits this persecution to afflict His Church because of the sins of men, especially of the priests and prelates of the Church. For certainly the hand of the Lord has not been shortened so that He cannot save, but sins separate us from Him and hide His face from us so that He does not hear. Scripture proclaims that the sins of the people are a consequence of the sins of the priests, and therefore (as Chrysostom says) our Savior, about to cure the ailing city of Jerusalem, first entered the Temple to chastise first the sins of the priests, like the good doctor who cures a sickness at its source. We know that for many years many abominable things have occurred in this Holy See, abuses in spiritual matters, transgressions of the commandments, and finally in everything a change for the worse [et omnia denique in perversum mutata]. No wonder that the illness has spread from the head to the members, from the Supreme Pontiffs to the prelates below them. All of us (that is, prelates and clergy), each one of us, have strayed from our paths; nor for a long time has anyone done good; no, not even one.[10] Therefore, we must all give glory only to God and humble our souls before Him, and each one of us must consider how he has fallen and judge himself, rather than await the judgment of God with the rod of His anger. As far as we are concerned, therefore, you will promise that we will expend every effort to reform first this Curia, whence perhaps all this evil has come, so that, as corruption spread from that place to every lower place, the good health and reformation of all may also issue forth. We consider ourselves all the more bound to attend to this, the more we perceive the entire world longing for such a reformation. (As we believe others have said to you)

[10] Psalm 13 (14), 3.

we never sought to gain this papal office. Indeed we preferred, so far as we could, to lead a private life and serve God in holy solitude, and we would have certainly declined this papacy except that the fear of God, the uncorrupt manner of our election, and the dread of impending schism because of our refusal forced us to accept it. Therefore we submitted to the supreme dignity not from a lust for power, nor for the enrichment of our relatives, but out of obedience to the divine will, in order to reform His deformed bride, the Catholic Church, to aid the oppressed, to encourage and honor learned and virtuous men who for so long have been disregarded, and finally to do everything else a good pope and a legitimate successor of blessed Peter should do. Yet no man should be surprised if he does not see all errors and abuses immediately corrected by us. For the sickness is of too long standing, nor is it a single disease, but varied and complex. We must advance gradually to its cure and first attend to the more serious and more dangerous ills, lest in a desire to reform everything at the same time we throw everything into confusion. All sudden changes (says Aristotle) are dangerous to the state. He who scrubs too much draws blood.

As to what you write in your last letter about those princes who had complained to you that their agreements had been infringed by the Holy See, you will say: We can not and should not be blamed for matters which occurred before our pontificate. Infringements of this kind always greatly displeased us, even while we were in lesser offices. Accordingly, we give our word, even if those men may not require it, that we shall completely abstain from this practice during the time of our pontificate, partly to observe the rights of each party, partly because equity and humanity demand it, so that not only may we not give offence to our illustrious country, but that we may also extend special favors to her.

Concerning the cases which they ask to have withdrawn from the Rota and returned to their places of origin, you will say: We desire to please them in this matter, as far as we honestly can. But due to the absence of the auditors [i.e., the judges or officials of the court] from the city because of the plague we cannot at present be informed about the nature and status of those cases. When these men have returned, which we hope will be soon since the plague is now subsiding, we shall do whatever we reasonably can to please the said princes.

You will also diligently seek out the responses to our letters and ask those to whom we write to inform us in their letters how in their opinion this most evil sect can be better resisted, so that those measures which we must take can be more quickly taken. And you will also inform us, most diligent son, about this same matter and give us the full details in writing.

Also, because we have known that there are in Germany many good and learned men in poverty, even some of outstanding ability, who have been estranged from the Holy See because of the character of apostolic appointments which have been customarily given to actors and tavern-keepers rather than to learned men, we desire you to find out who they are and to send their names to us, so that we can provide for them on our own initiative when a vacancy occurs in a German benefice. For we know how prejudicial it has been to the honor of God and the salvation and edification of souls that ecclesiastical benefices, especially those involving the care and direction of souls, for so long have been given to unworthy men.

We do not give you information concerning the procuring of aid for Hungary other than we gave you on your departure, except that we exhort you to attend to that matter with the greatest zeal (as you do). We shall also solicit the princes and the Italian republics through ambassadors, so that each may help to the best of his ability.

Pope Adrian VI   *T. Hezius*[11]

---

[11] T. Hezius is Dirk van Heeze, Adrian's private secretary.

CHAPTER X

The Theatine Rule
of 1526

The Theatines were an Order of Clerks Regular founded in 1524 by four members of the Roman Oratory of Divine Love.[1] Their intention was to be neither monks nor friars but a society of priests, engaged in pastoral work, who would profess the monastic vows of poverty, chastity, and obedience and live in a community under a superior. They were a new kind of religious association, dispensing with many of the externals and practices of the existing monastic Orders and aiming chiefly at the perfection of their own priestly life and at raising the standard of clerical life in general. As such they represent a reform most urgently needed, and they are the first of a number of new Orders—the Somaschi, the Barnabites, the Jesuits—based on a similar concept, who helped effect a revitalization of the Church's pastoral mission.

Gaetano da Thiene (1480–1547), a native of Vicenza, curial official, and devout priest, later canonized and venerated as St. Cajetan, is generally acknowledged as the founder of the society.[2] The cofounder and most dynamic force in the new Order was Gian Pietro Carafa (1476–1559), a Neapolitan noble and nephew of Cardinal Oliviero Carafa, Bishop of Chieti in 1505 and subsequently Archbishop of Brindisi, sometime papal nuncio to Naples, England, and Spain, and an ardent, active ecclesiastical reformer whose long career was to be climaxed by his reign as Pope Paul IV.[3] Both men were members of the Roman religious confraternity known as the Oratory of Divine Love, and in 1524 to give greater depth to their priestly vocation and to establish a more formal and permanent organization designed primarily for priests (the Oratory was essentially a lay confraternity), together with two other members of the Oratory, Bonifacio de' Colli and Paolo Consiglieri, they launched a society of Clerks Regular. Clement VII gave approval to their plan

---

[1] Brief accounts of the foundation and early years are given in Pastor, X, 397–419, and XI, 515–21, and *The New Cambridge Modern History,* Vol. II: *The Reformation, 1520–1559,* pp. 285–87. Fuller accounts are Pio Paschini, *S. Gaetano Thiene, Gian Pietro Carafa e le origini dei Chierici Regolari Teatini* (Rome, 1926), and P. A. Kunkel, *The Theatines in the History of Catholic Reform before the Establishment of Lutheranism* (Washington, 1941). The basic history is Guiseppe Silos, *Historiarum clericorum regularium a congregatione condita* (3 vols.; Rome-Panormi, 1650–66). On the Oratory of Divine Love, see Chap. II.

[2] On Gaetano, see *Le Lettere di San Gaetano da Thiene,* ed. D. F. Andreu (Rome, 1954), which contains an excellent bibliography.

[3] The early standard life is Carlo Bromato, *Storia di Paolo IV* (2 vols.; Ravenna, 1748–53). Also important is A. Caracciolo, *De Vita Pauli IV* (Cologne, 1612), which also contains *vitae* of Gaetano da Thiene and the other two founders of the Order.

and purpose in June, and in September the four founding members solemnly professed their vows in a ceremony at St. Peter's and inaugurated the new Order. The name Theatine, derived from Carafa's bishopric of Chieti or Theate, became their common designation, and it was soon a byword in Italy for an austere and reformed priesthood.

The Theatines remained, in numbers at least, a small Order—fourteen members by 1527, twenty-one by 1533. Their importance, however, is far greater than their numbers indicate. As Pastor points out, they were a "carefully chosen circle of men . . . a corps d'élite," and the Order was "not so much a seminary for priests, as at first might have been supposed, as a seminary for bishops who rendered weighty service to the cause of Catholic reform."[4] After the terrible sack of Rome by mutinous imperial troops in May, 1527, they moved to Venice, where they had close ties with Contarini and other Venetian reformers and with the reforming Bishop of Verona, Gian Matteo Giberti. In 1533 Gaetano established a second community in Naples. And when Carafa returned to Rome in 1536 at the summons of Paul III to play an active role in curial reform, their influence became even more expanded, and "their example pointed the way with irresistible force to the reform of the clergy throughout Italy."[5]

The following document is the original Theatine Rule. More a brief statement of the new Order's practices and guiding principles than a Rule in the traditional sense, it was written by Carafa (who had become the first Superior) in 1526 and was later incorporated in a letter sent by Bonifacio de' Colli to Giberti at Verona.[6] Especially noteworthy are its concluding words on the preeminence of the virtue of charity—words which recall the purpose and spirit of the Oratory of Divine Love.

[4] Pastor, X, 418. According to Broutin, op. cit., p. 44, n. 2, "the Theatines have furnished more than two hundred bishops to the Church."

[5] Pastor, XI, 521.

[6] Silos, op. cit., I, 73, and D. F. Andreu, "La regola dei Chierici Regolari nella lettera di Bonifacio de' Colli a Gian Matteo Giberti," Regnum Dei, II (1946), 38–53. The Latin text is in Silos, I, 73–75, and in Kunkel, op. cit., pp. 166–69. The present translation has been made by the editor.

LET ALL LIVE in the ordinary dress and in the way of life of clerics according to the Sacred Canons and the profession of the three vows, Poverty, Chastity, and Obedience. Of Poverty, so that no one may possess anything of his own, but that all may live in and of the community, not by begging, because the Canons forbid this, but by the gifts of the faithful freely offered. Also by tithes and first fruits, where it is just, as servants without recompense of the altar and the Gospel. We are forbidden neither by the Canons nor by our own profession to hold in common annual ecclesiastical revenues; nevertheless we care little about having them for many reasons, especially because of what we have been taught by experience itself. Of Chastity, by safeguarding not only bodily purity, but also the senses and speech, and as far as possible by purity of thought and desire, and also by frugality with food and sobriety. Talk and conversations with women, even the most upright and holy, should be avoided, as the Canons also prescribe, but where there is an unavoidable necessity or the law of charity prescribes otherwise, let the Superior decide and the others obey. Obedience is owed first of all to the Superior and the Elders, as to the Vicar and ministers of God; then to the brothers, obedient to one another and serving one another in charity; and this in such a way however that all may be done in due order, as the Apostle says, and that no one may usurp either the office of Superior or of another or the authority to command. The Superior also will bear in mind that a command is in no way regarded among us as binding under the pain of sin, when it is not a command of God or of the Church or the nature of one's own profession does not bind one.

The Superior is elected annually and is confirmed up to a three-year period, if it shall be so agreed, the electors being only those who have a voice in the Chapter. And the election and confirmation take place according to the Canons either by the entire Chapter or by the majority of its full membership, with these having previously been summoned and the absent awaited as long as it is necessary.

No novice is admitted for probation or profession unless he has been first prepared and tested for a long time and with much effort and patience and with at least two or three years having elapsed. And admission requires the consent of the whole Chapter. Let the novice be assigned from the beginning to one of the brothers who with God's help will instruct him and form him to the new life.

The divine office, both night and day parts, is customarily said continuously in choir only by clerics and priests according to the custom of the Roman Church and with the usage also preserved of the church or diocese in which we may happen to be staying, provided it does not run counter to the Catholic Church. The sacraments are administered without charge by those whom the Superior shall select and those whom he shall allow; they are administered with care and purity, faithfully keeping to the limits set by the privileges and exemptions of the Apostolic See, and by not abusing an immunity that has been granted, but with a sound respect for the decisions of the Superior and the Ordinary. The method of celebrating Mass and the divine office, and of reading, reciting, and singing in choir and in church, in addition to the genuine and ancient rubrics of the Missal and the Roman Breviary, are described separately for you in certain very brief and simple rules that have been handed down, where you are advised even when you should include or omit some Proper of the Saints.

No color of dress or specific habit is prescribed among us, nor is any prohibited, provided it becomes respectable clerics and is not contrary to the Sacred Canons or inconsistent with the common usage of the city or diocese in which we may happen to be staying.

No priest or cleric goes outside the house alone, but only after taking a companion and first offering a prayer before the altar and receiving the Superior's blessing. The same is observed on returning. But a lay brother and one who has the indispensable care of managing the household, even if he is a cleric, is not forbidden to go out at times alone, when the prescribed prayer has been offered and the blessing received.

At a given signal we fall down to prayer twice during the day, each in his own place or remaining in the cell and praying in silence—in the early morning after Lauds have been finished and in the evening at the outset of night, but in summer at midday.

The fasts proclaimed by the Church are observed most conscientiously. We add however from custom the Friday fast through the whole year and the Advent fasts, observing these not because of any precept, but freely and of our own accord. Sacred reading, taken either from divine Scripture or from the books of the holy Fathers, is never absent at the common table, and it is heard with great silence by all, nor does anyone except the Superior dare to speak about it.

We do not permit any custom, mode of living, or ceremony, pertaining either to divine worship and taking place in church or to what we have customarily observed in our common life within or without the house, to have the force of a precept; nor do we wish that anyone be bound in conscience, unless a precept of God or a constitution of the Church at the same time concur, or unless a person is held to the observance before God by his own profession of the three vows.

For the rest it would take much too long to continue item by item about all the remaining features of life among us. Whoever wishes to know about this, however, should do as the Lord says and hearken to His invitation: "Come and see." For among other things he will see how guests are received among us, how novices are tested and trained and at length lawfully admitted to profession, and in what way some specific occupation or duty is entrusted to the already professed lay brother, cleric, or priest, whereby he will serve for the love of Christ either the common benefit or the needs of individuals. Moreover he will understand how devotedly and faithfully each one must conduct himself in his [vow of] obedience by mastering himself and looking toward the advantage and obeying the will of another, as becomes servants of God, not only in those things which are customarily done in choir or in church or together in the community, but also in those matters which pertain to the private obligation of each, namely, of the sacristan, the librarian, the keeper of the wardrobe, the porter, the gardener, and the attendant of other things, even the most commonplace; and also what care must be taken with respect to literary studies. He will also understand what is greatest and most beneficial of all, namely, the meaning of vows and the purpose in taking them, on which account we have come together in the name of the Lord Jesus Christ; and he will be taught daily through experience the word of the Lord and the worth of his saying: "If anyone wishes to come after me, let him deny himself and take up his cross and follow me." And entering through the narrow gate and walking amidst the sorrow of repentance until he comes to the haven of the fullest charity, he will judge all to be vanity, even among those who have renounced the world, unless one makes every effort to conquer concupiscence and attain the charity of the Fathers; which charity, as blessed Augustine says, is then especially preserved, if the manner of life, the language, the general appearance are all appropriate to charity, and, let us add, if the vow, the profession, the entire religious life all zealously serve charity. And let us consider it as wrong to dishonor this virtue alone as we would consider it wrong to dishonor God, knowing that charity has been so commended by Christ and the Apostles that, if it is absent, as I have said, everything is empty, but if it is present, all things are full. What remains to be said you will learn far better by seeing and hearing than by the written word.

CHAPTER XI

Giberti's *Constitutions,* after 1527

"The bishop *par excellence* of the Catholic reform" is the designation that can best introduce the person and work of Gian Matteo Giberti, Bishop of Verona from 1524 to 1543.[1] A member of the circle of Church reformers which included such notables as Gasparo Contarini and Gian Pietro Carafa, he stands as the embodiment of the ideal described in Contarini's *De officio episcopi,* and his reforming activities are closely linked with Carafa and the Theatines.[2] Since he also had a great influence on others during and after his life, he affords a significant example of the development and extension of Catholic reform, as well as of its effective realization in the practical life of the Church. And he represents in full measure that revival of the Church's pastoral mission and that dedication to the *cura animarum* which gave the Catholic Reformation its essential meaning.

Giberti, born in Palermo in 1495, was the illegitimate son of a Genoese admiral. He came to Rome in 1513, became a secretary to Cardinal Giulio de' Medici, and when that prelate was elected Pope Clement VII in late 1523 was made his Datary and first minister. He is credited with playing a major role in the fateful pro-French diplomacy of the Pope which culminated in the devastating sack of Rome in May, 1527,[3] and he suffered a harsh imprisonment with his master in the Castel Sant' Angelo in the months that followed. After this disaster he left the Curia and took up residence in his see of Verona (he had been made bishop in 1524) where he remained till his death in 1543.

The terrible events of 1527 did not initiate a sudden conversion on the part of Giberti. He has been a young man of devout and upright life, and in the

---

[1] The phrase is that of Wilhelm Schenk in his *Reginald Pole, Cardinal of England* (London, 1950), p. 54, but it expresses an opinion generally shared by other historians of the era. See Paul Broutin, *L'évêque dans la tradition pastorale du XVIe siècle* (adaptation of *Das Bischofsideal der Katholischen Reformation* by Hubert Jedin; Bruges, 1953), Chap. IV, and Pastor, X, 424–42, where a brief account of Giberti's life, work, and influence is given. The fullest study in English is M. A. Tucker, "Gian Matteo Giberti, Papal Politician and Catholic Reformer," *The English Historical Review,* XVIII (1903), 24–51, 266–86, 439–69. The standard biography is G. B. Pighi, *Gianmatteo Giberti* (2d ed.; Verona, 1924). A recent account, dwelling mainly on the reforms, is Angelo Grazioli, *Gian Matteo Giberti* (Verona, 1955). There is a Giberti *Opera,* eds. P. and H. Ballerini (Verona, 1733), which contains a long *vita* and Francesco Zini's contemporary *Boni pastoris exemplum.*

[2] See Chaps. VII and X. On the Carafa-Giberti relationship, see G. M. Monti, *Ricerche su Papa Paolo IV Carafa* (Benevento, 1925), Part II.

[3] Tucker, *op. cit.,* p. 37.

early years of Clement VII's pontificate he was, in Pastor's words, "the animating spirit of all that was good in Rome."[4] He backed the early Theatines and in 1525 provided them with a house on the Pincian hill.[5] And before he took up residence in Verona he sought to effect improvement and reform in that diocese.[6] After 1527, however, nothing could shake his determination to devote himself wholly to the discharge of his episcopal duties. The document here presented—the *Constitutiones Gibertinae*—is a witness of his purpose as reformer and Bishop in Verona.

Giberti's action in the face of a situation characterized by laxity, neglect, and general religious decline was rigorous. As Marino Sanuto reported in his *Diarii* in late 1528: "The priests in this diocese are marked men; all are examined; the unworthy or unsuitable suspended or removed from their offices; the gaols are full of *concubinarii*; sermons for the people are preached incessantly; study is encouraged; the bishop, by his life, sets the best example."[7] Visitations of the parishes and convents were systematically undertaken, and close supervision was exercised to see that improvement was made and the conscientious cure of souls carried out. Two other projects must also be mentioned in connection with Giberti's reforms. He established a *Società della Carità*, with branches in every parish, for the material relief and moral guidance of the poor.[8] And he founded the *Accademia Gibertina*, a fraternity of humanist scholars and poets, to whom he gave hospitality and support. He himself had an excellent library with many Greek codices, and he installed in the episcopal palace a printing press which published, among other works, St. Paul's Epistles and St. John Chrysostom's Commentary on them.[9] His reforms essentially were popular and practical, but a Christian humanist culture certainly was one of their prime foundations.

Giberti's influence extended far and wide. He proved an inspiration and model for many other bishops, notably for Cardinal Ercole Gonzaga in Mantua and in the next generation for St. Charles Borromeo in Milan.[10] His ordinances also served as a pattern for many of the decrees of the Council of Trent.[11] In his own day his service was frequently sought in Rome. In 1536 Paul III made him a member of the important reform commission that drafted the *Consilium de emendanda ecclesia*,[12] and he subsequently offered him the Datary—a responsibility, which, however, Giberti declined.[13] Verona alone was to remain the chief concern of this effective reformer, this *boni pastoris exemplum*.

The text that follows consists of parts of three books or *tituli* (out of a total

[4] Pastor, X, 378–80, 427.

[5] *Ibid.*, X, 412.

[6] Tucker, *op. cit.*, p. 274.

[7] Quoted in Pastor, X, 430.

[8] The charter of this society may be found in Giberti, *Opera*, pp. 228–31. See also Grazioli, *op. cit.*, pp. 148–53.

[9] Tucker, *op. cit.*, pp. 280–81.

[10] Pastor, X, 440, and XI, 504–8, and Broutin, *op. cit.*, pp. 50–51.

[11] Grazioli, *op. cit.*, pp. 163–69.

[12] See Chap. XIII.

[13] Pastor, XI, 173–74.

of ten) from Giberti's *Constitutions,* the collection of ordinances and regulations pertaining to the religious life and discipline of his diocese which he published at Verona with the approbation of Paul III in 1542.[14] Though dated at the end of his episcopacy, they constitute a program he followed from the beginning of his residence. The passages selected are from Books I, III, and IV and give a good indication of the character and spirit of Giberti's disciplinary reforms.

[14] Subsequent editions appeared in 1563 and 1589, and the *Constitutions* are also included in the Giberti *Opera* of 1733, pp. 1–153. The translation into English was made for this volume by James F. Brady, Jr., from the Latin edition of 1542.

Book I

The Way of Life, Dress, Conversation and Character of the Clergy

Chapter 1: *Exhortation to a virtuous life.*

WHEN THE HIGH STATION of the clergy is being subjected to thorough scrutiny, it is fitting that all of us exert every effort to recognize, in view of the fact that we are in the place of the saints, that, mindful of our name and profession, we have the need to live well and have not gained a licence to do wrong. We must do this lest we give laymen any pretext to sin or cause them rightly to have a low opinion of the clergy and derive therefrom an excuse to persevere in their faults.

Therefore we must make a special effort to do the works of the saints and to make our deeds shine in the presence of men and to be watchful and solicitous of that evangelical salt in our ministry, planting, weeding, scattering, and with the greatest zeal building up what makes for holiness. Otherwise we who wish to correct others may readily be taunted: "Physician, cure yourself." Care must be taken therefore lest the complete opposite of that which is called for in us be found and lest anyone, in the realization that honor's place has been taken by dishonor, justifiably say that from head to toe there is no health in us.

Chapter 2: *Wearing of the tonsure.*

And since it has come in our day to such a pass that very many are ashamed to wear the tonsure, a crown fitting and proper, by which is marked the kingship which they ought to possess in God, we decree and instruct all the clergy of the church of the city and diocese of Verona, and all ecclesiastical persons, of whatever name or rank, always to wear the tonsure, the clerical crown, as it were, that befits their order, shaven and visible. Those who do not at present have the tonsure should at once resume it and wear it in the prescribed manner.

[Chapters 3 through 11 set down specific regulations concerning the tonsure and the dress of the clergy.]

CHAPTER 12: *The penalties for defiance of authority.*

Whoever is delinquent with respect to these regulations or of any regulations, if clergy of the first tonsure and of the four minor orders and not beneficed, shall automatically incur the special penalties of Pope Paul II of happy memory and of the decree granted by our most illustrious lord Pope Clement VII by his rescript *in forma brevis.* Clerics in sacred orders and the priesthood, not however beneficed, over and above a fine shall automatically incur a prison sentence to be imposed in accordance with our judgment and that of our Vicar, the duration of their imprisonment to be at our pleasure. Beneficed clergy in the city and our diocese in addition to the imposition of the penalties stated above shall automatically be suspended from the receipt of all the proceeds of said benefices for a period of six months, their suspension, moreover, to be extended as they remain recalcitrant toward bringing themselves into the prescribed state of conformity. They shall also be liable to other penalties to be determined and shall automatically be deprived of the proceeds of their benefices and the assignable property and vestments of their churches and other condemned ornaments and objects, considered unfitting by us, with which they are found or of whose possession two witnesses have convicted them.

CHAPTER 13: *Carrying of arms is prohibited.*

By the institutes of the Sacred Canons the clergy is prohibited from bearing military arms because they cannot be the soldiers of God and of the world at the same time, but they are not prohibited—and here the military is interdicted—from using their own proper arms, which are prayers and supplications, arms by which indeed the cause of God is advanced. For it was by means of such weapons, when Moses was waging his campaign with God's help, that his people won their victories, it was by means of such weapons that the elder Emperor Theodosius gained a miraculous victory over Eugenius and Arbogast.

Therefore following in the footsteps of our saintly fathers, we decree that any secular cleric, by whatever ecclesiastical rank he may be distinguished, who carries a sword and arms, unless he is by chance passing through dangerous places outside of the city, or for some other compelling reason, with our permission or that of our Vicar, is carrying them, shall forfeit his arms and for the first offence shall incur a fine to be imposed at our determination or that of our Vicar. For the second offence, whether they are liable to arrest by secular officers of the city or by diocesan officials, or whether in clerical garb or not, they are to be taken immediately upon apprehension to the episcopal prison, from which they will not be released, unless they pay in full the fine to be imposed at our determination or that of our Vicar and which is in part assignable to the arresting officials and in part convertible to pious uses. But religious and secular clerics who cannot be punished by a fine shall be condemned to prison by us or our Vicar, as seems best to us, and shall forfeit their arms.

No one whether on foot or riding shall presume to carry a crossbow or a pistol. If anyone dares to bear either of these weapons, no matter what the number of his offence, he shall be fined and made to serve a prison sentence.

CHAPTER 14: *The clergy is forbidden to go about at night.*

Indeed since by reason of the suspected time there arises a greater boldness for wrongdoing (for he who does wrong hates the light), no one of whatever status, rank, dignity or condition shall venture to go in the dark through the city after the town bell of Verona has sounded the curfew. We will impose a fine of six pounds on the person thus apprehended, if he is not carrying arms, no matter the number of his offence. But if he is apprehended carrying arms, he shall be liable to greater punishment to be imposed at our discretion, consideration being given to the nature of the incident and to the character of the person involved.

CHAPTER 15: *Going about with musical instruments is prohibited.*

Clerics ought to arise from their beds in the middle of the night to praise God, and seven times during the day they ought to utter His praises. They should also fulfill what they promise in singing to God together with the Prophet: "I shall meditate on your justifications, I shall not forget your words."[15] Therefore if it should happen that, adding evil to evil and going out at night, they even sing unseemly love or lewd songs, called 'Morning Songs' or serenades, or other songs whatever their name, or further give favor or aid to singers, whether apprehended with or without arms, in addition to a fine to be imposed at our discretion or that of our Vicar, they shall be sent to jail and shall be suspended from their priestly functions for a month.

CHAPTER 16: *The character of clerics and their position among the laity.*

The clergy would not have the occasion to complain because the laity does not accord them the proper respect and is exceedingly hostile in all things, if they themselves, weighing the burden placed on their shoulders, were fulfilling the command given them by our Saviour or at least trying to fulfill the command. We therefore urge and advise all the clergy, religious as well as secular, in our jurisdiction to remember that they have been set as a mark for the arrow, as it were, and therefore to be zealous especially to nourish by good example those over whom they have charge. The good odor of their own lives should induce others to live well and happily. And we hope this

---

[15] See Psalm 118 (119).

will be easy, if they are eager to do or avoid with God's help what according to our instructions they have the obligation to do or avoid with His help.

CHAPTER 17: *The cleric's carriage, conversation and eyes.*

Since therefore a lack of order in the body is an indication of a quality of the mind, we especially instruct all to exhibit a decorum in carriage so that they might manifest a maturity of understanding by the dignity of their bearing and reveal a sense of propriety, guardian of all virtues, and a modesty of the spirit by their demeanor. We further require that they be restrained in word, not given to disparagement, not unbridled in their language. Let them on the other hand abominate obscenity of word not less than of deed. Since it is often easy to ascertain the character of a person from the language he uses and since he who takes pleasure in the word is not far from the deed, let no dissolute laughter, no unseemly wandering of the eye be marked in a cleric. Since the unchaste eye is an indication of the unchaste heart, let them have a chaste eye of the mind, a chaste eye of the body, an eye that provides direction.

CHAPTER 18: *Attendance at public shows is forbidden.*

Whoever forgetful of his rank, order and profession participates in public dances and other performances or in public shows or other activities of this kind, or is present for an appreciable time thereat, or takes part in dances with women of whatever quality or rank, or is a member of a chorus shall be fined twenty-five pounds for his attendance and ten ducats for his active participation and shall be liable to a still greater punishment if any scandal follows therefrom. We wish also that they likewise avoid public banquets, especially of the laity, and that they not go to those places where they are held to refresh the minds of laymen by either their singing or playing. Indeed we condemn to the punishment of prison clerical singers who, disregarding our injunction and without making any request of us, as is required, venture to go to such places to sing. We suspend them from their priestly functions in accordance with our judgment, and we wish those clerics suspended—we also give them notice—who under pain of a punishment to be fixed by us and without our permission or that of our Vicar venture to go outside their own parishes to some other place under the pretext of singing masses or performing other priestly duties.

CHAPTER 19: *A demand for temperance in drinking.*

"Do not be drunk with wine, for in that is debauchery," says the Apostle.[16] For a priest must be sober and not given to drinking and must refrain from

---

[16] Ephesians 5, 18.

drunkenness and inebriation. For if drunkenness ill befits every man, it yet is most unbecoming to the clergyman not only because he may be subjected to ridicule but also because of the danger involved. For intoxicated clerics can neither perform their priestly duties nor administer the Sacraments, nor if there were need can they pronounce the priest's words in baptism, since wine banishes the understanding, and also when heated with wine men start quarrels and arguments and engage in altercations and fights and give utterance to insults in public. Therefore wishing to provide against so pernicious a disease out of the obligation our pastoral office imposes on us, we decree that if anyone is apprehended in a drunken condition he shall pay a fine of one ducat for the first offence and shall be suspended for fifteen days from his priestly functions, the fine to be doubled for the second offence. For the third offence he shall suffer a permanent suspension as incapable of reformation, and if he has a benefice in his care or one requiring residence, he can be assessed by us or our Vicar whatever stipend we please for the benefit of one chaplain serving in his place in the said benefice, according to the faculties granted us *in forma brevis* by our Holy Father, our Lord the Pope.

CHAPTER 20: *Taverns are not to be patronized.*

We also decree that no one, whether cleric or religious, under the pain of a penalty to be determined by us shall enter taverns or inns for the purpose of eating and drinking or shall eat or drink on the piazza of any tavern or other piazza adjacent thereto, or near the public road, unless forced by travel or some other compelling reason.

CHAPTER 21: *A respectable place is set aside in the city at which country priests ought to stop.*

We have learned by experience that very many country priests, when they come to the city, whether summoned by us or compelled by some other circumstance, have gone into taverns from bad motives or in innocence, seduced by the allurements of the innkeepers, procurers and prostitutes tarrying there and by various snares, just as fish by hooks or birds by bird lime, and have let loose the reins of indulgence and have committed vain and execrable wrongs. In view of this we are removing such obstacles, as it were, in the way of a blind man, and we have set aside one place, respectable, fitting and suitable, where poor rural clerics of our diocese, whose business in the city is not with an individual of unblemished reputation, when it happens that they are summoned to the city or come for some other reason, by all means ought to stop and take lodgings for the purpose of eating and drinking. If they refuse to stop there and fall into some wrongdoing, they will be punished severely in proportion to the seriousness of their offence and in accordance with our judgment.

CHAPTER 22: *The abuse of drinking parties is condemned.*

In our visitation, which with God's help we have made in past years, we have found in some parts of our diocese and especially in those parts near the German borders, a certain abuse maintained, once condemned in a General Council by Pope Innocent III of happy memory. By this custom men and women and even the priests themselves immediately after the conclusion of mass go to the taverns which are near the sacred building. They spend their time in clapping and boisterous laughter and in telling silly stories and singing. The drinkers pledge themselves not to be outstripped by their drinking companions in the amount of wine they consume. In the opinion of these people he is more praiseworthy who drinks and drains off more cups of a greater size. From all this the usual aftermath is much scandal. Therefore wishing to abolish completely that abuse and to counteract the scandal as far as we can, we decree that priests be zealous in urging the people to do away with such taverns if possible, since each person has his own house in which to eat and drink, and that it is not permitted to bring the Church of God into disrepute. But if the laity cannot be brought over to this point of view, we absolutely forbid, under pain of the penalties set forth above against intoxication, priests themselves at least from entering such taverns and mingling with the patrons. This may perhaps prevent the laity from drawing the conclusion from the example given by the clergy that they have the same licence. For the clergy's actions are readily taken as examples by the laity.

CHAPTER 23: *Monthly meetings of rural priests.*

Since we have abrogated the abuse of tippling in our previous chapter, we may now fittingly suggest a praiseworthy custom to be described below which has sprung up in certain parts of our diocese and which in the realization that it is a fruitful one we strongly desire to be publicized and observed throughout the diocese. This is the custom whereby country priests who are neighbors in a district (according to the appropriate division into sections we have made of the diocese itself) at least once a month come to a meeting place from their own localities and so assemble in regular sequence in each of the localities. There with the people of the locality convoked, those not under the interdiction of a legal impediment celebrate mass for the living as well as the dead, and one of them preaches, and attentive to wholesome practices, they perform with care the things that are God's and are, as it were, bright and blazing lights in the candelabra in the house of the Lord so that thus their people might be instructed in doctrine and molded in virtue and righteous action. Nor should the effort involved discourage some from this custom which is so beneficial. The example of the Apostle will be able to help them not a little, for the Apostle urges them not to shun such an effort, when he declares that on behalf of the salvation of men he has labored harder than the others.[17] In this rightly learning is preferable to silence, solicitude to contemplation, labor to rest.

Let the host of the convocation not strive for the glory of a splendid table, and while food is being taken let the mind be spiritually refreshed by pious readings and conversation. Let the same be done with respect to other meetings as is the practice and custom in certain chapters formed under this concept and approved by us. From these convocations indeed, if they are rightly managed, there will be, as every man of sound mind concedes, great progress along the road of God through these holy efforts, and many pious works, it is hoped, will be the issue.

CHAPTER 24: *The number of dishes to be served.*

Since the whole Church of God is supported by almsgiving and whatever is over and above the clergy's needs belongs entirely to the poor, it indeed seems ridiculous and scandalous that the clergy who ought to give an example of frugality and a standard of temperate living to the laity instead set a model for concocting vain and diverse seasonings of food in their meals, whereby the gluttonous belly may be sated. Therefore lest the patrimony of Christ be dissipated in luxurious living, we decree that no cleric, no matter how high the rank by which he is distinguished, may venture in private or public meals to set more than three courses before the diners. We permit this in view of the nature of the times more in toleration than in approval lest, if it were to be done otherwise, it be judged avarice rather than frugality, since we are the debtors even of foolish and petty men. For we live by almsgiving and are to provide an example of frugality and thrift to the laity, by whom nevertheless we are influenced to issue this decree, for the temporal rulers have already made provision under pain of the severest penalties for the elimination of table luxuries and of so many and such lavish courses at meals that after they have been prepared with much labor and consumed they fill us with regret.

CHAPTER 25: *The difference between public and private meals.*

Now by private meals we understand those meals which the clerics are accustomed to take with each other with the intention of paying a debt of charity. Such meals are then recognized as truly springing from charity, if the character of no absent person is attacked, if no fault is found with anyone in mockery. By public meals we understand those which one gives out of courtesy because of some obligation or because of his post in a church. At these we direct that not frivolous stories but the words of a sacred reading be heard. For by this means souls are edified for good, and needless stories are barred. The clergy acting thus, whether summoned to the office of the

17 I Corinthians 15, 10.

dead or to solemn feasts, will edify the laity more than if the laity hears that they are disparaging those absent or grumbling at them or injecting obscene talk.

As often as there are more than six persons at table this constitution should be fully observed. Let them also remember, after the blessing has been given, to sit down at table according to rank, when one comes before the other in honor. Similarly after the completion of the meal let them offer thanks to God, the giver of all good things, according to the example of the Lord, as we read that He did at the Last Supper.

CHAPTER 26: *The meals of religious.*

We also forbid the religious, no matter what order or status, from venturing to alter in any way the above constitution according to which the clergy must beware of setting more than three dishes during any meal before the diners under the penalty stated therein. We add that it is not fitting on the feasts of their churches to admit to dinner local residents, except the physician who tends those in the monastery and two or three other upright citizens. And by no means shall they bring flute-players and clowns into their refectory or cloister.

CHAPTER 27: *Absence without the consent of the bishop is forbidden.*

We decree that no one without our permission or that of our Vicar may absent himself an appreciable distance from the church entrusted to his care or leave the city and diocese of Verona. Within the purview of this constitution we intend to include pastors as well as non-pastors and those ordained in sacred orders as well as those in minor orders. For it is not very fitting that a bishop, the father as it were, not know where his dear and beloved sons are tarrying, and it is important also for a shepherd not to be ignorant where and in what pasture his sheep are to be found and at what times they are to be found, since the shepherd can have no excuse if a wolf devours them and he is ignorant. Such is my decree, custom perhaps and any other factors to the contrary notwithstanding.

CHAPTER 28: *The obligation to report the excesses of clerics and the punishment for failure to report them.*

We are human and cannot be everywhere. It very often happens that serious violations which are committed by priests, clerics and other persons of the Church in the city and diocese of Verona and in remote places do not get the attention of the superiors involved. They ought to correct the excesses of their subordinates. It is of importance to the public good that crimes not go unpunished lest the iniquitous become more iniquitous through the boldness impunity breeds. In view of this we have instructions for all rectors, vicars and chaplains, of whatever benefice, collectively and individually, and other superiors by whatever name they are called. These instructions are binding under the obligation imposed by the virtue of holy obedience as well as under the pain of a fine of twenty-five pounds. Once a cleric does something not in consonance with his rank and order and improperly commits any of the above mentioned infractions, and it has been brought to the attention of a superior or he has witnessed it, the superior should admonish the delinquent cleric once or twice in a brotherly spirit. If after this the clergyman refuses to come to his senses, the superior has the obligation within three days, or as soon thereafter as possible, to report, notify and make known the delinquency to us and our office. And let the pledge be given—given also to informers—that it will not be divulged.

CHAPTER 29: *Cohabitation of clerics and women is forbidden.*

Since there is absolutely not a place in women in which there has not been set a snare to entrap the eyes of men, therefore in compliance with the directions of the Sacred Canons and speaking from a full heart rather than from a sense of present necessity and looking more to future cases than to present ones, since by the grace of God no one in our city and diocese is at present found who publicly or clandestinely (and may any instance come to my attention) keeps concubines, we forbid any cleric, whether in minor or sacred orders or in any rank, from venturing to admit any woman of any rank or condition, whether suspect or not, to live with him in his house or to permit her to dwell with him at all without the express permission in writing obtained from us or our Vicar under the pain of a fifty pounds fine to be incurred as often as an infraction takes place. Indeed in granting this permission, especially in the case of those women who are of good repute and in whom a natural tendency to good and other qualities of understanding do not permit the suspicion of any serious wrongdoing, we will not show ourselves difficult.

If, however, the woman involved had been one with whom on another occasion the cleric had had carnal dealings, he will be sentenced to prison, the duration of the sentence to be at our discretion. And we have said "whether suspect or not" because it is our intention to examine thoroughly and carefully beforehand who the woman is and what her character, reputation and name are. For if she were to be some one already accustomed to lustful embraces, even if she were now seventy years of age, we will by no means allow her to live in the same house as a cleric.

Therefore we instruct all the clergy and religious of whatever class, if any are living with a concubine, to evict the concubines themselves and to have no further dealings with them. But those who at the prompting of the devil after a period of three days dare to keep publicly declared concubines, if they have a benefice, shall incur the loss of their benefices which they hold in the city and in our diocese. And if they do not have a benefice, they shall remain in the episcopal prison for as long a term as we deem best. This prison sentence can be terminated only on the payment of a fine of twenty-five ducats, of which one third will go to the accusers, one third to the officials holding him in detention, and one third to the Society of Most Holy Charity.

CHAPTER 30: *The illegality of letting a part of the house to women or to married men.*

To eliminate all occasions as well as suspicions of sin we decree that no cleric should let any part of his house to a woman or to a man and wife or keep in his home any servant or steward or sexton with a wife or permit them to dwell on the property adjoining the church or the priest's domicile.

BOOK III

PREACHING THE DIVINE WORD

CHAPTER 1: *No one is to be allowed to preach without a letter from the lord bishop.*

Since the devil is a sower of cockle ever envious of human salvation and because he cannot directly enter the Lord's field of himself, he sometimes tries to achieve that objective by carefully calculated means through his own people whom he possesses, inflamed as they are with the fire of cupidity. Therefore we must very carefully scrutinize the kind of life they lead who disseminate the Word of God among the people, lest pretending to plant they rather destroy. For this reason therefore to prevent the possibility of parish priests being duped and that function of preaching being usurped by anyone stealing in under the guise of a preacher or a clerical fund raiser [*quaestor*] or under the sometimes false appearance of a feigned piety, we, supported also by a faculty sufficient for this purpose through an Apostolic letter *in forma brevis* to be cited below, instruct all rectors of parish churches, individually and collectively, and others to whom this concern pertains not to admit any one, no matter what his status, order or condition is, to preach or raise funds in their parishes and other churches, unless they have been presented first to us or our Vicar through letters bearing the official seal of their superiors and approved by us and sent expressly by name for this purpose with our letters patent. For—attending to the words of the Apostle, "How will they preach unless they are sent?"[18]—we shall not send religious to preach in our diocese unless obedience to their superiors has first been witnessed by us. We also wish to examine them to the best of our ability to determine whether they

---

[18] Romans 10, 15.

are mature in age, serious in habits and adequately grounded in sacred literature, always asking the Lord of the harvest to send good workers to the fields, since the harvest is plentiful and the workers few.

[The Apostolic letter referred to above follows in the Latin text.]

CHAPTER 2: *The instruction on which preachers should stand firm.*

We ask all religious, after they have received permission from us to preach in the city and our diocese, by the compassion of our Lord Jesus Christ to preach and proclaim His Gospel sincerely to the people and to follow in His footsteps when He taught the Apostles "Preach the Gospel to every creature" and again "Teach all nations to observe whatever I have commanded you." Let them put their reliance in the interpretations of the holy doctors of the Church of old, as has also been decreed in the Lateran Council under pain of excommunication. Let them avoid in those holy sermons citations of profane laws not at all necessary, the superfluous appeal to the authority of poets, the advancing of subtle themes very often worthless. Let them be ever mindful that he who teaches and instructs uneducated minds ought to be able to adapt himself to the intelligence of those being taught and to keep the level of his speech in line with the capacity of his audience. Let them instruct the people to observe the precepts of God so that they may firmly keep the faith and obey all the commands of God and the Church. Nor let them deviate from the decrees and ordinances of the same Church. Let them urge parents to educate their children while still in their tender years, since that age is the principle and foundation of the other ages. Let them not be ashamed to preach to Christians Christ Crucified, and let them be zealous to impress His love upon the stony hearts of men. Let them be discreet in word, chaste, thoughtful, let their eloquence be the Lord's, let their eloquence be chaste. Let them also read with fitting charity about those abuses in the city and our diocese which out of the obligation imposed by our pastoral and paternal office we have caused to be collected and—more importantly—printed for the convenience of the preachers themselves so that thus, in season and out of season dealing vigorously with them every day, they might draw the people to the love of God and vice might be abominated, as they entice their listeners to embrace virtue. Like a target let them have the honor of God and the salvation of souls in their sights, doing nothing for glory and display, intent not upon gain, seeking not their own ends but those of Jesus Christ, so that thus next to truth they might give food at the right time and break bread for those who are hungry.

[The remaining chapters of Book III, Chapters 3 to 6, contain further regulations regarding preachers: they should preach against the vices prevalent in the areas where they are preaching; they must not preach false or scandalous doctrine; they should report back to the bishop, etc.]

BOOK IV

THE DUTIES OF THOSE IN CHARGE OF CHURCHES

CHAPTER 1: *The Gospel is to be explained on every feast day.*

Since our Lord and Redeemer will settle accounts with us when He returns, rewarding those who labor well in proportion to the profit they have earned but condemning servants who are listless in their work, we must take care lest we bury the talent given us in the earth. We must give ourselves in full measure to those beseeching us, so that having been found trustworthy with a few talents we may be able to be put in charge of many. Therefore, for this reason, since priests serve as teachers to the people of God (priests, that is, *sacerdotes*, are, as it were, men teaching sacred doctrine, that is, *sacra docentes*), we order all priests to explain forcefully the Gospel of Christ after the celebration of Mass on every Sunday and feast day and to do this with charity and simplicity of heart, as the Lord who is wont to give the Word to those spreading the Gospel with much power permits them to do so. And let them explain the Gospel by drawing out every action of our Lord Jesus Christ for the instruction of men.

And if they do not know what to say, let them exclaim with the Prophet: "Turn from evil and do good. Love God with your whole heart, your whole mind, your whole soul, and with all your strength, and your neighbor as yourself. What you do not wish to be done to you, do not do to others." Those priests, however, who are ignorant, let them learn from neighboring priests, and let them give explanations in common language, and let them borrow from the works of St. Antoninus which are useful to the people.[19]

[Only the first and last chapters of Book IV are presented here. The intervening chapters are in the vein of Chapter 1 and deal primarily with devotional matters and with the pastoral duties of the parish priests: they should reverence the Holy Name of Jesus; they should urge their parishioners to receive the sacraments; they should see to the instruction of the young, etc. It is interesting to note that the last chapter—Chapter 29— was excluded from the *Constitutions* when they were reprinted in the *Opera* in 1733.]

[19] St. Antoninus (1389–1459), Archbishop of Florence, was the author of a *Summa theologica* and of many treatises, manuals, and abridgments in the vernacular which were widely published in the fifteenth and sixteenth centuries. See *Dictionnaire de théologie catholique*, I, 2d part, cols. 1450–54.

CHAPTER 29: *Exhortation to be made by pastors to the people to rid themselves of superstitions.*

To destroy superstitions and certain devotions of the uneducated let the pastors try to make them grasp the truth by showing them how they ought to trust in God alone and ought to direct all things to God and ought to keep the devotion which they have for some holy person with the intention of venerating God in that saint, since all the saints are members of Christ and the temple of God and since we win the favor of the saints for ourselves especially by the idea of imitating the saints' own virtues in the service of God and since imploring the saints we should at the same time implore God that He might permit the saints' own prayers to benefit us, for we are unworthy. And this will be done not on account of the saints themselves (they do not have the power), but on account of Jesus Christ our Lord, just as the universal prayers of the Church called Collects express the idea that all might understand that neither Christ nor the saints suffered in order that we might acquire an abundance of temporal possessions, but that their sufferings might effect in us a faith in eternal possessions. And so as often as the people supplicate one or several saints to gain some favor, let them implore God also to whom the saints themselves will appeal. And let them always make their petitions in the way Christ taught us, namely that whatever we pray for we wish to obtain in so far as it is not repugnant to His will, so that not our will but His will be done who knows everything and loves us more than we love ourselves. In our ignorance we often anxiously pray for what is destined later to do us harm.

CHAPTER XII

The Capuchin Constitutions of 1536

The Capuchin movement represents a return to the original ideal of St. Francis of Assisi, to the strict observance of the Rule he had left his followers.[1] It was, and it saw itself to be, a reform of the Franciscan Order within whose confines it arose. As such it was in the tradition of the Spirituals and of many earlier attempts to restore the primitive ideal of the Poverello. There is, however, a broader significance to Capuchin reform in the early sixteenth century than its role in Franciscan history, important as that may be. The Capuchins raised the question, to use Father Cuthbert's terms, "of the supremacy of the spirit in religion as against the worldliness which had invaded the Church and had sapped the vitality and sincerity of the faith men professed."[2] Within the context of the Franciscan Rule they are witnesses then to a Christian dedication that stands in sharp contrast to the secularism and corruption of their age. Their struggle is a manifestation of Catholic reform in the deepest and most general sense, and their achievement a measure of the vigor of the forces of renewal wihin the Church at large.

The Capuchins have their origin in the decision of Matteo da Bascio (c. 1495–1552), a simple young Franciscan Observant, to leave his friary at Montefalcone in the Marches of Ancona so that he might live more strictly and faithfully according to the Rule of St. Francis. The decision indeed was a reaction to the growing relaxation of the Rule among the Observants (who themselves in former days had opposed the modifications and laxity of the Conventuals, the other great branch of the Franciscan Order), and it coincided with the desire of many sons of St. Francis for a stricter observance. Leaving his friary in early 1525, Matteo came to Rome and won the approval

---

[1] The best and most extensive study of the early Capuchins is Father Cuthbert, *The Capuchins* (2 vols.; New York, 1929). Also most useful is the collection of articles and documents in *Round Table of Franciscan Research*, Vol. VII: *The Birth of the Capuchin Reform* (Reprint; St. Anthony Friary, Marathon, Wis., 1949). There is a modern general history (in Latin): Melchior a Pobladura, *Historia Generalis Ordinis Fratrum Minorum Capuccinorum, 1525–1940* (4 vols.; Rome, 1947–51), of which only Vol. I treats the early period. *Monumenta Historica O.F.M.C.* (8 vols.; Rome, 1937–60) contains the early chronicles of the Order, which are briefly discussed and evaluated in Cuthbert, *op. cit.*, II, Appendix I. There is also a *Bullarium O.F.M.C.* (10 vols.; Rome-Innsbruck, 1740–1884). For a convenient collection of earlier Franciscan writings, including St. Francis' Rule of 1223 and his Testament, see *The Little Flowers of St. Francis and Other Franciscan Writings*, ed. and trans. Serge Hughes (New York, 1964).

[2] Cuthbert, *op. cit.*, I, 85, and also Preface. This particular point perhaps should be kept in mind as we read the Constitutions and observe the austerity and the spiritual intensity of the life they describe.

of Pope Clement VII for the solitary life in strict obedience to the Rule he now hoped to live. Defended then and later by Caterina Cibo, Duchess of Camerino and niece of the Pope, he survived the opposition of his superiors which his action provoked, and he was in fact soon joined by three fellow Observants, Ludovico and Raffaele da Fossombrone and Paolo da Chioggia, who likewise desired to follow the original Franciscan ideal. In July, 1528, in reply to the petition of the brothers da Fossombrone and the intercession of the Duchess of Camerino, the Pope formally authorized the austere mendicant life the four now professed and permitted them to receive additional members.[3] The *Cappuccini*, as they were soon called, with their distinctive coarse habit with its large square hood, or *cappuccio*, thus came into being as a separate branch, a reformed branch, of the Franciscan Order.

The growth of the movement, despite the hostility and intrigue of the Observant authorities, was phenomenal and represented in the early days a very serious secession from the ranks of the Italian Observants. They numbered some seven hundred by 1536, some two thousand five hundred at midcentury.[4] In 1529 the group's first general chapter was held at their hermitage at Albacina with twelve members in attendance. There they drew up their first constitutions, emphasizing the complete austerity and poverty of the life they wished to embrace. Meanwhile they worked among the poor and sick of the diocese of Camerino, ravaged at this time by plague and famine. As is the case with the Theatines, what they stood for and what they undertook to do signified a new departure, the beginning of that revival and reform the Church had so long awaited.

Matteo da Bascio was elected superior or Vicar General at the Albacina meeting, but very shortly thereafter he resigned his post to Ludovico da Fossombrone, under whose energetic and aggressive leadership the young Order began its great expansion throughout Italy.[5] Ludovico's autocratic rule, however, evoked considerable dissatisfaction, and at the second general chapter in 1535 he was replaced, much to his chagrin, by Bernardino d'Asti, the third founder of the Order, as he is sometimes called. At the next chapter in 1536 the constitutions were rewritten in view of the experience and needs of the burgeoning Order. It is this document that is presented here.[6] That same year Pope Paul III confirmed the Order and renewed the privileges his predecessor had grantd in 1528.[7] This action, prompted by the defense of the Capuchins by Vittoria

[3] In the bull *Religionis zelus*, in *Bullarium O.F.M.C.*, I, 3–4, and in English translation in *Round Table of Franciscan Research*, VII, 110–12. See also Pastor, X, 464–65.

[4] Pobladura, *op. cit.*, I, 97. Up to 1574 the movement was not permitted to expand outside of Italy. After that date its growth throughout Europe was very rapid.

[5] Until 1619 the Capuchins were not, strictly speaking, an independent Order. The election of their Vicar General was subject to the confirmation of the General of the Conventuals.

[6] The English text is the translation of Father Mark Stier, O.F.M.Cap., reprinted with Father Mark's kind permission from *Round Table of Franciscan Research*, VII, 113–42. It is a translation from the original Italian text edited by Edouard D'Alençon, in *Liber Memorialis O.F.M.C.* (Rome, 1928), pp. 356–419.

[7] In the bull *Exponi nobis*, in *Bullarium O.F.M.C.*, I, 18–20.

Colonna, marks in a sense the end of the initial period of trial and tribulation when the course of Capuchin reform was in constant danger of suppression.

One last great trial, however, remained. In 1542 the Order's fourth Vicar General, Bernardino Ochino, a former Observant and the greatest preacher in Italy of his day, apostatized and took flight to Geneva.[8] This startling event, dramatizing the thrust and danger of Protestantism in Italy, almost led to the Order's destruction, but the movement weathered the storm of suspicion and distrust that temporarily arose, and it soon resumed its progress as an instrument as well as a sign of Catholic revival.

The document that follows certainly casts a significant light on the spirit and intensity of this revival, and in this regard its evangelical stress is most noteworthy. The Capuchins were continually to read and study Holy Scripture, particularly the Gospels (paragraphs 1 and 4), and they were to preach from it, that being "evangelical preachers" they might fashion an "evangelical people" (paragraph 117).

[8] Cuthbert, op. cit., I, Chap. IV. Ochino (1487–1564) had been elected Vicar General in 1538 and reelected in 1541. His career after his apostasy was checkered, and his exile ended with his death in an Anabaptist community in Moravia.

IN THE NAME OF OUR LORD Jesus Christ begin the Constitutions of the Friar Minor Capuchins. To the end that our Order, as the Vineyard of the Most High Son of God, may the better stand fast in the spiritual observance of the Evangelical and Seraphic Rule, the General Chapter held at Rome in our monastery of St. Euphemia, the year of the Lord 1536, deemed it advisable to draw up certain statutes which might serve as a fence for our Holy Rule, in order that, like the unconquerable tower of David, it might have a means of protection from whatever might injure the spirit of our Lord Jesus Christ, and keep out all relaxations opposed to the fervent and seraphic zeal bequeathed to us by our Father St. Francis.

CHAPTER ONE

1. In the doctrine of the Gospel, wholly pure, heavenly, supremely perfect and divine, brought down to us from heaven by the most sweet Son of God, and promulgated and preached by Him in word and deed, approved and authenticated by His Heavenly Father in the river Jordan and on Mt. Thabor, when he declared that "This is My Beloved Son in Whom I am well pleased; hear ye Him," alone teaches and points out the straight path of going to God. Hence, all men, especially all Christians who have professed the Gospel in Baptism, and much more we Friars, are obliged to observe this holy Gospel. St. Francis, therefore, in the beginning and end of his Rule, expressly mentions the observance of the Holy Gospel; nay, his Rule is simply the Incarnation of the Gospel. In his Testament he also declares it was revealed to him that he should live according to the manner of the holy Gospel. In order that the Friars may always keep the doctrine and life of our Lord Jesus Christ before the eyes of their mind, and that like the saintly Virgin Cecilia always bear the holy Gospel in the interior of their hearts, it is ordained that in honor of the Most Blessed Trinity the four Evangelists be read three times a year, namely, one every month.

2. And since the Rule of St. Francis is like a little mirror in which evangelical perfection is reflected, it is ordained that every Friday in all our Friaries, it be read distinctly, with due reverence and devotion, so that being impressed upon our minds, it may be the better observed. Some other pious book shall also be read to the Friars, exhorting them to follow Christ crucified.

3. In order that the love of God be enkindled in our hearts, the Friars shall always strive to speak of God. Desiring that the evangelical doctrine should bear fruit in our hearts and that all chaff which might suffocate it be extirpated, it is ordained that in no wise shall books that are useless, or frivolous and dangerous to the spirit of Christ, our Lord and God, be kept in our Friaries.

4. And since the flames of divine love proceed from the light of divine things, it is ordained that some lesson from the Holy Scripture be read, expounding it by means of saintly and devout Doctors. And though the infinite and divine Wisdom be incomprehensible and elevated, still it has humbled itself in Christ, our Savior, to such an extent, that by means of the pure, simple and unaffected eye of faith, even the simple can understand it. It is forbidden, however, that the Friars read or study anything irrelevant or frivolous. Let them read and study the Holy Scriptures, nay, Christ Jesus, in Whom, according to St. Paul, are all treasures of wisdom and knowledge.

5. And because it was the desire, not only of our Seraphic Father, but of Christ, our Redeemer, that the Rule should be observed to the letter, with simplicity and without gloss, as it was observed by our first Fathers, we renounce all privileges and explanations that relax it, detract from its pure observance and wrest it from the pious, just and holy intentions of Christ, our Lord, Who spoke in St. Francis. We accept only as a living and authentic commentary thereon, the declarations of the Supreme Pontiffs, and the most holy life, doctrine and example of our Seraphic Father himself.

6. In order that we, as true and legitimate sons of Jesus Christ our Father and Lord, begotten again by Him in St. Francis, may have an abundant share in His inheritance, it is ordained that all observe the Testament made by our Father St. Francis when, near death, adorned with the sacred Stigmata, full of fervor and the Holy Ghost, he most ardently desired our salvation; and this we accept as spiritual commentary and gloss of our Rule, because it was written by him to the end that we may in a more Catholic manner observe the Rule we have promised. We are sons of the Seraphic Father so far as we imitate his life and example, for our Savior said to the Jews: "If you be the children of Abraham, do the works of Abraham." Hence, if we are sons of St. Francis let us do the works of St. Francis. Wherefore, it is ordained that everyone strive to imitate our Father who was given us as Rule, standard and example, nay, even our Lord Jesus Christ in him, not only in his Rule and Testament, but also in his fervent words and holy deeds. For this reason they shall frequently read his life and the lives of his blessed companions.

7. Our Father, being wholly divine, contemplated God in every creature, especially in man, and more so in the Christian, but above all in the priest, and in a very singular manner in the Supreme Pontiff, who is the Vicar of

Christ our Lord on earth and head of the whole Church Militant. He, therefore, wished his Friars, in accordance with the apostolic teaching, to be subject to the divine Majesty in every creature, out of love for Him Who humbled Himself so much for us. Wherefore, he called them Friars Minor in order that they should, not only in their hearts deem themselves inferior to all, but that, being called in the Church Militant to the Marriage-feast of the Most Holy Spouse, Jesus Christ, they should always take the lowest place, in accordance with His counsel and example.

8. Considering that to be free from subjection to the Ordinaries by privileges and exemptions is not only proximate to pride, but the enemy of the humble subjection of a Friar Minor, and because such liberty very often disturbs peace and begets scandal in the Church of God, and in order to conform ourselves to our humble crucified Savior, Who came to serve us, becoming obedient, even unto the bitter death of the Cross, and not being subject to the law yet wished to subject Himself to it by paying the Temple-tax, and finally, to avoid scandal, the General Chapter renounces the privilege of being exempt from Ordinaries. By the highest privilege we accept, with our Seraphic Father, to be subject to all. Furthermore, it is ordained, that all Vicars, each in their own Province, go to their respective Ordinary and Prelates who are members humbly subject to the Supreme Pontiff, the head and superior of all. In their name and in the name of all the Friars let them renounce all contrary privileges and humbly offer obedience and reverence in all divine and canonical matters.

9. And according to the desire of our Father, we exhort every Friar to treat all priests with due reverence, We further exhort the Friars to obey with all possible reverence all Prelates and the Supreme Pontiff, the Father of all Christians; to be subject even to all human creatures which show us the way to God. Let them remember that the lower the person is whom we obey for the love of Jesus Christ, so much more glorious and pleasing is our obedience in the sight of God.

10. We further ordain that the Friars be subject, not only to their Vicars, Custodes and Guardians, but that the Vicar General, when elected, will humbly present himself or write to the Very Reverend Father General of the Conventuals, by whom he must be confirmed.

11. And since to avoid similar privileges our Father St. Francis in his Testament commands his Friars that they shall not dare to ask letters from the Roman Court on account of bodily persecution, the General Chapter renounces all privileges which relax the Rule and, enervating the way of the spirit, lay the foundation of a sensual life.

CHAPTER TWO

12. As to the second chapter: Desiring that our Order grow more in virtue, perfection and spirit, than in numbers; knowing also as the Infallible Truth teaches that "many are called, but few chosen," and that, as our Seraphic Father foretold when near death: nothing is a greater hindrance to the pure observance of the Rule than a multitude of useless, worldly and self-indulgent

Friars, we ordain that when any persons apply for admission the Vicars shall make careful enquiries as to their condition and character, and they shall not receive them if they do not manifest a very good intention and fervent will. To avoid all wonder and scandal, and that the candidate may know by experience what he must promise, no one shall be received until he is sixteen years of age, or if he should be sixteen but have a youthful face.

13. It is further ordained, that no one be received as a Cleric who has not sufficient literary education so that in chanting the Divine Office he may not offend but understand what he says.

14. We further ordain that those who are admitted in this mode of life shall for some days previous to their clothing, exercise themselves in one of our friaries in all those things which are observed by the Friars, so that their good will may be known, and that they may enter on so great an undertaking with greater light, maturity and deliberation. The same is to be understood of those Religious who desire to be admitted to our life. In order that this be well observed, it is ordained that the Vicars shall not receive any one without the counsel and consent of the majority of the Friars dwelling in that place.

15. And since Christ, the wisest of Masters, charged that young man who desired to gain eternal life, that if he wished to become His disciple, he should first sell all that he had, give it to the poor and then follow Him; His imitator, Francis, not only observed that counsel and taught it by example in his own person and in those whom he received, but commanded it in his Rule. In order, therefore, to conform ourselves to Christ, our Lord, and to the will of the Seraphic Father, we ordain that no one shall be clothed, unless first, if able, he has distributed all to the poor as is becoming for one who freely chooses a mendicant life. In this way the Friars will be able to determine at least in part, the fervent or tepid spirit; and the candidates will be able to serve God with greater peace of mind and constancy of will. And the Friars, avoiding all interference in these matters, shall remain undisturbed in their holy peace.

16. We further ordain that the clothes of the novices who come from the world be kept until the day of profession; those of religious, for some days. If they persevere, the seculars shall give their clothes to the poor; those of religious shall be distributed by the Vicars themselves or by the medium of some spiritual person.

17. Lest that should be said of us which our most holy Savior said to the Scribes and Pharisees: "Woe to you, because you go about the sea and the land to make one proselyte, and when he is made, you make him the child of hell twofold more than yourselves," we determine that in every Province the novices shall be placed in one or two houses suited to the spiritual life, chosen for this purpose by the Chapter. And they shall be given Masters who are most mature, refined, and enlightened in the way of God. The Masters shall take diligent care to teach the novices not only the ceremonies, but those spiritual matters necessary for the perfect imitation of Christ, our Light, our Way, our Truth, and our Life. By word and example they shall show them in what the life of a Christian and a Friar Minor consists. No one shall be received to

profession unless he know beforehand what he must promise and observe. The Masters shall take diligent care that the Cleric novices learn the Rule by heart during the time of the novitiate.

18. In order that the novices may in quiet, peace and silence be better strengthened in the spirit we ordain that no one speak much with them except the Father Guardian and their Master. Nor shall anyone enter their cells, nor they the cells of others, without special permission.

19. And in order that they may better learn to bear the yoke of the Lord, we determine, that after their profession, they shall remain under the discipline of a Master for at least three years, so that they may not easily lose the newly acquired spirit, but growing in strength, may become more fixed and rooted in the love of Jesus Christ, our Lord and God.

20. And since the Doctors of the Church hold that those novices who make their profession with proper dispositions are restored to their baptismal innocence, we ordain that they prepare themselves before their profession with great care, by confession, communion and much prayer, their general confession having been made when they entered religion to put on the new man. And before receiving the said novices into religion, as well as admitting them to profession, the prescriptions and ceremonies customary and approved of in the Order shall be observed.

21. And since it was not without reason that Christ commended St. John the Baptist's austerity in clothing when He said: "They that are clothed in soft garments are in the houses of kings," it is ordained that the Friars who have chosen to be menials in the house of God, clothe themselves with the more common, abject, austere, coarse and despised cloth that can conveniently be had in the Province where they shall be. And let the Friars remember that the sack-cloth with which St. Francis would have us mend our habits, and the cord with which he would have us girt, are not suited to the rich ones of this world.

22. The General Chapter also exhorts all the Friars to be content with the habit alone, as expressed by St. Francis in his Testament, when he said: "And we were content with one tunic, patched inside and out." But should any of the Friars be weak in body or in spirit, then, according to the Rule, a second tunic may be given them; and to these a mantle shall not be given without necessity and permission of the Prelate; knowing that for a healthy Friar to use three pieces of clothing is a manifest sign of lax spirit.

23. In order that poverty, so loved by the Son of God, and given to us as a mother by the Seraphic Father, may shine forth in everything we use, it is decreed that the mantle shall not extend beyond the tips of the fingers and shall be without a hood, except when making a journey; and it shall not be worn without necessity. The habit shall not go beyond the ankles in length and shall be ten feet wide, twelve feet for the corpulent Friars. The sleeves shall be no wider than is necessary to put in and draw out the arms, and long enough to reach the middle of the hand or a little longer. The tunics shall be

very plain and coarse, eight or nine feet wide, and at least a half foot shorter than the habit. The hood shall be square, like those of St. Francis and his companions which still exist as relics, and as may be seen in ancient pictures, and as is described in the *Book of Conformity:* so that our habit be in the form of a cross to remind us that we are crucified to the world and the world to us. The girdle of the Friars shall be a plain and coarse cord, with very simple knots, without any art or singularity; so that being despised by the world we may have occasion to mortify ourselves the more. Neither birettas, hats, nor anything ornamented or superfluous shall be worn.

24. In each of our houses there shall be one small room where the community clothes are to be taken care of by a Friar appointed for that purpose; and he shall keep them clean and mended for the use of the brethren who, having used them according to their needs, shall return them *cum gratiarum actione.*

25. In order that our beds may resemble somewhat that on which He died Who said: "The foxes have holes and the birds of the air nests, but the Son of Man hath not where to lay His head"; and also that we may be the more watchful and solicitous in prayer and be the more like our Father St. Francis, whose bed was often the bare ground, and even like Christ, the Saint of Saints, especially in the desert, it is ordained that all the Friars, except the sick and the very weak, shall sleep on a bare board, rush mat, or upon a little straw or hay; and they shall not sleep upon quilts.

26. In accordance with the example of Christ it is ordained that the young Friars, and those who can, shall go barefooted, as a sign of humility, testimony of poverty, mortification of sensuality and as a good example to our neighbor. And those who cannot do this may, in conformity with evangelical teaching and the example of our primitive Fathers, wear sandals with the permission of the Prelate; but they shall be simple, plain and poor, without any ornamentation.

27. In order that the Friars reach the summit of most high poverty the queen and mother of all virtues, the spouse of Christ our Lord, and of our Seraphic Father, and of our most beloved Mother, we exhort all the Friars not to have any attachment on earth, but always to fix their affection in heaven, using the things of this world sparingly as if by constraint, and in so far as their weakness will allow, deeming themselves rich with all their poverty. Let them be content with one spiritual book, or even with Christ crucified, and with two handkerchiefs and two drawers. And let them remember, as our Seraphic Father said, that a Friar Minor should be nothing but a mirror of every virtue, especially of poverty.

28. In order that we may run more expeditiously in the way of the divine precepts, it is decreed that no animal for riding be kept in any of our houses, neither shall the Friars ride on horseback. But in case of necessity, after the example of Christ and His imitator, St. Francis, they may ride upon an ass, so that our life may always preach the humble Christ.

29. The tonsure shall be cut every twenty days, or once a month, with a

pair of scissors. The Friars shall wear the beard, after the example of Christ most holy, and of all our first Saints, since it is something manly, natural, severe, despised and austere.

CHAPTER THREE

30. As regards the third chapter: Our Seraphic Father, thoroughly Catholic, Apostolic, and enlightened by the Holy Spirit, always held the Roman Church in special veneration, as the judge and mother of all other Churches. Hence he laid down in the Rule that the clerics should say the Office according to the order of the Holy Roman Church, and in his Testament forbade them to alter it in any way. We therefore ordain, that the Friars, united in spirit under the same standard and called to the same end, shall observe the same rites as those used by the Holy Roman Church in all that regards the Missal, Breviary and the Calendar. And the clerics as well as the lay-brothers shall say the five Offices of the dead, as prescribed in the calendar.

31. The clerics and priests who are not very lettered shall look over beforehand whatever they have to read publicly in the Mass and Divine Office, lest their unworthy treatment of divine things should disturb the hearers and provoke against themselves the angels who are present at the divine praises. And in the Mass and Divine Office they shall say only what is in the Missal and Breviary, observing the prescribed ceremonies.

32. We exhort the priests when celebrating Mass, not to have the eye of their intention turned toward human favor or glory or anything temporal, but with a simple, pure and clean heart they shall attend solely to the divine honor, celebrating for mere charity, with humble reverence, faith and devotion. They shall prepare themselves as well as their frailty will allow, for he is denounced as accursed who doth the work of the Lord with negligence; and as this is, of all actions, the most sublime, its irreverent performance is exceedingly displeasing.

33. And let them, after the example of Christ, High Priest, Who offered Himself for us on the Cross without recompense, not be anxious to receive any earthly reward for celebrating, but rather let them understand that thereby their own debt to God is increased. We exhort the other Friars who are present at Mass to assist at these divine mysteries with the greatest reverence, in the spirit of the angels, keeping themselves in the presence of God, endeavoring spiritually to celebrate and communicate, and offer to God this most acceptable sacrifice.

34. And since the celebration of Mass is an action of the greatest importance, we ordain that, according to the canonical regulations, no cleric may be ordained priest until he is twenty-four years of age, and those who have been ordained shall not celebrate Mass until they have reached the prescribed age. We further ordain that no cleric shall be promoted to the priesthood, unless over and above a good spirit, he has also sufficient knowledge to understand and pronounce well the words which he utters when celebrating. And in all their

Masses and prayers they shall remember our benefactors, imploring God to reward them abundantly in the present and future life.

35.   The clerics and priests, not legitimately impeded, on hearing the first sound of the bell for the Divine Office shall promptly betake themselves to the choir to prepare their hearts for the Lord. There in devotion, composure, mortification, recollection and silence, they shall remember that they are in the presence of God, about to engage in the angelic function of singing the divine praises.

36.   The Divine Office shall be said with all due devotion, attention, gravity, uniformity of voice and harmony of mind, neither protracted nor disjoined and the voice pitched neither too high nor too low, but moderately. The Friars shall endeavor to sing the praises of God more with the heart than with the lips, lest that be said of them which our Most Sweet Savior said to the Jews: "This people honored Me with their lips, but their heart is far from Me."

37.   The lay-brothers shall assemble at the beginning of Matins, of Vespers, of Compline, and during the *Te Deum laudamus;* and when the general preparation is over and the Office commenced, they shall retire into some devotional place, to say the *Pater Nosters,* commanded by the Rule. On all Festivals the lay-brothers and clerics, not legitimately impeded, shall assist at Vespers and be present at as many Masses as they can.

38.   In order to maintain most high poverty, spiritual peace and undisturbed humility, to foster good relations between ourselves and other clerics and priests, and to avoid anything which might in time leave a blemish on our Order, we ordain that the dead shall not be buried in our Places, unless one be so poor as not even to have someone to bury him. In such cases we must show the greatest charity.

39.   No burials, neither of seculars nor of the Friars, shall be performed in our Places, since in our Churches, due to the presence of Christ most pure, there must be no defilement, but they shall be buried in some becoming place near the Church, or within the convent grounds. When the Friars visit the sick they shall guard not only against inducing them to be buried in our Places, but rather dissuade them from this. And lest this should be a cause of scandal they shall inform and instruct them regarding this matter.

40.   When one of our Friars dies, the others shall be careful, with loving charity, to commend his soul to God. And in the province where he dies each priest shall apply one Mass; the clerics shall say the Office of the dead; the lay-brothers one hundred Our Fathers. And every week each priest shall apply one Mass for our deceased brethren.

41.   Since holy prayer is the spiritual mistress of the Friars, in order that the spirit of devotion may not decrease in the Friars, but, continually burning on the sacred altar of our heart, may be enkindled more and more, as our Seraphic Father wished, we ordain that, although the true spiritual Friar Minor should always pray, two special hours shall be appointed for the tepid Friars, one after Compline during the whole year, the other, from Easter until the Exaltation of the Cross, immediately after None, except on days of fast

when it shall be after Sext, and from the Exaltation of the Cross until Easter, after Matins.

42. Let the Friars remember that prayer is nothing else than speaking to God with the heart. Consequently, he does not pray who speaks to God with the lips. Each one, therefore, should endeavor to pray mentally, and according to the teaching of Christ, taking diligent care to enlighten the mind and enkindle the affections far more than to frame words. Before the morning meditation, after None or Matins, or on the days of fast, after Sext, they shall recite the Litanies imploring all the Saints to pray to God with us and for us. And no other Offices shall be said in choir except that of the Blessed Virgin, so that the Friars have more time to devote to private and mental prayer which is far more fruitful than vocal prayer.

43. Our Seraphic Father, as appears in the beginning and end of the Rule, wished that special reverence should be paid to the Supreme Pontiff as the Vicar of Jesus Christ, and to all Prelates and priests. We ordain, therefore, that, over and above the prayers said in common, every Friar shall, in his private prayers, beseech the Divine Goodness for the Welfare of the Church Militant and for His Holiness the Pope, that grace may be given him clearly to see, efficaciously to will and successfully to carry out all that may redound to the honor and glory of the Divine Majesty, the salvation of the Christian people, and the conversion of infidels. They shall also pray for the Most Eminent Lord Cardinals, for Bishops and Prelates in communion with the Supreme Pontiff, for the Most Excellent Emperor, for all Kings and Christian Princes, and for all others, especially for those to whom we are most indebted.

44. Since silence is the safeguard of the religious spirit, and that according to St. James, the religion of the man who does not refrain his tongue is vain, we ordain that the evangelical silence be always observed, as far as our frailty will permit, knowing that as the Infallible Truth, Jesus Christ, says for every idle word we shall render account. So great indeed is the abundance of divine favors, that it is no trivial fault for a Friar, dedicated to the service of God, to speak of worldly things.

45. As regards the regular silence, it shall be perpetual in the Church, cloister and dormitory; but in the refectory silence shall be kept from the first sign given at table until grace after meals has been said. In like manner, silence shall be observed everywhere after Compline until Prime, and from Easter until the Exaltation of the Cross, the sign for silence shall be given after Sext until the close of meditation after None. And he who breaks it shall say five *Paters* and *Aves* in the refectory with his arms extended in the form of a cross. The Friars are exhorted to accustom themselves to speak always and in every place in a subdued and humble tone, with modesty and charity.

46. We further ordain that the Friars shall not leave the Friary alone, but they shall have a companion, after the example of the holy disciples of our Most Holy Savior. They shall correct each other fraternally, and if the advice be not taken, then let them make known each other's faults to their Prelates. And they shall not travel without the obedience of their Prelate in writing and

stamped with the seal of the Father Vicar, or of the local Superior; for that reason each house shall have, in accordance with the ancient custom of Religious, its own seal. They shall not part company on the way nor quarrel, but as brothers in Christ, they shall endeavor with all humility and charity to obey and serve each other spiritually.

47. Since St. Francis says in his Testament that it was revealed to him by the Lord that in saluting anyone we should say, after the example of Christ: "The Lord give you His peace," we ordain that the Friars always use this evangelical greeting.

48. As true Friars should depend with a lively faith on their kind and bountiful Heavenly Father, we ordain that on their journeys they shall not take wine, nor flesh meat, nor eggs, nor delicate or rich food, but leave all care of themselves to God, Who feeds not only the irrational animals, but even those who are constantly offending Him. The Friars shall not stop in cities or towns to sleep or eat, if our Friaries are near, except in case of great necessity.

49. Since delight in worldly feasts easily brings spiritual defilement, we ordain that the Friars shall not go to festivals, unless it be to preach the Word of God, after the example of Christ, Who, being invited to a feast, desired rather to preach. Let them remember that according to the Apostle St. Paul, they are made a spectacle to the world, to the angels and to men; and they should strive to live such exemplary lives that through men God may be glorified and not blasphemed.

50. Since abstinence, austerity and mortification are highly commended by the Saints, and since we have chosen a severe life, after the example of Christ our Lord and St. Francis, we exhort the Friars to observe the holy Lents St. Francis was wont to keep, even though the mortified Friar always fasts. The Friars shall not delight in excessive or superfluous collations, not even the customary ones. On Wednesdays they shall abstain from flesh meat.

51. To safeguard the spirit of mortification not more than one course of soup shall be served at table. But during the fast a warm or cold salad shall be added. And let the Friars remember that whereas little is needed to satisfy necessity, nothing can content sensuality.

52. And in order that, according to the teaching of Our Most Holy Savior, our hearts may not be overcharged with surfeiting and drunkenness, but that our minds may be clear and our senses mortified, we ordain that wine shall not be served at table, unless it has been mixed with a fair amount of water; even then it ought to appear a luxury when we recall that according to the Seraphic St. Bonaventure our Father St. Francis hardly ventured to quench his thirst, and used to say that it is difficult to satisfy necessity without yielding to sensuality. It will appear sweet to the Friars if they recall that water was denied Christ on the Cross and vinegar and gall given Him instead. St. Jerome writes, that in his time the monks, however weak, drank but water, and to eat anything cooked was considered a luxury.

53. We ordain that no partiality shall be shown at table, unless in the case of the sick, of travellers, of the aged and delicate Friars, when charity demands

it. Should any of the Friars wish to abstain from wine, flesh meat, eggs or other food, or to fast more than usual, the Prelate shall not prevent him when he sees that it will not prove injurious to his health, rather he shall encourage him to do so, provided he eats with the other Friars. In token of poverty, tablecloths shall not be used, but a plain napkin shall be allowed each Friar. During meals some spiritual book shall be read, so that not only the body, but much more the spirit may be nourished.

54.   We further ordain that the Friars, in accordance with our poor state, shall not ask for, or receive, dainty food. Likewise, they shall not use special food, unless in the case of the sick to whom the greatest charity must be shown, as is prescribed in the Rule, and by every just law, after the example of our Seraphic Father who was not ashamed to make public quest of flesh meat for the sick. And should superflous food be given us, with humble thanks let the Friars return it, or, with the consent of the benefactors, distribute it to the poor.

55.   As some of the ancient Patriarchs merited by their hospitality the privilege of entertaining angels, we ordain that in each of our Friaries a Friar shall be appointed who shall be very careful to receive strangers with the greatest of charity. And after the example of the humble Son of God, shall wash their feet, assembling all the Friars for this act of charity, they shall recite the while some devout hymn or psalm, always deeming themselves useless servants even when they have done everything in their power.

56.   In order that our body may not rebel against the spirit, but be in all things subject to it, and in memory of the most bitter Passion and especially of the cruel scourging of our Most Sweet Savior, it is ordained that the customary disciplines on Mondays, Wednesdays and Fridays shall not be omitted even on the Great Festivals. The discipline shall be taken after Matins except when it is very cold; in such case it shall be taken in the evening. During Holy Week the discipline shall be taken every night. And the Friars, while they chastise themselves, shall think with compassionate hearts of the Sweet Christ, Son of God, bound to the pillar; and endeavor to feel within themselves a little of His cruel sufferings. And after the Salve Regina they shall say five devout prayers.

Chapter Four

57.   Our Father St. Francis, aware of the Apostolic teaching, was convinced that the desire of money is the root of all evil; and wishing to eradicate it completely from the hearts of his children, commanded the Friars in the Rule on no account to receive money, either by themselves or through others. And the better to impress it upon their minds, as a thing he had much at heart, he repeated it three times in the Rule. Christ, Our Lord, also said: "Beware of all covetousness." Desiring, therefore, to carry out entirely and fully the pious desire of our Father, who was inspired by the Holy Ghost, we ordain that the Friars shall in no way have a Procurator, or any other person—by whatever name he may be called—to receive or hold money for them, either at their

instigation, request, or in their name, for whatever interest or cause. But our Procurator and Advocate shall be Jesus Christ, and all the Angels and Saints shall be our spiritual friends.

58.   As sublime poverty was the chosen spouse of Christ, the Son of God, and of His humble servant, our Father St. Francis, the Friars should remember that they cannot injure her without highly displeasing God, and that to offend her is verily to touch the apple of His eye. The Seraphic Father was accustomed to say that his true Friars ought to value money no more than dust, and to dread it as a venomous serpent. How often our pious and zealous Father, foreseeing in spirit that many, neglecting this pearl of the Gospel, would become lax by accepting legacies, inheritances and superflous alms, wept over their downfall, saying that the Friar was nigh to perdition who esteemed money more than dirt.

59.   Experience teaches us that no sooner does a Friar drive away from himself holy poverty than he falls into every great vice. Let the Friars, therefore, after the example of the Savior of the world and His Most Beloved Mother, strive to be poor in earthly things that they may be rich in divine grace, holy virtues and heavenly treasures. Above all, when visiting any sick person, let them beware of inducing him, directly or indirectly, to leave us any temporal goods. Nay, even should he wish to do so of his own accord, let the Friars dissuade him as far as they reasonably can, remembering that they cannot possess at the same time both riches and poverty. Legacies shall not be accepted.

60.   To possess more securely this precious treasure of poverty, we forbid the Friars to have recourse to Spiritual Friends, even for necessary things when these can be procured conveniently in some other way permitted by the Rule. In order to be less burdensome to our friends, no Friar shall buy, or cause to be bought, anything of great value without the permission of the Vicar Provincial. Recourse to Spiritual Friends is not forbidden for necessary things that cannot be procured in any other way. In all cases of recourse there must be real necessity and permission of the Superiors.

61.   And since we have been called to this life to mortify the outward man and to quicken the spirit, we exhort the Friars to accustom themselves to endure privations in earthly things after the example of Christ, Who, though Lord of all, chose for our sakes to be poor and to suffer.

62.   Let the Friars beware of the noon-day devil who transforms himself into an angel of light. This happens when the world, out of devotion, applauds us and rejoices, pampering us with earthly comforts, which were very often the cause of many evils in religion. Let them not desire to be of the number of those false poor who, in the words of St. Bernard, wish to be poor in such a way as to want for nothing.

CHAPTER FIVE

63.   Mindful that our ultimate end is God, to Whom each of us ought to tend and aspire, and into Whom we should strive to be transformed, we exhort

all the Friars to direct their every thought to that end and to turn to it, with every possible yearning of love, all their intentions and desires, so that with their whole heart, mind and soul, power and strength, with actual, continuous, intense and pure affection, they may unite themselves with their supremely good Father.

64.   Since it is impossible to reach the end without the means, let each one cast aside as useless and disastrous, whatever could mislead or preclude us from the way of salvation. Let the Friars not be solicitous about irrelevant matters, but choose those things that are useful and necessary to lead us to God. Such are the highest poverty, spotless chastity, humble obedience, and the other evangelical virtues taught us by the Son of God, by word and example, in His own Person and in His Saints.

65.   Forasmuch as it is very difficult for man to have his mind always raised to God, and to avoid idleness, the root of all evil, to give good example to our fellow-men, to be less burdensome to the world, to follow the example of St. Paul who worked while he preached, and of many other saints, to observe the admonition to labor, given us by our Seraphic Father in his Rule, and to conform ourselves to his will, expressed in his Testament, we ordain that the Friars, when not engaged in spiritual exercises, shall occupy themselves in some honest manual labor. They shall not fail, as far as human frailty will permit, to occupy their minds in some spiritual meditation. We further ordain that during the hours of labor they shall speak of God, or have read to them some devout book.

66.   Let the Friars take heed not to make work their sole object, nor to set their affections upon it, nor to become so engrossed in it as to extinguish, diminish or weaken the spirit to which all things should be subservient. With their eyes fixed always on God, let them take the highest and shortest road, so that labor imposed on man by God, accepted and commended by the Saints as a means of preserving interior recollection, may not become an occasion of distraction and laxity.

67.   Let every Friar remember that evangelical poverty consists in not having any affection for earthly things, using the goods of this world most sparingly, as if by constraint, forced by necessity and for the glory of God to Whom we are indebted for all. Whatever is over and above their own needs, they shall for the honor of poverty, give to the poor. We should also remember that we dwell in an inn and "eat the sins of the people," and that we shall be called upon to render a strict account of everything.

68.   The devout St. Bernard was wont to say that nothing is more precious than time, and that nothing is less esteemed. He also warns us that we shall be rigorously examined as to how we have spent our allotted time. We exhort all our brethren never to be idle, nor to spend their time in matters of little or no importance, much less in vain or useless conversations. Let them always bear in mind the fearful warnings of the Infallible Truth, that for every idle word we speak we shall render an account on the Day of Judgment. Let the Friars, therefore, spend all their time in praiseworthy, honest and useful oc-

cupations, either of mind or of body. Let them do this for the honor and glory of the Divine Majesty, and for the edification and good example to all our brethren and fellow-men, religious and secular.

CHAPTER SIX

69. Our Seraphic Father St. Francis, contemplating the most high poverty of Christ, the King of Heaven and Earth, Who, at His birth, could not find even a little place at the inn; Who, during His life, lodged like a pilgrim in the houses of others, and Who, at His death, had nowhere to lay His head; reflecting moreover, that in all other things He was most poor, and wishing to imitate Him, commanded the Friars in the Rule not to possess anything of their own, so that, unencumbered, like pilgrims of earth and citizens of Heaven, they might run with alacrity of spirit in the way of God. Desiring to imitate in truth this lofty example of Christ, and really to put into practice the Seraphic precept of celestial poverty, we wish it to be understood that we have, in fact, no jurisdiction, ownership, juridical possession, usufruct nor legal use of anything, even of the things we use through necessity.

70. We ordain that in every Friary an inventory be kept in which an account be given of the more valuable things bestowed upon us by benefactors for our necessary and simple use. Within the Octave of the feast of our Seraphic Father, every Guardian shall go to the owner of the Friary, thank him for the use of it during the past year, and humbly beg him to grant the Friars the use of it for another year. Should he consent, then the Friars may dwell there with a quiet conscience. Should he refuse, then, without any sign of sadness, nay, with a joyful heart, accompanied by divine poverty, let them depart, feeling themselves indebted to their benefactor for the time they were permitted to dwell there, and not offended because it is his property and he is not obliged to offer it to them. Thus they shall also do with other valuable things, carrying the articles, such as chalices and similar things, to the benefactor, when this can be conveniently done. They shall, at least, promise to return them should the owner so desire. When the articles can no longer be used, they shall return them to the owners, or ask them for permission to give the articles to the poor.

71. We also ordain that when the Friars wish to establish a new Friary, they shall first go to the Ordinary of the place, or his Vicar, and ask to open a House in his diocese. When the permission has been obtained, and with his benediction, they shall go to the civic authorities, or to the benefactors, and ask them for a site.

72. Let the Friars guard against accepting any place with the obligation of retaining it. Should this be demanded, they shall not accept the place without the express protest that they are free to leave whenever this should prove expedient for the pure observance of the Rule. Thus they shall not give scandal when they leave.

73. And as we ought, like pilgrims and after the example of the Patriarchs of old, live in humble dwellings or huts and quiet places, we exhort the Friars

to remember the words of our Seraphic Father in his Testament where he forbids them to accept on any account Churches or Houses built for them, unless they are in keeping with most high poverty. Still less shall the Friars themselves erect, or consent to the erection of, sumptuous buildings. Nor should the Friars in order to please the great ones of this world, displease God, violate the Rule, scandalize their neighbor, and offend against the evangelical poverty they profess. There should be a wide distinction between the palatial residences of the rich and the mean dwellings of poor Mendicants, pilgrims and penitents. It is therefore ordained that no place built for us or for others shall be accepted, nor shall the Friars build, or permit to be built, any House, unless it be in keeping with most holy poverty.

74. In order to proceed more securely, the Friars shall agree on a small model building according to which they shall build. The cells shall not be more than nine feet in length and width, and ten in height; the doors seven feet high and two and a half feet wide; the dormitory corridor six feet wide. In like manner the other offices shall be small, humble, poor and unpretending, so that everything may preach humility, poverty and contempt of the world. The Churches shall be small, poor and devotional. The preachers shall not desire that our Churches be spacious, for, as St. Francis says, we give a better example by preaching in other Churches than in our own, especially if thereby we offend against holy poverty.

75. To avoid whatever might transgress poverty the Friars are expressly forbidden to interfere with the building except it be to draw the attention of those charged with the management to the simple form of the model, or to offer them manual aid. Let the Friars strive, as far as possible, to use twigs and clay, reeds, tiles and common material, after the example of our Father, and as a mark of humility and poverty. Let them take as their models the humble dwellings of the poor, and not the modern mansions.

76. To avoid every disorder, it is ordained that no place be accepted or abandoned, built or destroyed without the permission of the Provincial Chapter and the Vicar-General. No Guardian shall make additions or pull down without the permission of the Vicar Provincial who, with a few other competent Friars, shall determine the plan of our Friaries.

77. In order that seculars may avail themselves of our spiritual services, and that they may assist us in our temporal needs, we ordain that our Friaries shall not be built in places too far removed from cities, towns or villages, nor yet too near them, lest we suffer from too frequent intercourse with seculars. The Friaries shall be, as a rule, a mile and a half or so distant, always preferring after the example of our venerable Fathers and especially of our own Holy Father, to dwell in solitary and unfrequented places, rather than in pleasurable cities.

78. It is also prescribed that in our Houses there shall be a modest room with a fire-place, so that, as charity demands and as far as our poverty will allow, we may receive pilgrims and strangers when necessary.

79. It is also prescribed that wherever convenient there shall be one or two

modest cells in the woods or other places consigned to the Friars. The cells shall be somewhat removed from the common dwelling of the Friars and in a solitary place, so that if any Friar desire to lead an eremitic life, when judged fit by his Prelate, he may in peaceful seclusion, and like the angels, surrender himself entirely to God, as the Spirit of God may inspire him. In order that the Friars who are thus in retirement may enjoy God in quiet, it is ordained that the other Friars shall not speak with them except their Spiritual Father who shall provide for them as a mother, according to the pious wish of our Seraphic Father and as we read in the Book of Conformity.

80. It is further ordained that if in the places the Friars have accepted, there be vines or superfluous trees, they shall not be cut down. With the consent of the owners let them give the fruit to the poor. The vines shall be cultivated, and if they bear fruit, they shall be planted in other places, or be given to the poor.

81. According to the doctrine of the Gospel, Christians, and therefore much more Friars Minor who have chosen to follow more closely Christ, Supreme Ruler and spotless mirror, in the path of most high poverty, are bound to remember that their Heavenly Father is able and willing to govern and provide for them. Unlike the heathens, who disbelieve in Divine Providence, they shall not seek with anxious and excessive solicitude to procure the things of this world which the all-bountiful God bestows with generous Hand, even on irrational creatures; but as children of the Eternal Father, putting aside all carnal solicitude, they shall trust for everything to that Divine Liberality and abandon themselves to His Infinite Goodness. We, therefore, ordain that no provision shall be made in our Houses, even of such necessaries of life as can be obtained from day to day by begging, except for two or three days, or at the most for a week, according to the needs of times and places. Fruit shall not be stored up except for a short time, according to the judgment of the Provincial.

82. To preclude the way to excessive provisions, we ordain that no barrels shall be kept in our Houses, but only a few small vessels or flasks. In winter, wood may be supplied for two or three months.

83. And lest our poverty be rich and delicate, lest it be a poverty in name and not in deed, we ordain that, except it be for the sick, the Friars shall not, even during the week preceding Lent, ask alms, such as meat, eggs, cheese, fish, or any other food unbecoming our humble state. Should such things be offered to the Friars, they may accept them provided they do not violate poverty.

84. Let the Friars beware above all things, lest through the abundance of alms bestowed on them through the favor of the great, the faith of the people, and the devotion of the world, they should become illegitimate sons of St. Francis, and forsake their most holy mother poverty. Let them call to mind those beautiful words our Seraphic Father was wont to repeat in transports of love: "I give thanks to God that through His goodness I have always been faithful to my beloved spouse, Poverty; nor was I ever a robber of alms, because I always accepted less than I needed, so that other poor might not be deprived of their share. To have done otherwise would have been theft before God."

85.   We further ordain that during a famine the Friars, appointed to this task by their Prelates, shall go in quest for food to succour the poor, after the example of our most devoted Father who showed great compassion for the poor. When an alms was given to him for love of God, he would not accept it save on condition, that he be allowed to give it to the poor, should he find one poorer than himself. We read that often times, lest he be found without the nuptial and evangelical garment of charity, he would divest himself of his own clothes and give them to the poor, rather than be deprived of the ardent flame of divine love.

86.   Since voluntary poverty possesses nothing, and yet is rich in all things, is happy, has no fear, no desire, and can lose nothing, because its treasure is in the safest keeping, we determine, in order to root out verily and effectively all occasions of proprietorship, that the keys of cells, chests, desks and so forth shall not be kept by any Friar except by the officials who have charge of the things to be dispensed to the community, as is just and reasonable.

87.   And as we possess nothing in this world, no Friar is allowed to give anything to seculars without the permission of the Guardians, who themselves may not give away or permit others to give, save with regard to trifling or valueless things, without the permission of their Vicar Provincial.

88.   To relieve the wants of the sick, as reason dictates, the Rule commands, and fraternal charity requires, we ordain that when any Friar falls sick, the Father Guardian shall immediately appoint a Friar qualified to attend to him in all his needs. Should the invalid require a change of climate, this shall be immediately provided for. Let each Friar consider what he would have done for himself in case of sickness. No mother, as our affectionate Father expresses it in the Rule, is so tender and devoted to her only son as each one of us ought to be to our spiritual brother.

89.   And since they who are detached from this world find it sweet, just and charitable to die for love of Him Who died for us on the Cross, we ordain that during a plague the Friars shall succour the afflicted according to the regulations of their Vicars. The Vicars, however, shall always have the eye of prudent charity open to such occasions.

CHAPTER SEVEN

90.   To remove every danger from subjects and Superiors, no Friar shall hear the confessions of seculars without the permission of the Chapter, or of the Father Vicar General. Since this office demands not merely a good and sufficient understanding but a ripe experience, it shall not be exercised save by those who are qualified. The Friars appointed to hear confessions shall do so only in particular cases, when charity demands. Thus they shall avoid every danger and mental distraction, and remain composed and recollected in Christ so that without any obstacle they may walk more securely on the road to their heavenly home.

91.   Let the Friars confess at least twice a week, and receive Holy Com-

munion every fortnight, or oftener if they wish, and their Superiors deem it expedient. During Advent and Lent they shall receive Holy Communion every Sunday. And let the Friars, according to the Apostolic admonition, carefully examine themselves beforehand, remembering on the one hand their own nothingness and unworthiness, and on the other hand, this sublime gift of God given to us with such great charity, so that they may not receive it to the injury of their souls but rather to their increase in light, grace and virtue. And this most august and Divine Sacrament, wherein our dearest Savior so lovingly condescends to abide with us always, shall be reserved in all our churches in a place of great cleanliness and shall be regarded by all with the greatest reverence. Let the Friars remain before It and pray as if they were already in their heavenly country with the holy angels.

92.   When the Friars happen to be absent from the monastery they may confess to other priests.

93.   To foster charity, the mother of every virtue, it is ordained that, with every possible Christian charity and as our Father exhorts us in his first Rule, the Friars shall receive any poor pilgrim or stranger, especially religious, devoted to the service of God.

94.   It is also ordained that in reserved cases the transgressors shall have recourse, with all humility, to their Vicars, in whom they may and must confide. If the Superiors see that they are really contrite and humble, have a firm purpose to amend, and are ready to submit to a suitable penance, then they shall receive the offenders with tenderness, after the example of Christ, our true Father and Shepherd, even as the prodigal son was received by his most compassionate father. Like Christ, let them with joy carry back on their own shoulders the lost sheep to the evangelical sheepfold.

95.   Let the Vicars also bear in mind what our Father, St. Francis, used to say: that if we would raise up one who has fallen, we must bend down to him with compassion, as Christ our most merciful Savior did when the adultress was brought before Him, and not treat the accused with rigid justice and cruelty. Christ, the Son of God, descended from heaven and died on the cross for our salvation. He always showed every possible tenderness to repentant sinners. The Superiors shall bear in mind that if God were to judge us rigidly, few or none would be saved. When they impose a punishment let their whole aim be to save and not to lose the soul and the good name of the erring Friar. Let no Friar be scandalized on account of the sin of a brother, nor avoid him or regard him with repugnance. On the contrary, they should feel compassion for him and love him all the more, as he has greater need of it, always remembering that, as our Seraphic Father says, each one of us would certainly be far worse if God did not prevent us by His grace. When Christ left St. Peter to the world as its universal Pastor, He told him to forgive the sinner even to seventy times seven. Our Seraphic Father has left recorded in one of his letters that it was his wish, that when a Friar, no matter how great a sinner he had been, appeared before his Superior and humbly asked for mercy, he should not depart unpardoned. He even wished that the Superior offer him forgiveness though

he did not ask for it. And if a sinner came to him a thousand times, it was his wish that the Superiors should never become angry or show themselves mindful of his sin, but the better to win him to Christ, Our Most Merciful Lord, should love him in all truth and sincerity, knowing that a contrite and humble heart together with a firm purpose to amend and to lead a virtuous life is sufficient before God. Christ used to say when imposing a penance: Go in peace and sin no more.

96.   Nevertheless, since to allow transgressors to go unpunished is to open wide the door to all the vices of the ill-disposed, and entice them to similar transgressions, the Superiors, in accordance with the Rule, shall with mercy impose on them a penance. In order to preserve this heritage of our Lord, we ordain that in all things, particularly in the correction and the punishment of the Friars, discipline be observed without recourse to excessive severity or juridical artifices.

97.   According to the concessions of Boniface VIII, Innocent and Clement, no Friar shall be allowed to appeal from his Superiors to others outside our Congregation under penalty of excommunication *latae sententiae,* of imprisonment, and of being expelled from our Congregation. We have not entered the religious life to wrangle, but to weep over our sins and amend our lives, to obey, and to carry the cross of penance after Christ. Lest in the future the delinquent be an obstacle to the good Friars, the former shall with mercy be punished by their Superiors.

98.   And since all Christians, and much more we, Friars Minor of St. Francis, must keep the Apostolic faith of the Holy Roman Church in its integrity and purity, steadfastly hold it and sincerely preach it, nay, be ready to shed our life's blood in defense thereof, we ordain that if any Friar be found, by the temptation of the devil, which God forbid, to be imbued with any error contrary to the Catholic Faith, he shall be perpetually imprisoned. To punish such and similar culprits an appropriate prison, withal humane, shall be provided for in some of our monasteries.

99.   Lest any Friar, disliking our secluded and quiet life, should return to the flesh-pots of Egypt, after having been once set free from the fiery furnace of Babylon, we determine that he shall be excommunicated by the Father Vicar General and the whole Chapter. The present Constitutions also decree that all apostates from our Congregation are *ipso facto* excommunicated, leaving it to the Vicar General and to the Vicars Provincial to determine the quality and quantity of punishment to be inflicted upon apostates and upon all other transgressors. The Vicars, however, shall punish them according to the quality of their sins and the humility of the penitent. Let the Vicars treat them with charitable discretion according to the ancient practices and laudable customs of our Order. But, as the illustrious Doctor, St. Augustine, says, both punishment and pardon tend always to the same end—reformation of life—so in corrections let justice be tempered with mercy, in such a manner, that discipline be not relaxed without recourse to excessive severity. Thus the transgressors will be reformed in such wise that mercy and truth may meet. For this reason, the Superiors shall be

chosen from among the Friars who are most distinguished for mature judgment, prudence, wisdom, and experience. In all things let the Friars seek counsel from the senior brethren.

100.   Lest the punishments we inflict from holy zeal may be impeded or misconstrued; and also that we may have greater freedom in proceeding against transgressors, we command that no one shall disclose the secrets of the Order. Let the Friars strive to uphold the good name of all, seeking always those things that are to the praise and glory of God, and to the peace and edification of our neighbors.

CHAPTER EIGHT

101.   As Christian Prelates, according to the teaching of Christ our humble Lord, should not resemble the Princes of the Gentiles, who lord it over their subjects; but on the contrary, the greater burden they bear on their shoulders, the more they ought to humble themselves and to reflect that, whereas, other Friars are bound to obey their Prelates, the Prelates themselves should obey all the brethren. The Chapter which elects them lays it upon them by obedience to serve and minister to the Friars in all things, especially in their spiritual needs, after the example of Christ Who came to serve and minister to us and to lay down His life for us. We therefore exhort all our Prelates to be the ministers and servants of all their brethren; this they will be, if in accordance with the teaching of our Seraphic Father, they administer spirit and life to their subjects by word and example.

102.   In every election the Friars shall proceed purely, simply, holily and canonically. Let them endeavor, according to the counsel of Christ, Our Gracious Lord, when invited to His marriage-feast, to take the lowest place with Him, rather than seek the first place with Lucifer, remembering that the last shall be first and the first last. Let them shun dignities as Christ did, and accept them only when, like Aaron, they are called by God through holy obedience.

103.   With regard to the General Chapter it is ordained that it be held every three years, about the Feast of Pentecost, as this time is most fitting for so important a matter and as is indicated by our Seraphic Father. The Provincial Chapter shall be held every year on the second or third Friday after Easter.

104.   As a sign of humility and to show sincere detachment from every kind of ambition, the Vicar General in the General Chapter and the Vicar Provincial in the Provincial Chapter shall spontaneously resign their offices and all authority into the hands of the Definitors elected by the Chapter. In proof of their entire resignation they shall place the seals into the hands of the aforesaid Definitors.

105.   Should the Father Vicar General die during his term of office it is ordained that the first definitor of the last Chapter shall become Commissary General. But should he have died, the second Definitor shall be Commissary

General and so of the others. And the Commissary General, with the consent of the Definitors, shall be bound to convoke the Chapter about the Feast of Pentecost, or in September, where it shall have been so determined, or prove expedient.

106. In order to provide for a secure and simple method of removing the Vicar General from office if at any time it should appear that he is not qualified, and in accordance with the wish of St. Francis expressed in the Rule, the first three Definitors of the preceding Chapter, having probable and sufficient evidence as to the Vicar General's unfitness, can and must convoke the Friars to a General Chapter when this proves advisable. At this Chapter they shall discuss the question of his removal from, or retention in, office. Should the Vicar General in any way endeavor to prevent the convocation of the Chapter we determine that he shall be 'ipso facto' deprived of office. Should the General Chapter decide that the Vicar General shall not be removed and that the three aforesaid Definitors have caused all this disorder in the Congregation without a just cause, they shall be severely punished at the discretion of the Chapter for having proceeded so rashly.

107. We also ordain that in the election of the Definitors all the vocals of the Chapter shall have a passive vote. In this election the Vicar General in the General Chapter and the Vicar Provincial in the Provincial Chapter shall have only an active vote. It is further ordained that in the General Chapter six Definitors shall be elected of whom not more than two may be from amongst those elected in the preceding Chapter. In the Provincial Chapters four Definitors shall be elected of whom likewise not more than two may be from those elected in the preceding year.

108. When the three years have expired the Vicar Provincials shall remain free from office for at least one year. But the Father Vicar General may, for just reasons, give them a passive vote.

109. During the celebration of the General Chapter, continual and fervent prayers shall be offered up by all the Friars of our Congregation, and during the Provincial Chapter by those of the Province. They shall beseech the Divine Clemency to deign to dispose all our affairs according to His good pleasure, to the praise and glory of His Majesty and the welfare of Holy Church.

CHAPTER NINE

110. Preaching the word of God, after the example of Christ, the Master of life, is one of the most honorable, useful, exalted and divine duties in the Church of God, on the fulfillment of which the salvation of mankind largely depends. We therefore ordain that no one shall be promoted to the office of preaching unless he has been examined and approved, as the Rule desires, by the General Chapter or by the Father Vicar General. Nor shall the office of preacher be conferred upon anyone unless it is evident that he is of holy and exemplary life, of clear and mature judgment, of strong and ardent will, because knowledge and eloquence without charity tend in no

way to edification but often to destruction. Let Superiors take diligent care that in granting faculties for preaching they be not acceptors of persons, nor swayed by human friendship or favor, but have in view simply and solely God's honor, make it their aim to have a few virtuous preachers, rather than many useless ones. Thus they will follow the example of Christ, the Supreme wisdom, Who from the whole Jewish nation chose only twelve Apostles and seventy-two Disciples, and that after long prayer.

111.   In addition it is ordained that the preachers refrain from introducing into their sermons trifles, foolish stories, useless questions, curious and far-fetched opinions, but after the example of the Apostle St. Paul, let them preach Christ crucified, in Whom are all the treasures of wisdom and knowledge of God. This is that Divine Wisdom which St. Paul preached to the perfect after he had become a Christian; for as a Hebrew youth, he thought as a child, and understood as a child, and spoke as a child, of the shadows and types of the Old Testament. Let the preachers, besides quoting the holy Doctors, chiefly cite Christ, Whose authority carries more weight than that of all other persons and reasons in the world.

112.   The preachers shall abstain from difficult and affected phrases as unworthy of Him Who died naked and humble on the Cross. Their language shall be plain, pure, simple and humble, withal holy, full of charity and aflame with zeal, after the example of St. Paul, the Vessel of Election, who preached, not in loftiness of speech and human eloquence, but in the power of the Holy Ghost. The preachers, therefore, are exhorted to do their utmost to imprint the Blessed Jesus on their own hearts and give Him peaceable possession of their souls, so that it may be He Who moves them to speak from the fullness of love, not merely by word but much more by their deeds, after the example of St. Paul, the Doctor of the Gentiles, who did not dare to preach anything to others until Christ had enabled him first to practice it. So, also, did Jesus, our most perfect Master teach us not only by words, but by deeds. They are great in the kingdom of heaven who first do, and then teach and preach to others.

113.   The preachers should not think that they fulfill their duty by preaching during Advent and Lent. Let them assiduously endeavor to preach at least on all Feast-days, after the example of Christ, mirror of all perfection, Who passed through Judea, Samaria and Galilee, preaching in the cities and villages, at times even speaking to one, as in the case of the Samaritan woman.

114.   And while preaching to others, should they feel the spirit weakening, let them return to solitude, and there let them remain, till once again, full of God, the impulse of the Holy Spirit may move them to go forth to spread divine grace over the world. Thus engaged, now like Martha, now like Mary, they shall follow Christ in His mixed life, Who, after praying on the mountain, went down to the temple to preach, nay, descended from Heaven to earth to save souls.

115.   We strictly forbid preachers to receive delicate food. They shall live like poor men and mendicants, as they have voluntarily promised for the love

of Christ. Above all, let them guard against every kind of avarice, so that preaching Jesus Christ freely and sincerely, they may gather fruit in greater abundance. When they preach, let them not beg either for themselves or for their brethren; so that, according to the teaching of the Apostle, all may know they seek not their own interests, but those of Jesus Christ.

116. Since he who does not know how to read and imitate Christ, the Book of Life, cannot have the learning necessary for preaching, preachers are forbidden to carry with them many books, so that they find all things in Christ.

117. In order that the sacred office of preaching, so precious and most pleasing to Christ, our God, Who has proved it by preaching the most salutary evangelical doctrine with so much ardor of divine charity for the welfare of our souls; in order also the better to impress on the hearts of preachers the norm and method they are to follow in the worthy exercise of preaching Christ Crucified and the kingdom of heaven, in effectively procuring the conversion and the spiritual welfare of the faithful, by reproducing, as it were, and implanting Christ in their souls, we counsel and command them to use the Sacred Scriptures, especially the New Testament and in particular the Gospels, so that being evangelical preachers, we may fashion an evangelical people.

118. Let them refrain from profane and useless questions and opinions, or such theories and subtleties as few understand. But after the example of the most holy Precursor, John the Baptist, the most holy Apostles and other saintly preachers aflame with divine love, nay after the example of our most sweet Saviour Himself, let them preach: "Do penance for the kingdom of heaven is at hand." As our Seraphic Father exhorts us in the Rule, let them discourse of vices and virtues, of punishment and glory, in few words, not desiring or seeking anything but the glory of God and the salvation of souls redeemed by the most precious blood of the spotless Lamb, Christ Jesus.

119. Let their discourses be well considered and so discreet as not to point to any particular person, because, as the glorious St. Jerome says, a general discourse will offend no one. Let them indeed denounce every vice, but glorify the image of the Creator in the creature. And as our Seraphic Father exhorts us in his Testament let them endeavor to respect, love, and honor all priests, bishops, cardinals, and above all the Holy and Supreme Pontiff, Vicar of Christ on earth, the Supreme Head, Father and Shepherd of all Christians and of the entire Church Militant. Let them also love and honor all other ecclesiastics who live according to the manner of the Holy Roman Church and are humbly subject to the Head, Father and Lord, the Supreme Pontiff. Let all the Friars bear in mind the admonition left by our Seraphic Father in his Testament, that all theologians and those who minister to us the Most Holy and Divine Word, we must honor and revere as those who minister to us spirit and life.

120. And in order that, while preaching to others, the preachers themselves may not become castaways, they shall sometimes leave the multitude, and, with our most sweet Savior, ascend the mountain of prayer and contem-

plation. There let them endeavor to become inflamed as the Seraphim, with divine love, so that, all aflame themselves, they may enkindle others.

121. As mentioned above it is enjoined on preachers not to carry with them many books, so that they may attentively study the most excellent book, the Cross. And as it was always the intention of our beloved Father that the Friars have the necessary books in common and not individually, and the better to observe poverty and to remove from the hearts of the brethren all feeling of attachment, it is ordained that in each House there shall be a small room where the Holy Scriptures and some of the Holy Doctors shall be kept. But books that are really useless and make a man worldly rather than Christian (as stated above in the first chapter) shall not be kept in our houses. Let such as are found be disposed of according to the injunction of the Vicars General or Provincial.

122. And since in him who would preach worthily and in a befitting manner there is required, together with a religious and exemplary life, some knowledge of the Holy Scriptures, which cannot be acquired except by literary study; lest so noble and useful a function as preaching should, to the greater loss of souls, decline in our Congregation, we enact that there shall be devout and holy studies, abounding in charity and humility, both for the humanities and sacred letters. To these studies only such Friars shall be admitted, as the Vicar Provincial and the Definitors judge to be distinguished for fervent charity, praiseworthy behavior, humble and holy conversation, and at the same time, so capable of learning that they may afterwards, by their life and doctrine, be useful and productive in the House of the Lord.

123. Let the students not seek to attain that knowledge which only puffs up, but let them endeavor to acquire the illuminating and enkindling charity of Christ, which quickens the soul. They should not be so absorbed in literary pursuits as to neglect the study of holy prayer; otherwise they would act against the express wish of our Seraphic Father, who desired that prayer should never be omitted for any study whatever. The better to acquire the spirit of our Lord Jesus Christ, let both Lectors and Students strive to deepen the spiritual life even more than to cultivate letters. Thus they shall derive more profit from their studies; for without the spirit the true sense is not attained, but the mere letter which blinds and kills.

124. The students should strive, while maintaining holy poverty, never to leave the royal road which leads to heaven—holy humility. Let them often call to mind the saying of Blessed Giacapone: "Acquired knowledge without humility of heart gives a deadly wound." It will be an occasion of humbling themselves, if they realize that they have contracted further obligations towards God, by being promoted to study and by being counted worthy to be introduced to the true and pleasing knowledge of sacred letters, under which lies hidden that Supreme Good Whose Spirit is sweet above honey to them that taste it.

125. At the beginning of every lesson we exhort the students to raise their minds to God, and in a spirit of humility and with a contrite heart to say:

"Domine, iste vilissimus servus tuus et omni bono indignus, vult ingredi ad videndum thesauros tuos. Placeat tibi ut ipsum indignissimum introducas, et des sibi in his verbis et sancta lectione tantum te diligere, quantum te cognoscere, quia nolo te cognoscere nisi ut te diligam, Domine Deus Creator meus. Amen."

CHAPTER TEN

126.   We ordain that the Father Vicar General shall endeavor during his term of office, to visit personally all the House and Friars of our Congregation. The Vicar Provincials shall do the same in their Provinces. They as well as the Guardians shall continually urge their subjects with all charity to the perfect observance of the divine and evangelical precepts and counsels, of the Rule they have vowed, of these present Constitutions, but especially of most high poverty, the solid foundation of all regular observance. With all humility and charity let them correct transgressors, always mingling the wine of rigorous justice with the oil of soothing mercy.

127.   And the Friars who are subjects shall obey their Superiors with all humility in all things which they know are not sinful. They shall duly reverence their Superiors as vicars of St. Francis and even of Christ our God. And when they are reprehended and corrected by them, let the Friars, according to the praiseworthy custom of our first and humble Fathers and Brothers, kneel and patiently endure every admonition and correction. They shall not answer in a proud manner, or, indeed, reply at all to the Superior, especially in the Chapter or the refectory, unless they have first asked and obtained permission. He who does otherwise shall take the discipline publicly for the duration of a *Miserere.* And let all the Friars strive diligently to correct their faults; and by virtuous acts to acquire heavenly virtues, and by good habits to overcome evil inclinations. Let the Superiors beware of binding the souls of their subjects by precepts of obedience, unless they are forced to do so by religious piety or loving necessity.

128.   It is also ordained that visiting Friars shall be received with all fraternal charity. As true sons of the Eternal Father they shall first visit the Church, and having made a short adoration, they shall present themselves to the Superior, showing him their obedience without which no Friar may leave our Friaries. When the Friars leave the Friary for some useful purpose they shall, on leaving and returning, ask the blessing from their Superior.

129.   In order that all things be done with the merit of holy obedience and with due devotion, no Friar shall venture to take a repast, whether within or without our Friaries, without the permission and blessing of the Superior or senior Father or Brother.

130.   Let all the Friars endeavor to avoid superfluous and trivial conversation; and let them not desire to visit other churches in order to gain indulgences since many Supreme Pontiffs have granted a greater number in our own churches.

131. We also ordain that no fugitive Friar of one Province shall be received into another without the written permission of the Father Vicar General. Without this permission the admission is declared null and void, and the receiving Vicar Provincial shall be severely punished according to the judgment of the Father Vicar General.

132. To avoid all possible irregularities it is ordained that a Junior Friar shall not send or receive letters without the permission of the Superior.

133. All the Friars, after the example of our Lord Jesus Christ, and of our Seraphic Father, should prefer to be subjects and to obey, rather than to be Superiors and to command others. Nevertheless, those upon whom prelacies are imposed by obedience must not be obstinate in refusing them; but with all humility and solicitude shall fulfill the ministry entrusted to them.

134. We also exhort all the Friars, in accordance with the admonition of our Father in the tenth chapter of the Rule, to beware of all pride and vain glory, envy and avarice, of all care and solicitude about this world, of all detraction and murmuring against any person, especially Prelates, the Clergy, and Religious, particularly of our Congregation. Let them show respect to everyone according to his state, looking upon all as our Fathers and Superiors in Christ Jesus, Our Savior.

CHAPTER ELEVEN

135. According to the opinion of the holy Doctors, especially St. Jerome, familiarity with women, however holy, should be avoided with seraphic prudence, by the servants of God. Therefore, the entire General Chapter with the greatest consideration, and after due consultation and deliberation, have framed these present Constitutions to be observed inviolably by our entire Congregation. The Friars shall in nowise nor under any species of doing good or promoting the sanctification of souls, or at the request of the people or of nobles, accept the charge of monasteries or other religious houses of men or of women. They shall not provide them with Confessors nor have any concern about them, following the striking examples of Christ, Our Savior, and the salutary instruction of the Saints, rather than the teaching of the world.

136. As it behooves true religious and servants of Christ to avoid not only what is manifestly evil and sinful, but even whatever might have the appearance thereof; we desire that the Friars should not frequent any convent or other houses of religious women without the permission of the Vicar Provincial. The Vicar Provincial shall take heed not to grant such permission readily to any one, save tried and mature Friars, and in cases of necessity or charity, because, as our Father, St. Francis, was want to say, God delivered us from a wife and the devil has provided us with the nuns.

137. That clean of heart we may see God with the eye of a sincere faith and be more fitted for heavenly things, the Friars shall not have any suspicious intercourse or dealings with women, or long and unnecessary interviews with them. When obliged to speak with them, they shall remain where they can

always be seen by their companion, so as to give good example to the world and everywhere be a sweet odor to Jesus Christ. They shall converse with purity, discretion and religious decorum. Let them remember the memorable example, related in our Chronicles, of that Friar who burning a wisp of straw said: "What the straw gains by the fire, the same doth the religious servant of God gain by conversing with women." Pope John XXII, in the Bull of Canonization of St. Louis, Bishop, one of our Friars, says of him: "So deeply rooted in heart, even from childhood, was the love of chastity, that to guard it faithfully he avoided all intercourse with women, never having spoken to any woman alone, except his mother and sister, understanding that woman is more bitter than death." And St. Bernard says that there are two things which defile and ruin religious: familiarity with women and daintiness in food.

138. We also desire that women shall not enter into our Friaries except in case of real necessity or of extraordinary devotion, and when they cannot be refused without giving scandal. If they enter, they must always be accompanied by trustworthy men and women. Before admitting them, the approval of the Friars dwelling in the Friary must be obtained. Two mature and saintly Friars shall accompany them, always speaking of edifying subjects in Christ our Lord, and of their spiritual welfare, with all religious decorum and good example. No only with women, but even with laymen, our intercourse should be infrequent, since undue familiarity with them is injurious to us.

Chapter Twelve

139. In order to safeguard the pure observance of the Rule, as well as to ensure the proper performance of the divine services, and at the same time to observe most high poverty, we ordain that in our Friaries there shall not be less than six nor more than twelve Friars, who, united in the sweet name of Jesus, shall be of one heart and one soul ever striving to arrive at greater perfection. And if they would be true disciples of Christ, let them cordially love one another, bearing with each other's defects, exercising themselves in divine love and fraternal charity, studying to give a good example to one another and to everyone, doing constant violence to their own passions and evil inclinations, because as our Savior says: "The Kingdom of Heaven suffereth violence, and the violent, that is, those who do violence to themselves, bear it away."

140. We also ordain that in our churches there shall be only one small bell, about one hundred and fifty pounds in weight. In our churches there shall be no other sacristy but a case, or chest, with a good key which shall be kept by a professed Friar. In this case or chest shall be stored all requisites for divine worship. They shall have two small chalices, one of tin and the other with only the cup of silver. They shall not have more than three simple vestments without gold, silver, velvet or silk, or anything costly or superfluous, but everything must be neat and clean. The altar linens shall be plain; the candlesticks shall be of wood. Our missals, breviaries, and other books shall

be plainly bound and without any ornate book-marks, so that in everything we use holy poverty is seen resplendent, which will make us yearn after the riches of heaven where are all our treasures, our joys and our glory.

141. Since it is impossible to lay down laws and statutes for every individual case that may arise, the number thereof being indefinite, we exhort all our Friars, in the charity of Christ, to keep before their minds in all their actions the Holy Gospel, the Rule they have promised, the holy and praiseworthy customs and examples of the Saints, by directing their thoughts, words and actions to the honor and glory of God and the salvation of their neighbor. Thus will the Holy Spirit enlighten them in all things.

142. To maintain uniformity in the divine services, both in choir and in every other place, the teaching of St. Bonaventure and the ordinances of our first Fathers shall be read. To better understand the mind of our Seraphic Father, the Friars shall read his "Fioretti," the "Book of Conformity," and the other books that speak of him.

143. As our Seraphic Father had the conversion of unbelievers very much at heart, in accordance with the Rule, it is ordained that if any Friars, inflamed with love for Christ and zeal for the Catholic Faith, wish through divine inspiration to preach to the infidels, they shall have recourse to their Vicar Provincials or to the Vicar General. Should the Superiors judge them fit, they shall send them with their permission and blessing on such an arduous mission. Let the subjects not rashly presume to judge themselves competent for such dangerous and difficult works, but with all fear and humility, let them submit their wishes to their Superiors' judgment. It is well, indeed, to draw a distinction between unbelievers who are gentle, docile, and well disposed to receive the Christian Faith, as are those recently discovered by the Spaniards, or Portuguese in the Indies, and the Turks and Agarenes who, by force of arms and cruel persecution, maintain and defend their pernicious sect. The Superiors shall not refrain from sending out missionaries because the Friars are few in number, but casting all care and solicitude on Him, Who has unceasing care of us, let them act in all things as the Spirit of God will inspire them, and arrange all with charity which worketh no evil.

144. In order that beloved poverty, the holy spouse of Christ our Lord and of our Father, remain ever with us, let the Friars be careful not to allow any costliness, rarity or superfluity to appear in the things appertaining to divine worship, or in our buildings or in the furniture we use, remembering that God wishes from us rather our obedience promised in holy poverty, than sacrifices. And as Pope Clement says in his declaration, God desires a pure heart and holy deeds rather than costly and richly adorned things. Nevertheless, cleanliness must shine forth in our poverty.

145. And as our Savior first began to do and then to teach others, in like manner our Prelates shall be the first to comply with these Constitutions, and then with all holy and efficacious zeal, induce their subjects to observe them inviolably. And should certain things appear somewhat difficult in the beginning, habit will make them easy and pleasant. To impress them more deeply

on the minds of the Friars, and that they observe them, all the Guardians shall have them read at table once every month. And although we have no intention by these Constitutions to bind the Friars under pain of any sin, yet it is our wish and command that transgressors of them be severely punished. And if the Guardians are remiss in their observance or in causing them to be observed they shall be still more severely punished by the Vicar Provincials, and these latter by the Father Vicar General.

146.   Since the present Constitutions were drawn up with the greatest care and mature deliberation, and approved by our whole General Chapter and by the Apostolic See, we enact that they be not changed without the consent of the General Chapter. We also exhort all our Fathers and Brothers present and to come, not to change these Constitutions—even in the Chapters. Experience has proved that great injury has been done to Religious Orders by the frequent alteration of their Constitutions. Nor shall Provincial Constitutions be framed, but if particular cases arise they shall be provided for by General Chapters. These Constitutions shall be left intact and in accordance with them our Congregation should live and be governed with a holy uniformity.

147.   As our Seraphic Father, when on the point of death, bequeathed the fruitful blessing of the Most Holy Trinity, together with his own, to the zealous and true observance of the Rule; let us all, therefore, shaking off all negligence, assiduously apply ourselves with sincerity and devotedness to the observance of the perfection which the said Rule and our Order propose and inculcate.

148.   Let the Friars remember that to obey with no other intention than to escape punishment belongs solely to slaves and hirelings, but to obey for the love of God and for the glory and the pleasure of the Divine Majesty, and to give a good example to our neighbor and for other similar motives, pertains to the true children of God. Let the Friars beware of transgressing these Constitutions on the plea that they do not oblige under pain of sin; but, recognizing their spirit, let them observe inviolably the laws, ordinances, and statutes of our Congregation, that grace may be added to their head. Thus shall they, by this holy service, merit the Divine Mercy, and become conformable to the Son of God, Who though not bound by the laws He himself made, nevertheless observed them for the salvation of others. Let them, therefore, uphold the sublimity of the Religious State and become the source of much benefit to their neighbors. Let them remember that it behooves good servants not only to fulfill the commands of their lords and masters, imposed under threats of punishment, but to please them in many other ways.

149.   Wherefore, in fulfilling these duties, let us keep our eyes upon our Redeemer, so that knowing His good pleasure we may strive to please Him, not only by not despising the present Constitutions (for contempt of them would be a grave sin), but through love of Him avoiding all negligence in their obedience. This observance will be a help to us to be faithful not only to the Rule, but to the divine law and Gospel counsels. The grace of God, through Jesus Christ, will deliver us from all dangers. As our labors abound so also

will our consolations in Christ Jesus. We can do all things in Him Who strengthens us, namely in Christ Who is omnipotent, and in everything shall we be given understanding by Him Who is the Power, Wisdom, and Servant of God, Who giveth abundantly to all men and upbraideth not. He Who upholds all things by the word of His power will supply the strength.

150. Let us, dearest Fathers and Brothers, frequently call to mind that sacred and memorable text, on which our Seraphic Father preached a most impressive sermon to more than 5,000 Friars: "Great things we have promised to God, but greater things has He promised unto us." Let us observe the things we have promised, and with ardent longing yearn after the things that have been promised to us. The pleasures of this life are short, but the pains of hell incurred by pursuing them are never ending. The sufferings which we bear for the love of Christ, and the penance which we do for His sake will last but a short time; but the glory, with which God will reward us, will never end. Many have been called to the kingdom of life eternal, but few have been chosen, because very few follow Christ in sincerity of heart. But on the last day God will give to each the reward of his deeds; to the good, the glory of Heaven; to the wicked, the confusion of everlasting fire.

151. Great, indeed, are the things we have promised, yet they are nothing in comparison with the eternal reward God will bestow upon us if we remain faithful. Let us therefore act manfully, and not distrust our strength, because that best of Fathers Who has created us and has called us to a life of evangelical perfection, knowing our condition, will give us not only strength by His aid, but also heavenly gifts in such abundance, that, surmounting all obstacles, we shall be able not merely to obey His Most Beloved Son, but even to follow and imitate Him with the greatest cheerfulness and simplicity of heart; utterly despising those visible and temporal things, and ever yearning after those which are heavenly and eternal.

152. In Christ then, Who is God and Man, the True Light, the Brightness of Glory and of Eternal Light, the Spotless Mirror and Image of God; in Christ, appointed by the Eternal Father to be the Judge, Lawgiver and Savior of men; in Christ, to Whom the Holy Ghost has given testimony; and from Whom are all our merit, example, help, grace, and reward; in Whom be all our meditation and imitation; in Whom all things are sweet, learned, holy, and perfect; in Christ, Who is the light and expectation of the Gentiles, the end of the law, the salvation of God, the Father of the world to come, our final hope, Who of God is fashioned the Wisdom and Justice, Sanctification and unto us Redemption, Who with the Father and the Holy Ghost, co-eternal, consubstantial, and co-equal liveth and reigneth one God, be everlasting praise, honor, majesty, and glory, world without end. Amen.

CHAPTER XIII

The *Consilium de emendanda ecclesia,* 1537

The pontificate of Paul III (October, 1534, to November, 1549) marks a turning point in the history of the Church and the Papacy during this troubled age. Now at last serious, competent leadership was exerted at Rome to stem the tide of disruption and effect the general reform so desperately needed. Paul III, the former Cardinal Alessandro Farnese and dean of the Sacred College, may indeed be a transitional figure wherein the old habits of the papal prince still contend with the new demands of this perilous time, but at least we can say these new demands were heard and a serious response was made. From the start he sought to convene the General Council that so many desired and to grapple with the problems of curial and ecclesiastical reform. Above all he brought many of the most able Catholic reformers to Rome and thereby infused new life into the Sacred College and a new spirit into the papal administration. "Under him," says Pastor, "a strong Catholic movement gained step by step a sure foothold, and herein lay the practical value and the real significance of his reign."[1]

The other major developments of this long and eventful pontificate that bear directly on the Church's recovery and revival—the foundation of the Jesuits (1540), the convening of the General Council at Trent (1545), the establishment of the Roman Inquisition (1542)—are closely related to this gathering of reformers under papal auspices and this infusion of new life into the highest echelon of the papal regime. The latter event, however, remains primary and is our chief consideration here, and the remarkable document that is presented below, as well as the occasion for it, can serve well to announce the new era of the Farnese Pope and indicate its reform possibilities. These possibilities, let us add, if they were not immediately realized amid the

---

[1] Pastor, XI, 40. Pastor, XI and XII, and Carlo Capasso, *Paolo III* (2 vols.; Messina, 1924), afford the fullest account of this long pontificate. It is also of course treated in Jedin, *A History of the Council of Trent,* I and II, particularly in connection with the preparation and convening of the General Council which finally opened at Trent in December, 1545. *Concilium Tridentinum,* IV, 449–512, contains a number of documents pertaining to reform efforts under Paul III, and Stephan Ehses, "Kirchliche Reformarbeiten unter Paul III vor dem Trienter Konzil," *Römische Quartalschrift,* XV (1901), 153–74, 397–411, is a basic essay on this theme.

obstacles and difficulties of the time, nevertheless provide a standard for action and a guide for future accomplishment.[2]

In May, 1535, Paul III bestowed a cardinal's hat on the eminent Venetian Gasparo Contarini, "a layman whose name implied a programme of reform."[3] The appointment was highly indicative and began that revitalization of the Roman Court so badly needed. Coming to Rome and taking up his residence in the Vatican, Contarini became one of the Pope's closest advisers. Indeed it appears to have been his suggestion that the Pope, in view of the projected General Council scheduled to meet in Mantua in May, 1537, as well as of the urgent need to inaugurate reform, assemble at Rome a reform commission.[4] Invitations were dispatched in July, 1536, to a truly outstanding group of men, and by November they had gathered in Rome to begin their deliberations under the presidency of Cardinal Contarini. They were for the most part close friends of Contarini, and their names are a roster of some of the most prominent men in the history of the Catholic Reformation: Gian Pietro Carafa, the Theatine leader; Gian Matteo Giberti, Bishop of Verona; Jacopo Sadoleto, Bishop of Carpentras; Gregorio Cortese, Abbot of San Giorgio Maggiore in Venice; Reginald Pole, the English noble and scholar; Federigo Fregoso, Bishop of Gubbio; Jerome Aleander, nuncio and Archibishop of Brindisi; and Tommaso Badia, Dominican Master of the Sacred Palace.

This commission of nine, whose sessions were opened by a frank and moving address by Sadoleto, continued its discussions for three months, and in early March, 1537, Contarini formally presented its report to Paul III.[5] That report, the *Consilium delectorum cardinalium et aliorum prelatorum de emendanda ecclesia*, is the document at hand.[6] Its provenance, the boldness of its

---

[2] I make this point having in mind the critical judgments concerning the *Consilium de emendanda ecclesia* one finds, for example, in Preserved Smith, *The Age of the Reformation* (N.Y., 1920), pp. 382–83, and G. R. Elton, *Reformation Europe, 1517–1559* (N.Y., 1966), pp. 187–89. It seems to me quite incorrect to say, as Smith does, that the *Consilium* "led to nothing," or, as Elton does, that it contains "no sign at all of positive reform." Aside from its general significance or inherent value as a reform document, it certainly anticipates much of the legislation of Trent.

[3] Pastor, XI, 144. On Contarini, see Chap. VII. Paul at the same time elevated John Fisher, Bishop of Rochester, then prisoner of Henry VIII (and executed the following month), and several others. He thought too of nominating Erasmus. Huizinga, *op. cit.*, pp. 185–86, 253.

[4] Pastor, XI, 153, but also see R. M. Douglas, *Jacopo Sadoleto* (Cambridge, Mass., 1959), pp. 100, 269, n. 19.

[5] The discussions were secret, and no record survives. An account of the commission and its work will be found in Pastor, XI, 153–72, which should be supplemented by Jedin, I, 423–28, and Douglas, *op. cit.*, pp. 100–12. All are replete with bibliographical reference. The text of the report, the *Consilium de emendanda ecclesia*, will be found in *Concilium Tridentinum*, XII, 134–45, and in Kidd, *Documents Illustrative of the Continental Reformation*, pp. 307–18.

[6] The English translation presented here has been made by John Higgins and the editor from the Latin text in *Concilium Tridentinum*, XII. It is curious to note that a much earlier English version, *The State of the Church of Rome when the Reformation began, as it appears by the advices given to Paul III and Julius III by creatures of their own*, was published in London in 1688 as a polemical pamphlet in the campaign against James II.

9. Pope Paul III. Portrait by Titian.

attack on the curial system, the incisiveness of its recommendations in behalf of the pastoral ideal, all combine to make it one of the great documents of Catholic reform. As Pastor declares, "the wounds had been laid bare, and now the remedy could be applied."[7] Whatever the problems of this application, we cannot deny that a major step had been taken—that the gulf between the aspirations of the reformers and the practices of the institutional Church had begun to be bridged. And, as if to underline his support for the reform commission, in late December, 1536, Paul III elevated three of its members to the cardinalate: Carafa, Sadoleto, and Pole.[8]

The automatic translation of this collective report into the actual correction and improvement—*emendatio*—of ecclesiastical practice was hardly to be expected, given the deep-seated evils that prevailed and the unreconstructed attitude (and habits) of so many in the Curia and the papal bureaucracy.[9] But the significance of the *Consilium*, as we have indicated, lies on a different plane—that of raising the standard for action and of preparing the future. There was, however, an interesting repercussion that followed the presentation of this report. Copies of it were circulated among the cardinals, and in spite of its strictly confidential character, it soon found its way into print. It was published at Rome, Cesena, and Cologne in 1538,[10] and the German Protestants gave it further circulation as a confirmation of their own accusations against the Roman Church. Luther published a German text with a scornful preface and marginal gloss in March 1538,[11] and the following month Johann Sturm in Strasbourg brought out the Latin version with a more moderate but nevertheless critical open letter addressed to the authors of the *Consilium*. What was a most serious and vital declaration looking only toward the regeneration of the Church became unfortunately a weapon in the hands of the Protestants, but that of course was not its only fate.

[7] Pastor, XI, 171.

[8] The others too, with the exception of Giberti, were subsequently elevated by Paul III: Aleander in 1538, Fregoso in 1539, Cortese and Badia in 1542. Giberti, fully engaged in his diocese of Verona, apparently declined any such honor and service. *Ibid.*, XI, 189–90.

[9] Jedin, I, 427–45, gives an excellent analysis of this depressing situation and of the difficult course of curial reform in the months immediately following the *Consilium*. Particularly interesting are the reservations concerning it of the future cardinal Bartolomeo Guidiccioni, who defended curial practice and approached reform in a far more conservative and accommodating way (pp. 427–28). His critical judgment of the *Consilium* as well as his own reform views were expressed in a report (*c.* 1538) which may be found in *Concilium Tridentinum*, XII, 226–56.

[10] The Cologne edition, a very fine pocket-size book, also contains two important treatises, or *epistolae*, addressed to Paul III, by Contarini: "*De potestate pontificis in usu clavium*," and "*De potestate pontificis in compositionibus*."

[11] An English translation of Luther's edition is in *Luther's Works*, Vol. 34: *Career of the Reformer*, IV, ed. Lewis W. Spitz (Philadelphia, 1960), pp. 235–67.

MOST HOLY FATHER, we are so far from being able to express in words the great thanks the Christian Commonwealth should render to Almighty God because He has appointed you Pope in these times and pastor of His flock and has given you that resolve which you have that we scarcely hope we can do justice in thought to the gratitude we owe God. For that Spirit of God by whom the power of the heavens has been established, as the prophet says, has determined to rebuild through you the Church of Christ, tottering, nay, in fact collapsed, and, as we see, to apply your hand to this ruin, and to raise it up to its original height and restore it to its pristine beauty. We shall hope to make the surest interpretation of this divine purpose—we whom your Holiness has called to Rome and ordered to make known to you, without regard for your advantage or for anyone else's, those abuses, indeed those most serious diseases, which now for a long time afflict God's Church and especially this Roman Curia and which have now led with these diseases gradually becoming more troublesome and destructive to this great ruin which we see.

And your Holiness, taught by the Spirit of God who (as Augustine says) speaks in hearts without the din of words, had rightly acknowledged that the origin of these evils was due to the fact that some popes, your predecessors, in the words of the Apostle Paul, "having itching ears heaped up to themselves teachers according to their own lusts,"[12] not that they might learn from them what they should do, but that they might find through the application and cleverness of these teachers a justification for what it pleased them to do. Thence it came about, besides the fact that flattery follows all dominion as the shadow does the body and that truth's access to the ears of princes has always been most difficult, that teachers at once appeared who taught that the pope is the lord of all benefices and that therefore, since a lord may sell

[12] II Timothy 4, 3.

by right what is his own, it necessarily follows that the pope cannot be guilty of simony. Thus the will of the pope, of whatever kind it may be, is the rule governing his activities and deeds: whence it may be shown without doubt that whatever is pleasing is also permitted.

From this source as from a Trojan horse so many abuses and such grave diseases have rushed in upon the Church of God that we now see her afflicted almost to the despair of salvation and the news of these things spread even to the infidels (let your Holiness believe those who know), who for this reason especially deride the Christian religion, so that through us—through us, we say—the name of Christ is blasphemed among the heathens.

But you, Most Holy Father, and truly Most Holy, instructed by the Spirit of God, and with more than that former prudence of yours, since you have devoted yourself fully to the task of curing the ills and restoring good health to the Church of Christ committed to your care, you have seen, and you have rightly seen, that the cure must begin where the disease had its origin, and having followed the teaching of the Apostle Paul you wish to be a steward, not a master, and to be found trustworthy by the Lord, having indeed imitated that servant in the Gospel whom the master set over his household to give them their ration of grain in due time[13]; and on that account you have resolved to turn from what is unlawful, nor do you wish to be able to do what you should not. You have therefore summoned us to you, inexperienced indeed and unequal to so great a task, yet not a little disposed both to the honor and glory of your Holiness and especially to the renewal of the Church of Christ; and you have charged us in the gravest language to compile all the abuses and to make them known to you, having solemnly declared that we shall give an account of this task entrusted to us to Almighty God, if we carelessly or unfaithfully execute it. And you have bound us by oath so that we can discuss all these matters more freely and explain them to you, the penalty of excommunication even having been added lest we disclose anything of our office to anyone.

We have therefore made, in obedience to your command and insofar as it can be briefly done, a compilation of those diseases and their remedies—remedies, we stress, which we were able to devise given the limitations of our talents. But you indeed according to your goodness and wisdom will restore and bring to completion all matters where we have been remiss in view of our limitations. And in order to set ourselves some fixed boundaries, since your Holiness is both the prince of those provinces which are under ecclesiastical authority and the Pope of the universal Church as well as Bishop of Rome, we have not ventured to say anything about matters which pertain to this principality of the Church, excellently ruled, we see, by your prudence. We shall touch however on those matters which pertain to the office of universal Pontiff and to some extent on those which have to do with the Bishop of Rome.

---

13 Luke 12, 42.

This point, we believed, most Holy Father, must be established before everything else, as Aristotle says in the *Politics*, that in this ecclesiastical government of the Church of Christ just as in every body politic this rule must be held supreme, that as far as possible the laws be observed, nor do we think that it is licit for us to dispense from these laws save for a pressing and necessary reason. For no more dangerous custom can be introduced in any commonwealth than this failure to observe the laws, which our ancestors wished to be sacred and whose authority they called venerable and divine. You know all this, excellent Pontiff; you have long ago read this in the philosophers and theologians. Indeed we think that the following precept is not only most germane to this, but a greater and higher ordinance by far, that it can not be permitted even for the Vicar of Christ to obtain any profit in the use of the power of the keys conferred on him by Christ. For truly this is the command of Christ: "Freely you have received, freely give."[14]

These points having been established at the outset, then [it should be remembered] your Holiness takes care of the Church of Christ with the help of a great many servants through whom he exercises this responsibility. These moreover are all clerics to whom divine worship has been entrusted, priests especially and particularly parish priests and above all bishops. Therefore, if this government is to proceed properly, care must be taken that these servants are qualified for the office which they must discharge.

The first abuse in this respect is the ordination of clerics and especially of priests, in which no care is taken, no diligence employed, so that indiscriminately the most unskilled, men of the vilest stock and of evil morals, adolescents, are admitted to Holy Orders and to the priesthood, to the [indelible] mark, we stress, which above all denotes Christ. From this has come innumerable scandals and a contempt for the ecclesiastical order, and reverence for divine worship has not only been diminished but has almost by now been destroyed. Therefore, we think that it would be an excellent thing if your Holiness first in this city of Rome appointed two or three prelates, learned and upright men, to preside over the ordination of clerics. He should also instruct all bishops, even under pain of censure, to give careful attention to this in their own dioceses. Nor should your Holiness allow anyone to be ordained except by his own bishop or with the permission of deputies in Rome or of his own bishop. Moreover, we think that each bishop should have a teacher in his diocese to instruct clerics in minor orders both in letters and in morals, as the laws prescribe.

Another abuse of the greatest consequence is in the bestowing of ecclesiastical benefices, especially parishes and above all bishoprics, in the matter of which the practice has become entrenched that provision is made for the persons on whom the benefices are bestowed, but not for the flock and Church of Christ. Therefore, in bestowing parish benefices, but above all bishoprics, care must be taken that they be given to good and learned men so that they

---

[14] Matthew 10, 8.

themselves can perform those duties to which they are bound, and, in addition, that they be conferred on those who will in all likelihood reside.[15] A benefice in Spain or in Britain then must not be conferred on an Italian, or vice versa. This must be observed both in appointments to benefices vacated through death and in the case of resignations, where now only the intention of the person resigning is considered and nothing else. In the case of these resignations we think that it would have good effect if one or several upright men were put in charge of the matter.

Another abuse, when benefices are bestowed or turned over to others, has crept in in connection with the arrangement of payments from the income of these benefices. Indeed, the person resigning the benefice often reserves all the income for himself.[16] In such cases care must be taken that payments can be reserved for no other reason and with no other justification than for alms which ought to be given for pious uses and for the needy. For income is joined to the benefice as the body to the soul. By its very nature then it belongs to him who holds the benefice so that he can live from it respectably according to his station and can at the same time support the expenses for divine worship and for the upkeep of the church and other religious buildings, and so that he may expend what remains for pious uses. For this is the nature of the income of these benefices. But just as in the course of natural events some things occur in particular cases which are contrary to the tendency of nature as a whole, so in the instance of the pope, because he is the universal steward of the goods of the Church, if he sees that that portion of the revenues which should be spent for pious uses or a part of it may more usefully be spent for some other pious purpose, he can without a doubt arrange it. He is able therefore in all justice to set aside payment to aid a person in need, especially a cleric, so that he can live respectably according to his station. For that reason it is a great abuse when all revenues are reserved and everything is taken away which should be allotted to divine service and to the support of him who holds the benefice. And likewise it is certainly a great abuse to make payments to rich clerics who can live satisfactorily and respectably on the income they have. Both abuses must be abolished.

Still another abuse is in the exchanging of benefices which occur under agreements that are all simoniacal and with no consideration except for the profit.

Another abuse must be entirely removed which has now become prevalent in this Curia due to a certain cunning on the part of some experienced persons. For, although the law provides that benefices can not be bequeathed in a will, since they do not belong to the testator but to the Church, and

---

[15] Regarding this important question see Adrian VI's concluding remarks in his Instruction to Chieregati (in Chap. IX).

[16] Luther's gloss on this particular passage, which is characteristic of his remarks in general on the *Consilium*, reads as follows: "This Romish trick was invented by the popes and cardinals themselves, and it is doubtful that they will be reformed therein." *Luther's Works*, Vol. 34, p. 248.

this so that these ecclesiastical properties may be kept in common for the benefit of all and not become the private possession of anyone, human diligence—but not Christian diligence—has discovered a great many ways whereby this law may be mocked. For first the surrender of bishoprics and other benefices are made with the right of regaining them [cum regressu]; the reservation of the income is added, then the reservation of conferring benefices; the reservation of the administration is piled on top of this, and by this stipulation they make him bishop who does not have the rights of a bishop, whereas all the episcopal rights are given to him who is not made bishop. May your Holiness see how far this flattering teaching has advanced, where at length it has led, so that what is pleasing is permitted. What, I pray, is this except appointing an heir for oneself to a benefice? Besides this another trick has been devised, when coadjutors are given to bishops requesting them, men less qualified than they are themselves, so that, unless one wishes to close his eyes, he may clearly see that by this means an heir is appointed.

Also, an ancient law was renewed by Clement [VII] that sons of priests may not have the benefices of their fathers, lest in this way the common property [of the Church] become private property. Nevertheless, dispensations are made (so we hear) in the case of this law which ought to be revered. We have not been willing to be silent in the face of that which any prudent man may judge for himself to be absolutely true, namely, that nothing has stirred up more this ill-will toward the clergy, whence so many quarrels have arisen and others threaten, than this diversion of ecclesiastical revenues and income from the general to private advantage. Formerly everyone was hopeful [that such abuses would be corrected]; now led to despair they sharpen their tongues against this See.

Another abuse is in the matter of expectatives and reservations of benefices,[17] and the occasion is given to desire another's death and to hear of it with pleasure. Indeed the more worthy are excluded when there are vacancies, and cause is given for litigations. All these abuses, we think, must be abolished.

Another abuse has been devised with the same cunning. For certain benefices are by right "incompatible," and they are so designated. By virtue of that term our forefathers have wished to remind us that they should not be conferred on one single person. Now dispensations are granted in these cases, not only for two [such benefices] but for more, and, what is worse, for bishoprics. We feel that this custom which has become so prevalent because of greed must be abolished, especially in the case of bishoprics. What about the life-long unions of benefices in one man, so that such a plurality of benefices is no obstacle to holding benefices that are "incompatible"? Is that not a pure betrayal of the law?

Another abuse has also become prevalent, that bishoprics are conferred on the most reverend cardinals or that not one but several are put in their

---

[17] An expectative is the assignment of a benefice before it has become vacant. A reservation of a benefice is the retention of the right of assigning it.

charge, an abuse, most Holy Father, which we think is of great importance in God's Church. In the first place, because the offices of cardinal and bishop are "incompatible." For the cardinals are to assist your Holiness in governing the universal Church; the bishop's duty however is to tend his own flock, which he cannot do well and as he should unless he lives with his sheep as a shepherd with his flock.

Furthermore, Holy Father, this practice is especially injurious in the example it sets. For how can this Holy See set straight and correct the abuses of others, if abuses are tolerated in its own principal members? Nor do we think that because they are cardinals they have a greater license to transgress the law; on the contrary, they have far less. For the life of these men ought to be a law for others, nor should they imitate the Pharisees who speak and do not act, but Christ our Savior who began to act and afterwards to teach. This practice is more harmful in the deliberations of the Church, for this license nurtures greed. Besides, the cardinals solicit bishoprics from kings and princes, on whom they are afterwards dependent and about whom they cannot freely pass judgment. Indeed, even if they are able and willing, they are nevertheless led astray, confused in their judgment by their partisanship. Would that this custom be abolished therefore and provision be made that the cardinals can live respectably in accordance with their dignity, each receiving an equal income. We believe that this can easily be done, if we wish to abandon the servitude to Mammon and serve only Christ.

With these abuses corrected which pertain to the appointment of your ministers, through whom as through instruments both the worship of God can be properly directed and the Christian people well instructed and governed in the Christian life, we must now approach those matters which refer to the government of the Christian people. In this regard, most blessed Father, the abuse that first and before all others must be reformed is that bishops above all and then parish priests must not be absent from their churches and parishes except for some grave reason, but must reside, especially bishops, as we have said, because they are the bridegrooms of the church entrusted to their care. For, by the Eternal God, what sight can be more lamentable for the Christian man travelling through the Christian world than this desertion of the churches? Nearly all the shepherds have departed from their flocks, nearly all have been entrusted to hirelings.[18] A heavy penalty, therefore, must be imposed on bishops before the others, and then on parish priests, who are absent from their flocks, not only censures, but also the withholding of the income of absentees, unless the bishops have obtained permission from your Holiness and the parish priests from their bishops to be away for a short period of time. Some laws and the decrees of some Councils may be read in this regard, which provide that the bishop shall not be permitted to be away from his church for more than three Sundays.

---

[18] "The calamity of our age," says Contarini with reference to such widespread absenteeism and neglect in his *De officio episcopi* (see Chap. VII).

10. Cardinal Gasparo Contarini. A contemporary portrait.

It is also an abuse that so many of the most reverend cardinals are absent from this Curia and perform none of the duties incumbent on them as cardinals. Although perhaps not all should reside here, for we think it advantageous that some should live in their provinces—for through them as through some roots spread out into the whole Christian world the peoples are bound together under this Roman See—yet your Holiness therefore should call most to the Curia that they might reside here. For in this way, aside from the fact that the cardinals would be performing their office, provision would also be made for the dignity of the Curia and the gap repaired, if any should occur by the withdrawal of many bishops returning to their own churches.

Another great abuse and one that must by no means be tolerated, whereby the whole Christian people is scandalized, arises from the obstacles the bishops face in the government of their flocks, especially in punishing and correcting evildoers. For in the first place wicked men, chiefly clerics, free themselves in many ways from the jurisdiction of their ordinary. Then, if they have not arranged this exemption, they at once have recourse to the Penitentiary or to the Datary, where they immediately find a way to escape punishment, and, what is worse, they find this in consideration of the payment of money. This scandal, most blessed Father, so greatly disturbs the Christian people that words cannot express it. Let these abuses be abolished, we implore your Holiness by the Blood of Christ, by which He has redeemed for Himself His Church and in which He has bathed her. Let these stains be removed, by which, if any access were given to them in any commonwealth of men or any kingdom, it would at once or very soon fall headlong into ruin, nor could it in any way longer survive. Yet we think that we are at liberty to introduce these monstrosities into the Christian Commonwealth.

Another abuse must be corrected with regard to the religious orders, for many have become so deformed that they are a great scandal to the laity and do grave harm by their example. We think that all conventual orders ought to be done away with, not however that injury be done to anyone, but by prohibiting the admission of novices. Thus they might be quickly abolished without wronging anyone, and good religious could be substituted for them. In fact we now think that it would be best if all boys who have not been professed were removed from their monasteries.[19]

We believe that the appointment of preachers and confessors from among the friars must also be given attention and corrected, first that their superiors take great care that they are qualified and then that they are presented to the bishops, to whom above all others the care of the Church has been en-

---

[19] The *Consilium* quite clearly is not recommending "the abolition of monasticism," as H. R. Trevor-Roper states it is in his *Historical Essays* (New York, 1966), p. 50. It is simply a matter of doing away with the relaxed or less strict branches of the mendicant orders, notably the Franciscan Conventuals. In fact the reform of monasticism and the establishment of new orders—the Theatines, the Capuchins, and later the Jesuits—had major support among the authors of the *Consilium*.

trusted, by whom they may be examined either directly or through capable men. Nor should they be permitted to carry out these tasks without the consent of the bishops.

We have said, most blessed Father, that it is not lawful in any way in the matter of the use of the keys for him exercising this power to obtain any profit. Concerning this there is the firm word of Christ: "Freely you have received, freely give." This pertains not only to your Holiness, but to all who share your power. Therefore we would wish that this same injunction be observed by the legates and nuncios. For just as custom which has now become prevalent dishonors this See and disturbs the people, so, if the contrary were done, this See would win the highest honor and the people would be wonderfully edified.

Another abuse troubles the Christian people with regard to nuns under the care of conventual friars, where in very many convents public sacrilege occurs with the greatest scandal to all. Therefore, let your Holiness take this entire responsibility away from the conventuals and give it either to the ordinaries or to others, whatever will be deemed better.

There is a great and dangerous abuse in the public schools, especially in Italy, where many professors of philosophy teach ungodly things. Indeed, the most ungodly disputations take place in the churches, and, if they are of a religious nature, what pertains to the divine in them is treated before the people with great irreverence. We believe, therefore, that the bishops must be instructed, where there are public schools, to admonish those who lecture that they not teach the young ungodly things, but that they show the weakness of the natural light [of reason] in questions relating to God, to the newness or the eternity of the world, and the like, and guide these youths to what is godly. Likewise, that public disputations on questions of this kind should not be permitted, nor on theological matters either, which disputations certainly destroy much respect among the common people, but that disputations on these matters be held privately and on other questions in the realm of natural science publicly. And the same charge must be imposed on all other bishops, especially of important cities, where disputations of this kind are wont to be held.

The same care must also be employed in the printing of books, and all princes should be instructed by letter to be on their guard lest any books be printed indiscriminately under their authority. Responsibility in this matter should be given to the ordinaries. And because boys in elementary school are now accustomed to read the *Colloquies* of Erasmus, in which there is much to educate unformed minds to ungodly things, the reading of this book and others of this type then must be prohibited in grammar school.[20]

[20] Erasmus' *Colloquies* was first published in 1518 and saw numerous editions and enlargements in subsequent years. Originally intended as a school text, it became one of Erasmus' most popular works. Because of its ridicule and criticism of many common practices and notably of the monks and friars, it came under frequent attack. Its censure by the Sorbonne in 1526 elicited a defense of it by Erasmus, which may be read in *The*

Following these matters which pertain to the instruction of your ministers in the care of the universal Church and in its administration, it must be noted that with regard to privileges granted by your Holiness besides the former abuses other abuses have also been introduced.

The first concerns renegade friars or religious who after a solemn vow withdraw from their order and obtain permission not to wear the habit of their order or even the trace of a habit, but only dignified clerical dress. Let us omit for the moment any reference to gain. For we have already said in the beginning that it is not lawful to make a profit for oneself from the use of the keys and of the power given by Christ, but that one must abstain from this indulgence. For the habit is the sign of profession, whence a dispensation cannot be given even by the bishop to whom these renegades are subject. Therefore this privilege ought not to be granted them, nor should those, when they depart from a vow which binds them to God, be allowed to hold benefices or administrative posts.

Another abuse concerns the pardoners [of the hospital] of the Holy Spirit, [of the hospital] of St. Anthony, and others of this type, who deceive the peasants and simple people and ensnare them with innumerable superstitions.[21] It is our opinion that these pardoners should be abolished.

Another abuse is in connection with dispensing a person established in Holy Orders so that he can take a wife. This dispensation should not be given anyone except for the preservation of a people or a nation, where there is a most serious public reason, especially in these times when the Lutherans lay such great stress on this matter.

There is an abuse in dispensing in the case of marriages between those related by blood or by marriage. Indeed we do not think that this should be done within the second degree [of consanguinity] except for a serious public reason and in other degrees except for a good reason and without any payment of money, as we have already said, unless the parties previously have been united in marriage. In that case it may be permitted in view of the absolution of a sin already committed to impose a money fine after absolution and to allot it to the pious causes to which your Holiness contributes. For just as no money can be demanded when the use of the keys is without sin, so a money fine can be imposed and allotted to pious usage when absolution from sin is sought.

Another abuse concerns the absolution of those guilty of simony. Alas, how this destructive vice holds sway in the Church of God, so that some have no fear of committing simony and then immediately seek absolution from punishment. Indeed they purchase that absolution, and thus they retain the

---

Colloquies of Erasmus, trans. Craig R. Thompson (Chicago, 1965), Appendix I. In view of other condemnations the above prohibition, limited as it is to grammar schools, is rather mild.

[21] The pardoners mentioned were attached to two hospitals in Rome. There were many complaints about the kind of indulgence preaching these and similar pardoners conducted. See *Concilium Tridentinum*, XII, 142, n. 1.

benefice which they have purchased. We do not say that your Holiness is not able to absolve them of that punishment which has been ordained by positive law, but that he ought by no means to do so, so that opposition might be offered to a crime so great that there is none more dangerous or more scandalous.

Also permission should not be given to clerics to bequeath ecclesiastical property except for an urgent reason, lest the possessions of the poor be converted to private pleasure and the enlarging of a person's own estate.

Moreover confessional letters as well as the use of portable altars should not be readily allowed, for this cheapens the devotions of the Church and the most important sacrament of all. Nor should indulgences be granted except once a year in each of the principal cities. And the commutation of vows ought not to be so easily made, except in view of an equivalent good

It has also been the custom to alter the last wills of testators who bequeath a sum of money for pious causes, which amount is transferred by the authority of your Holiness to an heir or legatee because of alleged poverty, etc., but actually because of greed. Indeed, unless there has been a great change in the household affairs of an heir because of the death of the testator, so that it is likely that the testator would have altered his will in view of that situation, it is wicked to alter the wills of testators. We have already spoken often about greed, wherefore we think that this practice should be entirely avoided.

Having set forth in brief all those matters which pertain to the pontiff of the universal Church as far as we could comprehend them, we shall in conclusion say something about that which pertains to the bishop of Rome. This city and church of Rome is the mother and teacher of the other churches. Therefore in her especially divine worship and integrity of morals ought to flourish. Accordingly, most blessed Father, all strangers are scandalized when they enter the basilica of St. Peter where priests, some of whom are vile, ignorant, and clothed in robes and vestments which they cannot decently wear in poor churches, celebrate mass. This is a great scandal to everyone. Therefore the most reverend archpriest or the most reverend penitentiary must be ordered to attend to this matter and remove this scandal. And the same must be done in other churches.

Also in this city harlots walk about like matrons or ride on mules, attended in broad daylight by noble members of the cardinals' households and by clerics. In no city do we see this corruption except in this model for all cities. Indeed they even dwell in fine houses. This foul abuse must also be corrected.

There are also in this city the hatreds and animosities of private citizens which it is especially the concern of the bishop to compose and conciliate. Therefore, all these animosities must be resolved and the passions of the citizens composed by some cardinals, Romans especially, who are more qualified.

There are in this city hospitals, orphans, widows. There care especially is the concern of the bishop and the prince. Therefore your Holiness could properly take care of all of these through cardinals who are upright men.

These are the abuses, most blessed Father, which for the present, according to the limitations of our talents, we thought should be compiled, and which seemed to us ought to be corrected. You indeed, in accord with your goodness and wisdom, will direct all these matters. We certainly, if we have not done justice to the magnitude of the task which is far beyond our powers, have nevertheless satisfied our consciences, and we are not without the greatest hope that under your leadership we may see the Church of God cleansed, beautiful as a dove, at peace with herself, agreeing in one body, to the eternal memory of your name. You have taken the name of Paul; you will imitate, we hope, the charity of Paul. He was chosen as the vessel to carry the name of Christ among the nations.[22] Indeed we hope that you have been chosen to restore in our hearts and in our works the name of Christ now forgotten by the nations and by us clerics, to heal the ills, to lead back the sheep of Christ into one fold, to turn away from us the wrath of God and that vengeance which we deserve, already prepared and looming over our heads.

> Gasparo, Cardinal Contarini
> Gian Pietro [Carafa], Cardinal of Chieti
> Jacopo, Cardinal Sadoleto
> Reginald [Pole], Cardinal of England
> Federigo [Fregoso], Archbishop of Salerno
> Jerome [Aleander], Archbishop of Brindisi
> Gian Matteo [Gilberti], Bishop of Verona
> Gregorio [Cortese], Abbot of San Giorgio, Venice
> Friar Tommaso [Badia], Master of the Sacred Palace[23]

[22] Acts 9, 15.

[23] The question of who actually wrote the *Consilium* has been often discussed, and various attributions have been made (see *Concilium Tridentinum*, XII, 132-33). Given the state of the problem, however, it seems best to attribute it to the nine signatories as a collective work, though perhaps Contarini and Carafa may be viewed as the principal authors. A strong case can be made especially for the latter, in view of his energetic personality and of several important points of similarity between the *Consilium* and a reform memorial sent by Carafa to Clement VII in 1532. This latter document may be found in *ibid.*, XII, 67-77, and is discussed in G. M. Monti, *Ricerche su Papa Paolo IV Carafa* (Benevento, 1925), Part I, where (pp. 41-47) its correspondence with the *Consilium* is stressed.

CHAPTER XIV

St. Ignatius Loyola and the Founding of the Jesuits

1. The Bull of Institution, 1540
2. Rules for Thinking with the Church

One of the most important events in the story of the Catholic Reformation is the founding of the Society of Jesus. This was due above all to the inspiration and effort of a Spanish soldier, Don Iñigo Lopez de Loyola, one of the towering figures of the sixteenth century. The significance of the new Order, however, is a consequence not only of his striking personality and spiritual gifts but also of its own rapid expansion throughout Europe and of the activities and achievements of so many of its sons in the service of the Church and the faith they cherished. One can say—without fear of contradiction, I believe—that it became the most powerful instrument of Catholic revival and resurgence in this era of religious crisis. Yet the dynamic element in the Order was and remained the experience of a Spanish saint, and it is his life and spirituality that we must first seek to understand in any study of the role of the young Society.[1]

---

[1] The documentation and literature on Ignatius and the early Jesuits are very extensive. The works of James Brodrick, S.J., afford perhaps the best introduction: *The Origin of the Jesuits* (N.Y., 1940), *The Progress of the Jesuits (1556–79)* (N.Y., 1947), *Saint Ignatius Loyola, the Pilgrim Years, 1491–1538* (N.Y., 1956), *et al.* Standard biographies of Ignatius are Paul Dudon, S.J., *St. Ignatius of Loyola*, trans. William J. Young, S.J. (Milwaukee, 1949), and Paul Van Dyke, *Ignatius Loyola, the Founder of the Jesuits* (N.Y., 1926). Ignatius' autobiography (to 1538) as well as his famous letter on obedience (1553) may be found in *St. Ignatius' Own Story*, trans. William J. Young, S.J. (Chicago, 1956); a selection from his voluminous correspondence is in *Letters of St. Ignatius of Loyola*, trans. William J. Young, S.J. (Chicago, 1959); two recent translations of his *Spiritual Exercises* are by Louis J. Puhl, S.J. (Westminster, Md., 1951) and by Anthony Mottola (N.Y., 1964).

The great collection of sources on Ignatius and the early Society is the *Monumenta Historica Societatis Jesu* (93 vols.; Madrid-Rome, 1894–1965). It is divided into various sections, the most extensive and important of which is the *Monumenta Ignatiana*, containing the correspondence and writings of St. Ignatius. This in turn is divided into four series: the first series (12 vols.; Madrid, 1903–12) containing the letters of St. Ignatius; the second series (1 vol.; Madrid, 1919) the critical text of the *Spiritual Exercises*; the third series (4 vols.; Rome, 1934–48) the *Constitutions* of the Society of Jesus; and the fourth series (2 vols.; Madrid, 1904–18) early writings about Ignatius. The latter series is now replaced by the *Fontes narrativi de S. Ignatio de Loyola* (4 vols.; Rome, 1943–65), which contain the earliest *vitae*.

Attention should also be called to several recent studies of the character and historical context of Ignatian spirituality and of the new Society. The problems here involved are of the utmost interest for the historian, and perhaps the best introduction to them is H. O.

Iñigo, or Ignatius, to use the name he later adopted, was born in 1491 of a noble Basque family in the province of Guipuzcoa in the old kingdom of Castile. In his youth he served as a page at the royal court and then as a soldier under the banner of the Spanish kings. He was gravely wounded at Pamplona in May, 1521, at the time of the French invasion of Navarre–an event which proved to be a decisive turning point in his life. During his long and painful convalescence at the family castle of Loyola he underwent a conversion, and he forswore all ambition to serve an earthly king for a dedication and service to a higher Lord. Two books that he read during this time for want of any other are famous for the influence they had upon him: Ludolph of Saxony's *Life of Christ* and Jacopo de Voragine's *Golden Legend*. A third was soon to join their number: Thomas à Kempis' *Imitation of Christ*. It was from them that his conversion flowed and in them that his new devotion, his new chivalry, had its source.

Having recovered from his wound, he set out on a pilgrimage to the shrine of Our Lady at Montserrat, and he then retired to the little town of Manresa for several months, where the religious experience he there sustained completed his transformation into the "new man" and set the course of his great career. He found his life's aim in the service of God and the salvation of souls, and, as Hugo Rahner expresses it, "Ignatius, the pilgrim and penitent, was made over into the man of the Church," the visible Kingdom of Christ.[2] In view of the times and the needs of that Church this was indeed an auspicious moment.

After Manresa in early 1523 Ignatius went off to visit the Holy Land, and returning the following year, he undertook to gain an education which would enable him to work more effectively in the apostolate he desired to embrace. This carried him to Alcalá and Salamanca and finally to the University of Paris, where he studied from 1528 to 1535. The Paris years mark a most important phase: his zeal continued, his doctrine matured, and he gathered about him the disciples and companions with whom he was eventually to form the new Society. On August 15, 1534, in a small chapel on Montmartre

---

Evennett, *The Spirit of the Counter-Reformation*, ed. John Bossy (Cambridge, 1968), where Ignatius is closely linked to the *Devotio moderna* and the new Society to the currents and needs of the times. Quite a different (and more transcendent) approach is followed in Hugo Rahner, S.J. *The Spirituality of St. Ignatius Loyola*, trans. William J. Young, S.J. (Westminster, Md., 1953). Joseph de Guibert, S.J. *The Jesuits, Their Spiritual Doctrine and Practice*, trans. William J. Young, S.J. (Chicago, 1964), is a basic and comprehensive work on this subject. The possible *rapports* between Erasmian humanism and the Ignatian experience and foundation are explored in Marcel Bataillon, "D'Erasme à la Compagnie de Jésus," *Archives de sociologie des religions*, XXIV (1967), 57–81, and in John C. Olin, "Erasmus and St. Ignatius Loyola," *Luther, Erasmus and the Reformation: A Catholic-Protestant Reappraisal*, eds. John C. Olin, James D. Smart, and Robert E. McNally, S.J. (New York, 1969). The correspondence or relationship stressed in these two articles is countered by the thesis and argument in R. G. Villoslada, S.J., *Loyola y Erasmo, dos almas, dos epocas* (Madrid, 1965).

[2] Rahner, *op. cit.*, p. 55. See, however, the critical comments regarding Rahner's view by John Bossy in Evennett, *op. cit.*, pp. 126–30.

11. Profession of vows by Ignatius Loyola and companions, made at the basilica of St. Paul in Rome, April 22, 1541.

Ignatius and six others—Pierre Favre, Francis Xavier, Diego Laynez, Alfonso Salmeron, Nicholas Bobadilla, Simon Rodriguez—bound themselves by the vows of poverty and chastity and resolved to go to Jerusalem to labor for the conversion of the Turks.[3] If that latter intention could not be carried out, they planned to place themselves at the disposal of the Pope. Such indeed was the situation that developed. They subsequently gathered in Venice for passage to the East—three others meanwhile had joined the band: Claude Le Jay, Paschase Broet, Jean Codure—but, unable to embark on their mission overseas because of war, they ventured to work nearer home and by the spring of 1538 converged on Rome to fulfill their alternate proposal. There in the months that followed they decided to form a permanent religious organization, and they discussed the aims and character of the new Society they had agreed to establish.[4] Finally, in the summer of 1539 they submitted, through the good offices of Cardinal Gasparo Contarini, a brief statement of their plans for the approval of the Holy See. The bull *Regimini militantis ecclesiae,* issued in September, 1540, by Paul III—it is given below—is the formal approbation that Ignatius and his companions sought.[5] Delayed because of opposition in the Curia, notably by Cardinals Guidiccioni and Ghinucci, to the new Order, it had been preceded nevertheless by the oral approval of the Pope in September, 1539, and in the intervening months the group began to disperse on various missions (Francis Xavier left Rome for the Indies in March, 1540),[6] and several new members joined the ranks. The Society of Jesus had come into being—an event which Jedin hails, with specific reference to the papal approbation, as "the first, and perhaps the greatest, success" of the reform movement that had been developing in Rome under the auspices of Paul III.[7]

By 1540 Ignatius' other great work, his *Spiritual Exercises,* had also taken its definitive shape.[8] This systematic program which has as its purpose "the conquest of self and the regulation of one's life" proved to be a most effective instrument in the hands of Ignatius and other members of the young Society

[3] Brodrick, *The Origin of the Jesuits,* pp. 42–43.

[4] *Ibid.,* pp. 68 ff. The pertinent documents are in *M.H.S.J., Monumenta Ignatiana, series tertia,* I.

[5] This important bull contains nearly the entire statement submitted by Ignatius and his friends and thus gives the purpose and plan of the new Society in the words of the founding fathers themselves. The Latin text is in *ibid.,* I, 24–32, and also in Kidd, *Documents Illustrative of the Continental Reformation,* pp. 335–40. The English version presented here has been reprinted with permission from Robert Harvey, *Ignatius Loyola* (Milwaukee: The Bruce Publishing Company, 1936), Appendix.

[6] Pierre Favre, for example, along with Diego Laynez, had gone to Parma for pastoral work at the behest of Paul III in June, 1539. From there he proceeded into Germany in October, 1540, to attend the religious conferences at Worms and Ratisbon. Ignatius, who was elected General of the Society in April, 1541, alone of the original band remained in Rome. He died there July 31, 1556.

[7] Jedin, *A History of the Council of Trent,* 1, 439.

[8] The *Spiritual Exercises* have their origin in Ignatius' meditations and experience at Manresa. They developed over the years and assumed their final form around 1540. The oldest manuscript copy of the book as it exists today is that of 1541. The first printed edition was published in Rome in 1548—a Latin text of the Spanish original. For modern editions, see footnote 1. For background and commentary, see de Guibert, *op. cit.*

in bringing about the personal reform and dedication that must underlie any Catholic revival. Here in fact is the fundamental contribution of Ignatius to the Catholic Reformation: the spiritual ideal and method capable of changing lives and of creating an elite devoted to the Church and desirous of serving her.[9] The reform of the Christian and his commitment to active service under the banner of Christ in the Church of Christ was then the supreme Ignatian goal, and this in turn accounts both for the Society that was created and for its historic role in the age of the Reformation.[10]

The two documents that follow will help to clarify the purpose and character of this new Order, as well as the attitude of Ignatius and his companions toward the Church. Their achievements, which, as Lortz declares, "amounted to nothing less than the rescue of the Church at the time," still lay ahead, but the spirit and motivation for them are, in part at least, revealed.[11] The first document is the papal bull of 1540, *Regimini militantis ecclesiae*, formally establishing the Society of Jesus.[12] The second is the so-called "Rules for Thinking with the Church," the final section of the *Spiritual Exercises* and actually an addition or appendix to it.[13] It was composed by Ignatius during his stay in Paris (1528–35), and though it embodies his quintessential view of the Church, "the true Spouse of Jesus Christ," it quite obviously represents a response to the Protestant challenge and an affirmation of many long-established practices then under severe criticism and attack.[14] It is a most interesting document, characterized more perhaps by its balance and moderation than one may at first think—note, for example, Rules 11 and 17—and it should be read, of course, in the context of its own occasion, place, and time.

[9] On this important subject, see Candido de Dalmases, S.J., "Les idées de Saint Ignace sur la réforme catholique," *Christus*, XVIII (1958), 239–56, and Robert E. McNally, S.J., "The Council of Trent, the *Spiritual Exercises*, and the Catholic Reform," *Church History*, XXXIV (1965), 36–49.

[10] One need hardly point out that the Jesuits were not founded to combat Protestantism. Their devotion to the Church, however, made them her most vigorous defenders, just as the spirituality of Ignatius, whom Rahner calls "the mystic of the Church," made him in this sense the antithesis of Luther. But the explicit defense of the Church in the face of the Protestant challenge was not an original purpose or aim, and it is interesting to note that the words *ad fidei defensionem* were only added in 1550 to the Society's statement of purpose as expressed in the second bull of confirmation, *Exposcit debitum*, issued by Pope Julius III. *M.H.S.J., Monumenta Ignatiana, series tertia*, I, 373–83.

[11] Lortz, *The Reformation: A Problem for Today*, p. 183.

[12] See footnote 5.

[13] The English translation is reprinted with permission from *The Spiritual Exercises of St. Ignatius*, trans. Louis J. Puhl, S.J. (Westminster, Md.: Newman Press, 1951), pp. 157–61. The original Spanish and Latin texts may be found in *M.H.S.J., Monumenta Ignatiana, series secunda, Exercitia Spiritualia* (Madrid, 1919), pp. 548–63.

[14] Dudon, *op. cit.*, pp. 457–62, stresses the influence of the decrees of the synod of Sens of 1528 (as well as of the writings of Josse Clichtove) on the formulation of these Rules and points out the very striking parallelism that exists. See also Bataillon, *op. cit.*, 67–73, for a very interesting explanation of these Rules.

1. THE BULL OF INSTITUTION, 1540

PAUL, BISHOP, Servant of the Servants of God, for a perpetual memorial.

Presiding by divine dispensation over the government of the Church Militant, despite our own unworthiness, and filled with that zeal for the salvation of souls which our pastoral office lays upon us, we foster, by the token of apostolic favor, certain persons who express their desire for it, and we dispense further graces according as a ripe examination of times and places leads us to judge it useful and beneficial in the Lord.

As a matter of fact, we have lately learned that our beloved sons, Ignatius of Loyola, Pierre Favre, and Diego Laynez, as also Claude Le Jay, Paschase Broet, and Francis Xavier, and further Alphonso Salmeron, and Simon Rodriguez, Jean Codure, and Nicholas Bobadilla, all priests of the cities and dioceses respectively of Pamplona, Geneva, Siguenza, Toledo, Viseu, Embrun, and Placencia, all Masters of Arts, graduates of the University of Paris, and trained for a number of years in theological studies; we have learned, as we say, that these men, inspired, as is piously believed, by the Holy Ghost, have come together from various regions of the globe, and entering into association have renounced the pleasures of this world and have dedicated their lives to the perpetual service of our Lord Jesus Christ, and of ourselves and the other Roman Pontiffs who shall succeed us.

Indeed, they have already labored acceptably for a number of years in the vineyard of the Lord, publicly preaching the Word of God, having obtained the necessary permission to do so; privately exhorting the faithful to lead a blameless life worthy of eternal happiness, and inciting them to godly meditations; serving in the hospitals, instructing children and ignorant persons in the essentials of a Christian education; and finally, fulfilling with an ardor worthy of the highest praise, in all parts of the world where they have traveled, all the offices of charity and the ministries needful for the consolation of souls.

Having at length come to this illustrious city, and persevering constantly in the bond of love, they have now, in order to cement and conserve the union of their Society in Jesus Christ, adopted a plan of life conformable to the evangelical counsels and the canonical statutes of the Fathers, in accordance with what their experience has taught them to be most conducive to the purpose which they have set before themselves. Now this manner of life, set forth in the aforesaid formula, has not only merited the praise of good men who are zealous for the honor of God, but has so attracted some among them that they have resolved to embrace it.

We append herewith this plan of life already mentioned. It is as follows:

Whoever shall desire to bear the arms of God under the banner of the Cross, and to serve the one God and the Roman Pontiff, His Vicar upon earth, in our Society, which we wish to be called by the name of Jesus, having made a solemn of perpetual chastity, must purpose to become a member of a society principally instituted to work for the advancement of souls in Christian life and doctrine, and for the propagation of the faith by public preaching and the ministry of God's Word, by spiritual exercises and works of charity, more particularly by grounding in Christianity boys and unlettered persons, and by hearing the confessions of the faithful, aiming in all things at their spiritual consolation. He must also act so as to have always before his eyes, first God, and then the plan of this Institute which is a definite path that leads to Him, and he must use all his energies to attain this goal which God Himself sets before him, always according to the grace which each one has received from the Holy Spirit and the proper grade of his vocation, lest any might be carried away by a zeal without knowledge.

It shall be in the power of the Prepositus, or Prelate, whom we shall choose, to decide upon the rank suitable for each, as well as upon the activities of all, so that due and proper order, most necessary in very well-regulated community, may be observed. With the approval of his associates and in a council where all shall be decided by a vote of the majority, the Prepositus shall have the authority to make constitutions conformable to the purpose of the Institute. On matters of importance and permanence this council shall be the greater part of the Society which can conveniently be convoked by the Prepositus, and on the lighter and temporary affairs all those who happen to be present in the place where the Prepositus resides. But the right of issuing commands shall belong entirely to the Prepositus.

Let all the members of the Company know and bear in mind, not only in the early days of their profession but through all the days of their life, that this entire Company and all who compose it are engaged in a conflict for God under the obedience of the most sacred Lord the Pope, and his successors in the pontificate. And although we have learned from the Gospel, and know by the orthodox faith, and firmly profess that all the faithful in Christ Jesus are subject to the Roman Pontiff, as the Head and the Vicar of Jesus Christ, nevertheless, for the greater humility of our Society, and the perfect mortification of each, and the abnegation of our wills, we have deemed it to be very helpful to take upon ourselves, beyond the bond common to all the faithful, a special vow. It is meant so to bind that whatsoever the present Roman Pontiff and his successors may command us concerning the advancement of souls and the spreading of the faith, we shall be obliged to obey instantly as far as lies in us, without evasion or excuse, going to whatever country into which they may send us, whether among the Turks or other heathen, and even to the Indies, or among whatsoever heretics and schismatics, or among any believers whomsoever.

Wherefore let those who shall desire to join us consider well, before assuming this burden, whether they have sufficient spiritual riches to complete this tower, following in this matter the counsel of our Lord, that is to say, whether the Holy Spirit who impels them promises them so much grace as will enable them to support with His aid the burden of this vocation. And when, by the leading of the Lord, they shall be enrolled in this militia of Jesus Christ they must have their loins girded day and night, ever ready to discharge so great a debt. But in order that we may neither seek nor refuse these missions in different countries, let each and every one of us vouch that they will never make any solicitation directly or indirectly to the Roman Pontiff, but shall leave all such matters entirely to the will of God, to the Pope as His Vicar, and to the Prepositus of the Society. The latter himself shall promise, like the others, not to make solicitation of the Pope concerning his own mission in one way or the other, except with the concurrence of the Society.

All shall vow obedience to the Prepositus of the Society in all things which concern the observance of this our rule, and he, on his part, shall ordain what he may deem expedient for the attainment of the purpose which he shall know that God and the Society have set for him. In the exercise of his office let him always remember the kindness, the gentleness, and the love of Christ, and the prescriptions of Peter and Paul, and let him and his council zealously adhere to this rule. Above all things let them have at heart the instruction of boys and ignorant persons in the knowledge of Christian doctrine, of the Ten Commandments, and other such rudiments as shall be suitable, having regard to the circumstances of persons, places, and times. For it is very necessary that the Prepositus and his council watch over this business with the greatest diligence, both because without foundations the edifice of faith in our neighbors cannot be raised to a fitting height, and also because there is danger for our own members, lest the more learned they become, the more they may be tempted to belittle this field of work, as at first sight less attractive, although there is none more useful, whether for the edification of our neighbor, or for our own training in love and humility. As to the subjects, they shall be bound to obey the Prepositus in all things which pertain to the Institute, both for the resultant advantage to the Order and for the assiduous practice of humility, which is a virtue that cannot be too highly praised; and they shall recognize in him Jesus Christ as though present in him, and as far as is becoming revere him.

Since we have learned by experience that the more a life is remote from the contagion of avarice, and comfortable to evangelical poverty, the more it is

12. St. Ignatius Loyola. Copy of a portrait by Alonzo Sánchez Coello.

pure, agreeable, and edifying to our neighbor, and also since we believe that our Lord Jesus Christ will supply what is needful for the food and clothing of His servants who seek only the Kingdom of God, we desire that each and every one of them shall take a vow of perpetual poverty, declaring that they cannot acquire privately, nor even in common, for the maintenance or use of the Society, civil rights to any real property, or to any rents or incomes whatsoever, but let them be content to receive the use only of the alms given them in order to procure the necessities of life. However, they may have in the Universities a college or colleges holding revenues, estates, and funds, applicable to the use and needs of the students.

To the Prepositus and the Society shall be reserved the entire government or administration of the said colleges and aforesaid students, as regards the selection of the regent or regents, as also of the student body and their admittance, discharge, reception, exclusion; the rules regarding the instruction, erudition, edification, and correction of the students; the manner of supplying their food and clothing, and all other subjects of administration, regulation and general care. All this shall be done in such a way, however, that the students may not abuse the aforesaid properties, nor the Society convert them to its private use, but administer them solely for the needs of the students. And these students, when their progress in piety and learning has been assured, and after sufficient probation, may be admitted into our Society.

All the members who are in holy orders, although they hold no benefice and receive no ecclesiastical revenue, shall be bound to say the divine office according to the ritual of the Church, each one privately and individually and not in common.

Such are the plans regarding our profession which we have been able to draw up by the favor of our Lord, Paul III, and of the Apostolic See. This we have done with the view of instructing by this brief writing both those who are inquiring about us at the present time, and those who shall succeed us in the future, if it is God's will that we should have imitators in this way of life. It has great and numerous difficulties, as we know by our own experience, and so we have judged it right to order that no one be admitted into this Society except he shall have had long and diligent testing. Not until he has been found prudent in Jesus Christ, and distinguished in doctrine or in purity of Christian life, may he be received into the militia of Jesus Christ, who will be pleased to favor our humble enterprises for the glory of God the Father, to whom be glory and honor forever. Amen.

Now seeing that we find nothing in these premises which is not pious and holy, and in order that these same Associates, who have herein most humbly presented to us their petition, may follow with the more ardor their plan of life, because they feel that they enjoy the favor of the Holy See and behold the foregoing approved by us; We, in virtue of our Apostolical authority, according to the tenor of these presents, and of our certain knowledge, do approve, confirm, bless, and strengthen with a safeguard of perpetual stability the aforesaid premises, in whole and in part, as suitable to the spiritual progress of these

Associates and of the rest of the Christian flock. The Associates themselves we take under our protection and that of the Holy See Apostolic, granting to them, moreover, freely and lawfully to draw up such special Constitutions as they shall judge to be comfortable to the purpose of the Society, the glory of our Lord Jesus Christ, and the utility of our neighbor; the constitutions and apostolic ordinances of the general Council and of our predecessor of happy memory, Pope Gregory X, and any others to the contrary, notwithstanding.

It is our will, however, that persons who desire to make profession of this way of life be admitted into the said Society up to the number of sixty, and not beyond.[15]

Let no man therefore infringe upon nor contravene any of the points herein expressed of our approbation, confirmation, blessing, strengthening, acceptance, concession, and good will. If anyone should presume to attempt it, let him know that he will incur the wrath of Almighty God and of the Apostles St. Peter and St. Paul.

Given at Rome, at St. Mark's, the year of the Incarnation of the Lord, 1540, the fifth of the calends of October [September 27], the sixth year of our Pontificate.

The Bull *Injunctum Nobis* of March 14, 1544, removed this limitation of the number of sixty, placing no limits on the number of members. At the death of Ignatius in 1556 there were, according to Father Brodrick (*The Origin of the Jesuits*, p. 221), a thousand members. Pastor, XIII, 184, basing his figure on Polanco, puts the membership at "some 1500 as early as 1554."

2. RULES FOR THINKING WITH THE CHURCH

THE FOLLOWING *rules should be observed to foster the true attitude of mind we ought to have in the Church militant.*

1. We must put aside all judgment of our own, and keep the mind ever ready and prompt to obey in all things the true Spouse of Jesus Christ, our holy Mother, the hierarchical Church.

2. We should praise sacramental confession, the yearly reception of the Most Blessed Sacrament, and praise more highly monthly reception, and still more weekly Communion, provided requisite and proper dispositions are present.

3. We ought to praise the frequent hearing of Mass, the singing of hymns, psalmody, and long prayers whether in the church or outside; likewise, the hours arranged at fixed times for the whole Divine Office, for every kind of prayer, and for the canonical hours.

4. We must praise highly religious life, virginity, and continency; and matrimony ought not be praised as much as any of these.

5. We should praise vows of religion, obedience, poverty, chastity, and vows to perform other works of supererogation conducive to perfection. However, it must be remembered that a vow deals with matters that lead us closer to evangelical perfection. Hence, whatever tends to withdraw one from perfection may not be made the object of a vow, for example, a business career, the married state, and so forth.

6. We should show our esteem for the relics of the saints by venerating them and praying to the saints. We should praise visits to the Station Churches, pilgrimages, indulgences, jubilees, crusade indults, the lighting of candles in churches.

7. We must praise the regulations of the Church with regard to fast and abstinence, for example, in Lent, on Ember Days, Vigils, Fridays, and Saturdays. We should praise all works of penance, not only those that are interior but also those that are exterior.

8. We ought to praise not only the building and adorn-

ment of churches, but also images and veneration of them according to the subject they represent.

9. Finally, we must praise all the commandments of the Church, and be on the alert to find reasons to defend them, and by no means in order to criticize them.

10. We should be more ready to approve and praise the orders, recommendations, and way of acting of our superiors than to find fault with them. Though some of the orders, etc., may not have been praiseworthy, yet to speak against them, either when preaching in public or in speaking before the people, would rather be the cause of murmuring and scandal than of profit. As a consequence, the people would become angry with their superiors, whether secular or spiritual. But while it does harm in the absence of our superiors to speak evil of them before the people, it may be profitable to discuss their bad conduct with those who can apply a remedy.

11. We should praise both positive theology and that of the Scholastics.

It is characteristic of the positive doctors, such as St. Augustine, St. Jerome, St. Gregory, and others, to rouse the affections so that we are moved to love and serve God our Lord in all things.

On the other hand, it is more characteristic of the scholastic doctors, such as St. Thomas, St. Bonaventure, the Master of the Sentences, and others, to define and state clearly, according to the needs of our times, the doctrines that are necessary for external salvation, and that help to refute and expose more efficaciously all errors and fallacies.

Further, just because scholastic doctors belong to more recent times, they not only have the advantage of correct understanding of Holy Scripture and of the teaching of the saints and positive doctors, but, enlightened by the grace of God, they also make use of the decisions of the Councils and of the definitions and decrees of our holy Mother Church.

12. We must be on our guard against making comparisons between those who are still living and the saints who have gone before us, for no small error is committed if we say: "This man is wiser than St. Augustine," "He is another St. Francis or even greater," "He is equal to St. Paul in goodness and sanctity," and so on.

13. If we wish to proceed securely in all things, we must hold fast to the following principle: What seems to me white, I will believe black if the hierarchical Church so defines. For I must be convinced that in Christ our Lord, the bridegroom, and in His spouse the Church, only one Spirit holds sway, which governs and rules for the salvation of souls. For it is by the same Spirit and Lord who gave the Ten Commandments that our holy Mother Church is ruled and governed.

14. Granted that it be very true that no one can be saved without being predestined and without having faith and grace, still we must be very cautious about the way in which we speak of all these things and discuss them with others.

15. We should not make it a habit of speaking much of predestination. If

somehow at times it comes to be spoken of, it must be done in such a way that the people are not led into any error. They are at times misled, so that they say: "Whether I shall be saved or lost, has already been determined, and this cannot be changed whether my actions are good or bad." So they become indolent and neglect the works that are conducive to the salvation and spiritual progress of their souls.

16.   In the same way, much caution is necessary, lest by much talk about faith, and much insistence on it without any distinctions or explanations, occasion be given to the people, whether before or after they have faith informed by charity, to become slothful and lazy in good works.

17.   Likewise we ought not to speak of grace at such length and with such emphasis that the poison of doing away with liberty is engendered.

Hence, as far as is possible with the help of God, one may speak of faith and grace that the Divine Majesty may be praised. But let it not be done in such a way, above all not in times which are as dangerous as ours, that works and free will suffer harm, or that they are considered of no value.

18.   Though the zealous service of God our Lord out of pure love should be esteemed above all, we ought also to praise highly the fear of the Divine Majesty. For not only filial fear but also servile fear is pious and very holy. When nothing higher or more useful is attained, it is very helpful for rising from mortal sin, and once this is accomplished, one may easily advance to filial fear, which is wholly pleasing and agreeable to God our Lord since it is inseparably associated with the love of Him.

Bibliographical Postscript

In place of a lengthy listing of books on our subject or of the works already cited it would seem far more useful at this point to append a few remarks on the historiography of the Catholic Reformation and to indicate certain studies that have particular relevance and value for our theme. We have in each of the chapters of this book given a number of important bibliographical references for the specific topics, personalities and episodes treated. Our references here will be of a more general nature and are intended as a guide to the concept and movement of the Catholic Reformation as a whole.

The Catholic Reformation as a spontaneous reform movement within the Church has been comparatively neglected by historians. This at least would appear to be the case with regard to an overall synthesis or appraisal and with regard to an adequate analysis of its origins and historical development. What can and should be done is indicated in the posthumous publication of H. O. Evennett's Birkbeck Lectures at the University of Cambridge, *The Spirit of the Counter-Reformation*, ed. John Bossy (Cambridge, 1968). Its scope is limited, but its approach is new and most suggestive, and it affords perhaps the best single introduction to the historical phenomenon we are considering. Another work of comparable importance in opening up the subject and revealing something of its character and context is the superb study by the late Wilhelm Schenk, *Reginald Pole, Cardinal of England* (London, 1950). With grace and erudition it tells us much about the milieu of Italian Catholic reform. Third, the first volume of Hubert Jedin's *A History of the Council of Trent*, trans. Dom Ernest Graf (St. Louis, 1957), a work of impressive scholarship, must be mentioned. It is centered on the theme of Church and Council in the decades prior to the opening of Trent (1545), but it covers a wide range of religious and ecclesiastical history in the fifteenth and early sixteenth centuries, and it throws very great light on the whole issue of Church reform. Because of its factual content as well as its penetrating and judicious analysis it can truly be called indispensible for a study such as ours. Jedin's second volume (St. Louis, 1961), the only other one published to date, takes up the first sessions of Trent (1545–47).

In addition to these three works which can be recommended as basic introduction to our theme, the more general histories of the Church during this time are important. In the first rank here is Ludwig Pastor's monumental *The History of the Popes from the Close of the Middle Ages*, trans. F. I. Antrobus, R. F. Kerr *et al.* (40 vols.; St. Louis, 1891–1953), Volumes I to XVI of which cover the period from 1305 to 1565. Equally important are the relevant volumes in the Fliche and Martin series, *Histoire de l'Eglise depuis les origines jusqu'à nos jours* (21 vols.; Paris, 1936–64), that is, Volumes XIV to XVII covering the period from 1378 to 1563. Valuable too, especially for general background and context, are several single-volume works: Volume III of Philip Hughes' *A History of the Church* (New York, 1949), a substantial survey of Church history from 1270 to 1517; Erwin Iserloh, Joseph Glazik and Hubert Jedin, *Reformation, Katholische Reform und Gegenreformation* (*Handbuch der Kirchengeschichte*, Vol. IV; Freiburg, 1967); and Hermann Tüchle, C. A. Bouman and Jacques Le Brun, *Réforme et Contre-Réforme* (*Nouvelle Histoire de l'Eglise*, Vol. III; Paris, 1968). To these we can add the two essays of Robert E. McNally, S.J., *Reform of the Church* (New York, 1963), and *The Unreformed Church* (New York, 1965), which give background and perspective to the problem of Catholic reform in the sixteenth century.

There are of course some books, old and new, specifically devoted to the topic of the Catholic Reformation and/or Counter-Reformation, but these in general leave something to be desired. They are surveys, or they lack the adequate breadth and depth, or they approach their subject with too narrow and outmoded a perspective. The more recent and more acceptable of these are: Paolo Brezzi, *Le riforme cattoliche dei secoli XV e XVI* (Rome, 1945); Mario Bendiscioli, *La riforma cattolica* (Rome, 1958); Pierre Janelle, *The Catholic Reformation* (Milwaukee, 1949); and Henry Daniel-Rops, *The Catholic Reformation*, trans. John Warrington (New York, 1962). We might also mention in this company the article of Henry Lucas, "Survival of the Catholic Faith in the 16th Century," *Catholic Historical Review*, XXIX (1934), 25–52, which gives a competent though very sketchy *aperçu*. The older works of B. J. Kidd, *The Counter-Reformation* (London, 1933), and of A. W. Ward, *The Counter-Reformation* (New York, 1888), as well as G. V. Jourdan's *The Movement towards Catholic Reform in the Early XVI Century* (London, 1914), are inadequate and considerably out of date.

We cannot fail to call attention, however, particularly for historiographical reasons, to two classic works in the field: Leopold von Ranke's *Geschichte der Päpste*, which first appeared in 1834–37 (Eng. trans. by E. Fowler: *History of the Popes, Their Church and State*, 3 vols; New York, 1901), and Wilhelm Maurenbrecher's *Geschichte der katholischen Reformation*, the first and only volume of which was published at Nordlingen in 1880. Ranke's study, which has a majestic and dramatic sweep, is truly the work of a master, and to it is ascribed the earliest conceptualization of the Counter-Reformation as well as the origin of the term itself. The heart of Ranke's theme is the offensive launched by Rome against Protestantism (about 1563), but he is well aware of a preliminary reform and regeneration making possible the counterattack, and in his first volume he gives an interesting, if nevertheless inadequate, account of this reform development. Maurenbrecher, on the other hand, who seems to have introduced—or perhaps reintroduced—the expression "Catholic Reformation," concentrates more exclusively on the Catholic revival (to 1534) and views it of Spanish origin and beginning prior to the Lutheran revolt. To him we may attribute the early formulation of the concept of an independent Catholic Reformation as well as the employment of that significant label itself.

The historiographical problem that arose in this area, including the subsequent usage of these terms and the interpretations rendered by later historians, has been studied by Hubert Jedin in an extended essay entitled *Katholische Reformation oder Gegenreformation?* (Lucerne, 1946); by R. G. Villoslada, S.J., in his article "La Contrareforma: Su nombre y su concepto historico," *Saggi storici intorno al Papato* (Rome, 1959), pp. 189–242; and by P. G. Camaiani's "Interpretazioni della Riforma cattolica e della Controriforma," *Grande Antologia Filosofica*, ed. M. F. Sciacca, VI (Milan, 1964), 329–490. The latter, which appears in a remarkable collective work that contains much of relevance for our subject (Volumes VI through XI bear the title *Il pensiero della rinascenza e della riforma*), also includes many texts from historians exemplifying their interpretations. Finally there is a brief and perceptive analysis of the problem in Evennett's *The Spirit of the Counter-Reformation*, Chapter I.

With regard to the sources for the study of Catholic reform the several documents in this volume give some idea of the material at hand, and footnote references in each chapter indicate the collections and works whence these were drawn and where a great deal more can be found. There is, as far as I know, only one other "source book" comparable to the present work, namely M. Bendiscioli and M. Marcocchi, eds., *Riforma cattolica, antologia di documenti* (Rome, 1963). Its excerpts are rather brief, but it contains a representative selection. A few larger collections, however, should be noted, aside from such important works as the *Monumenta Historica Societatis Jesu* or the *Opus Epistolarum Erasmi*, which we have already cited in connection with the specific topics treated in the various chapters. Foremost here is the *Concilium Tridentinum: diariorum, actorum, epistolarum, tractatuum nova collectio* (13 vols.; Freiburg, 1901–38), a scholarly enterprise of the first magnitude undertaken by the *Görresgesellschaft* and containing a wealth of documentation for the period prior to Trent. There is also the *Corpus Catholicorum* (28 vols.; Münster, 1919–41), chiefly devoted to the theological and controversial writings of the Catholic defenders in the Reformation period. And there is the extensive *Reformationsgeschichtliche Studien und Texte* (94 vols.; Münster, 1906–66), now under the editorship of Hubert Jedin and concerned principally with German Catholic reform and counter-reform. Despite these multivolume collections, however, the sources for this immense field of study are widely scattered, nor are they always accessible or available in modern editions, nor have they yet been adequately charted or appraised. Indeed it has been one of the intentions in preparing this volume to assist, at least in a small way, in overcoming these difficulties. The task for the historian nevertheless remains very great, for, as Ranke said as he approached his narrative of the Counter-Reformation in his *History of the Popes*—the context is slightly different, it is true—"a boundless scene opens before us."

Index of Names